THE BLUESHIRTS

The Blueshirts

MAURICE MANNING

University of Toronto Press

Published by
GILL AND MACMILLAN LTD

First published in Canada and the United States
by University of Toronto Press
Toronto and Buffalo

ISBN 0–8020–1787–8
Microfiche ISBN 0–8020–0102–5

PRINTED AND BOUND IN THE REPUBLIC OF IRELAND BY THE BOOK PRINTING
DIVISION OF SMURFIT PRINT AND PACKAGING LIMITED, DUBLIN.

TO MY PARENTS

ABBREVIATIONS USED IN FOOTNOTE
REFERENCES

Walsh MS.—*General Eoin O'Duffy—His Life and Battle*, by Captain Liam Walsh, O'Duffy's private secretary. Loaned to author by Captain Jim O'Beirne.

D.D.—*Dail Debates*

S.D.—*Senate Debates*

I.I.—*Irish Independent*

I.T.—*The Irish Times*

I.P.—*The Irish Press*

C.E.—*The Cork Examiner*

U.I.—*United Irishman* and later *United Ireland*

An Phob.—*An Phoblacht*

R.T.—*The Round Table*

Contents

List of Illustrations

Foreword

LITTLE of substance has yet been written on the history and politics of Ireland during the decade 1930–40. This is rather surprising, for it was a turbulent and exciting decade, a decade of change, drama and bitter dissension with the passions and virulent forces aroused during the Civil War decade still to work themselves out of the nation's system. It was a decade which saw the peaceful transfer of power from Civil War victors to Civil War vanquished; a decade which saw the infant Free State lock in economic war with one of the world's most powerful states; it was a decade which saw the Irish state experiment with economic nationalism, adopt for itself a new Constitution and embark on the perilous course of neutrality. And perhaps most of all it was the decade of the Blueshirts—the only shirted movement the country has known and one which has left in its wake not only memories which are still bitter but also a host of controversial and unanswered questions.

This book is an attempt to tell the story of that Blueshirt movement—its origins, its development, its disintegration, to discuss the questions which the appearance of such a phenomenon must raise and to examine the relationship of the Blueshirts with the Fascism of the 1930s.

One of the biggest problems associated with a venture of this kind is that primary sources—personal papers, memos, official documents—are scarce and not easily accessible. There is an indefinite and unspecified embargo on Cabinet minutes, and the records of the political parties, where they exist, are scanty. As a consequence much of my research has had to be based on secondary sources, and especially on contemporary newspapers and parliamentary debates. Happily, however, many of the leading political figures of the 1930s are alive and it was possible to interview them.

Indeed one of the most pleasant aspects of writing this book was the excuse and opportunity it afforded me to meet these men. To do so was always an enjoyable experience— and on a few occasions a memorable one. I have learned much from meeting these men and if there was one quality above all others which was common to all of them, it was their courtesy. On every occasion I was made to feel welcome; each in his own way sought to be as helpful as possible and even the most foolish and irrelevant of my questions were treated with a respect they little deserved. I would like to take this opportunity of placing on record the very great debt of gratitude I owe them all.

Among those I would like to thank in particular are the following: Mr Frank Aiken, T.D., Colonel Austin Brennan, Mr Ernest Blythe, Mr Gerald Boland, Mr John A. Costello, Mr James Dillon, Mr Patrick McGilligan, Mr Frank MacDermot, General Richard Mulcahy, Dr Michael Tierney, Dr C. S. Andrews, Colonel David Neligan and Mr John L. O'Sullivan, T.D., the late Dan Breen, the late Dr James Ryan and the late Gerard Sweetman. Major Vivion de Valera, T.D., was particularly helpful and provided me with some valuable insights I might otherwise have missed.

I would also like to thank the very many individual Blueshirt, I.R.A. and Fianna Fáil veterans with whom I have discussed the period, in home and hostelry over the past few years. They are too numerous to thank individually, but to each and every one I am profoundly grateful.

I have received very considerable assistance from my academic colleagues. To Dr John H. Whyte of the Queen's University, Belfast, I owe a particular debt for the manner in which he guided me through earlier drafts of this work. My colleagues in the Politics department at University

College, Dublin, Mr Brian Farrell and Mr Thomas Garvin asked many useful questions; Fr Fergal O'Connor, O.P., and Dr Patrick Masterson were friendly gad-flies. Mr T. P. O'Neill of U.C.G. was of great help, especially in the earlier and more desolate stages. Sr Benvenuta, O.P., of the History department at U.C.D. was of help throughout. I owe a very special debt of gratitude to my head of department—Fr Conor Martin. His understanding and encouragement over some very difficult patches were invaluable.

Mr Tim Pat Coogan was particularly helpful throughout.

Mr Jim O'Beirne made available to me the very valuable MS. of Captain Walsh's *General Eoin O'Duffy—His Life and Battle*, for which I would like to thank him, and also Mr Oliver Snoddy, through whom I met Mr O'Beirne. Mr Joe Carroll made available to me some very useful interview material.

The staff of the National Library were painstakingly helpful. A special word of thanks here to Mr Michael O'Clery for his assistance.

My uncle, Fr Joseph Nolan, C.S.Sp., of Rockwell College, provided me with some very useful comment and criticism and was at all times encouraging.

To Gus and Claire Martin a special word of thanks for their hospitality during the writing of the final draft—and much more besides.

Miss Mary Thompson who typed the final draft was flawless in the execution of her work—and a very pleasant working companion.

A final word of thanks to Ann, Mary, Michael and Tom for their help in compiling the index.

To all of the above I am extremely grateful and without their very considerable help this book would not have been possible. It only remains for me to add that all opinions and errors are solely my own.

MAURICE MANNING

UNIVERSITY COLLEGE, DUBLIN
October, 1970

1 Setting the Scene: The 1920s

THE blue shirt made its first appearance in Irish politics in April of 1933 when it was adopted as the official uniform of the already existing Army Comrades Association. The impact of this new movement was immediate and dramatic. Within a matter of months, it had members and branches in all parts of the state. Nothing like it had been seen before. It was new and vigorous and colourful. It was also unpredictable. Its coming coincided with a point in time when shirted movements were fighting for power in virtually every country in Europe and had attained it in some—movements as varied as the Blackshirts of Italy, the Brownshirts of Germany, Mosley's British Union of Fascists, the Spanish Falange, the Austrian Heimwehr, the Rumanian League of the Archangel Michael, Action Française, the Mocidade Portuguesa, the Legio Portuguesa, Quisling's Najonal Sambling, the Belgian movements Action Nationale, Legion Nationale, Rex and VNV, and indeed many more.

For the next two years, the Blueshirts dominated and overshadowed the Irish political scene, making those years two of the most exciting, bitter and turbulent in the history of the state. And then, almost suddenly, the movement disintegrated, soon to disappear with a finality that is almost inexplicable. The Blueshirt phenomenon was unique in the Irish experience, and though its life was short and it is now no more than a folk memory, it has left in its wake a residue of bitterness and a host of interesting and unanswered questions.

Although the Blueshirt movement was essentially a product

of the thirties—indeed, it is hard to see it taking the form
it did in any other decade—it would be impossible to understand it or the fears and hopes which attended its birth and
gave it its impetus, without reverting to the events and issues
of the previous decade. In the early days of the 1920s, and
in the events of that unhappy decade, can be found some
of the origins and many of the explanations of the Blueshirt
movement. It was in that decade too that the patterns of
Ireland's subsequent political development were laid down,
and the controversies which were to cause such hatred and
implacable hostility first appeared and then hardened into
irreconcilable differences.

*   *   *

On 6 December 1921, the Anglo-Irish Treaty was signed in
London, and one month later it was formally ratified in
Dublin by Dáil Éireann, which voted by sixty-four votes to
fifty-seven in its favour. The ratification of the Treaty was
to mark the end of the conflict with England. More omin-
ously, it also marked the end of the spirit of national unity
and sense of shared purpose which had characterised the
Sinn Féin movement from 1916 on. The defeated minority
in the Dáil refused to accept the validity of the Treaty decision, and, led by Eamon de Valera and Cathal Brugha,
withdrew. In April 1922, the Four Courts building in Dublin
was seized by Republican soldiers under Rory O'Connor.
The Civil War had begun and was to continue until the
final surrender of the anti-Treaty forces in April 1923.

The Civil War was fought on the issue of the Treaty.
The question was whether or not to accept it, with its obvious
limitations on full sovereignty—Dominion status, the Oath
of Allegiance and Partition—as the basis for the new state,
or to repudiate it completely and continue to fight in the
hope of full independence and unfettered sovereignty. Those
who accepted the Treaty were fully aware of the limitations
which it contained, but were prepared to accept it as a

basis for further future development, as a 'stepping-stone' to full freedom. It was felt, moreover, that to continue to fight in face of increasing British strength and depletions in I.R.A. ranks was unrealistic, and could easily jeopardise gains already made.[1]

Around the divisions caused by the Treaty the two groups were to polarise which have dominated Irish politics since that day. Whatever hopes remained of healing these divisions were dashed by the advent of the Civil War—a conflict more bitter, more vindictive and more brutal than the earlier fighting had been. It was a time characterised by confusion and desolation, destined to cost the country dearly in terms of property, life and morale. It was a conflict unrelieved by grandness of purpose or nobility of execution and its legacy was to poison political debate and behaviour for a generation to come.

The divisions born of the Treaty and nurtured by the Civil War were to harden and crystallise as the 1920s progressed, and indeed were made even more permanent and more deep-rooted by the events of that decade. By the end of the 1920s, political activity was dominated by two groups which shared a common origin but were now distinctively different, and mutually hostile. These two groups were by now the main political parties in a situation which had seen the restoration of a fair degree of stability.

First, there was the Cumann na nGaedheal Party, the party which governed the state from its foundation until 1932. This party was based essentially on that part of the old Sinn Féin movement which had accepted the Treaty, and indeed this was the only really fundamental unifying principle at the founding meeting of the party in April 1923. This was the party of those who had looked for leadership to Michael Collins and Arthur Griffith, and after their deaths the task of leadership fell to William T. Cosgrave. The leaders of this party were, for the most part, men who had been active in 1916 and in the post-1916 period, and many of its Dáil members had first been elected as Sinn Féin

M.P.s in the 1918 election. Cosgrave had taken part in the
1916 Rising, had been imprisoned and elected Sinn Féin
M.P. for Kilkenny in 1917. He had been a minister in the
first Dáil Cabinet and close to the centre of Sinn Féin
activity during all of the Anglo-Irish conflict. He had become head of government after the death of Collins, and
was in some ways a strange enough choice at that very
perilous and unstable time. He had none of the commanding
presence or imposing appearance of Collins, his style of
leadership was quiet and unassuming, and as a public
speaker he was forceful but businesslike and unadorned.
There was little of the mystique of leadership about him,
and his handling of his sometimes difficult colleagues was
firm but unassertive. As President of the Executive Council,
he did not set out to dominate his colleagues. Rather did
he seek to co-ordinate, conciliate and to act as a chairman,
always regarding himself as a 'primus inter pares'.[2]

The other members of his Cabinet who had been involved
in Sinn Féin included General Richard Mulcahy, Ernest
Blythe, who became Vice-President after the assassination of
Kevin O'Higgins in 1927, and the Minister for Defence,
Desmond FitzGerald. Mulcahy had succeeded Collins as
Chief of Staff, and later became Minister for Defence. He
had resigned his Cabinet position following the Army Mutiny
in 1924, but returned to the Cabinet in 1927. He was one
of the architects of the government's victory in the Civil War
and as such was deeply hated by many on the Republican
side. Blythe, a northern Protestant, had as Minister for
Finance been associated with a number of extremely unpopular measures including a proposal to cut the salaries of
police, civil servants and teachers before the 1932 elections,
and, most famous of all, his decision to reduce old age
pensions by a shilling a week. His manner was northern in
its directness and bluntness and was little burdened with
finesse.

Desmond FitzGerald was also a 1916 veteran and was one
of the most able members of the administration, although

his somewhat difficult manner was to cause a certain amount of strain between him and the army leaders. His contempt for opponents, which he rarely bothered to conceal, antagonised the politicians of the other parties.

Patrick Hogan, Minister for Agriculture, was a Galway solicitor, and was regarded by contemporaries as one of the big successes of the administration. Direct and vigorous, he was probably the best platform speaker of his party. He was also extremely realistic and pragmatic, and during his period in office he introduced a number of important and far-reaching reform measures.[3]

Patrick McGilligan was the youngest member of the Cabinet, and was identified with the important constitutional advances which were made by the Free State from 1923 to 1931, in which he played a major part. He was also the minister largely responsible for the Shannon Scheme.[4]

During its ten years in power, the policies of Cumann na nGaedheal were neither radical nor revolutionary. The Cosgrave administration sought to develop the institutions of the state on the basis already laid down. It attempted to restore the forces of law and order, to re-open the channels of trade and to develop the state constitutionally on the lines laid down in the Treaty settlement. As a result of this attempt to return to conditions of normality and stability, the party attracted the support of the entrenched and established elements in the community and was generally regarded, by both its own supporters and its opponents, as a conservative party. It drew its support mainly from the business and commercial classes, the professions and the bigger farmers, whose values and attitudes it reflected. That is not to say that its support was exclusively middle-class. It certainly numbered among its supporters many who belonged to none of the above categories—some perhaps who tendered it allegiance because of their belief in the validity of the Treaty, others perhaps who were followers of some individual leader such as Collins or Griffith, and probably others who, by some quirk of fate or circumstance, had been placed on the

2

Treaty side during the tortuous days of 1922. Nevertheless, having made these allowances, it would seem that in terms of policy, personnel and image, Cumann na nGaedheal showed all the signs of being a solid, pragmatic and orthodoxly conservative political party. Certainly this was the appearance it presented.

Warner Moss, an American political scientist who spent part of the 1920s in Ireland studying the Irish parties, noted that the party drew upon the local business leaders, the priests and the prosperous farmers, and he perhaps unfairly characterised it as the 'party of age and complacency'.[5]

It was a party too which relied heavily on voluntary and ad hoc arrangements in its electioneering. Little attention was paid during the twenties to establishing a strong organisational framework. Perhaps the problems of office at a period of reconstruction left little time for this type of activity, but during this time the party's network of branches and its organisational efficiency never equalled that of its main rival, Fianna Fáil, nor did it ever appear to grasp the possibilities inherent in mass organisation.[6]

The other major political force which owed its origin to the Civil War split had, by the end of the 1920s, become firmly established as a constitutional political party, and, as Fianna Fáil, now provided the official Dáil opposition to its erstwhile Civil War opponents. This decision of the defeated minority to accept and work through the constitutional framework which had been imposed by the Treaty was one of the most interesting and far-reaching decisions of that decade.

After their Civil War defeat, the Republican forces were dispirited and disorganised, with most of their leaders and very many of their supporters either in prison or on board the emigrant ships. Against all the odds, this group decided to contest the 1923 general election. Republican candidates made it clear that, if elected, they would not take their seats in the Dáil, but in spite of this and in spite also of the chaotic and disrupted state of their organisation, they managed to

win forty-four of the 153 seats in the Dáil. This compared
very favourably, under the circumstances, with the sixty-
three seats which the government party had won. As they
had promised, the elected Republicans refused to sit in the
Dáil, and, ironically, this abstention greatly strengthened the
position of the government, which now had an artificial,
though effective, overall majority in the Dáil.

The sense of isolation and frustration imposed on the
Republicans by their acceptance of a policy of abstentionism
was increased by the smooth functioning and growing stability of the government. The first frontal assault on this policy
of abstentionism came in 1926 at the Republican Congress
of that year. A motion was put forward in de Valera's name
to the effect that if the Oath of Allegiance was abolished, it
would then be possible to enter and use the Dáil. This
motion was defeated by 222 votes to 218, and the result was
interpreted by de Valera as a vote of no confidence in his
leadership, and he resigned.[7]

Two months later, Eamon de Valera presided over the
foundation of a new political party—Fianna Fáil. Most of
those who had been elected as Republican T.D.s in 1923
followed de Valera into the new party, including Seán T.
O'Kelly, Dr James Ryan, Seán Lemass, Frank Aiken, Gerald
Boland, Seán MacEntee and P. J. Ruttledge. By the mid-
1920s, Eamon de Valera was the undisputed and commanding leader among this group, enjoying a personal ascendancy
which was to persist for a further thirty years.

Although the new party refused to take the Oath of
Allegiance necessary to enter the Dáil, it started to organise
itself energetically and thoroughly throughout the country,
beginning at local level and aiming at a nation-wide network of parish-based branches. This work was executed
partly on the basis of plans which had been formulated by
jailed Republicans towards the end of the Civil War and in
the immediate aftermath. The process of organisation appears to have been largely under the direction of Seán
Lemass, but the party was fortunate to have at its disposal

also the majority of the anti-Treaty T.D.s, who provided the nucleus around which the new party was built as well as a ready-made leadership structure.[8]

In 1927, Kevin O'Higgins, the Vice-President of the Executive Council and probably the strongest member of the Cabinet, was assassinated. The government, greatly shaken, reacted with a series of stringent public safety acts and an Electoral Amendment Bill, the effect of which was to force Fianna Fáil either to enter the Dáil or to face political extinction. After a lengthy and agonising debate, the party decided to enter the Dáil. This was in July 1927. By entering the Dáil, Fianna Fáil ensured that all its future activities would be directed along constitutional lines and within the structural framework laid down in the Treaty.[9] From now until 1932, Fianna Fáil was to form the official opposition to the Cosgrave government.

Although the two main parties in the Free State, Fianna Fáil and Cumann na nGaedheal, shared a common source, and although their original difference was on a constitutional question, by 1930 the differences between the two groups were very considerable. Cumann na nGaedheal, as we have seen, had attracted to itself the support of the men of substance and property and was largely representative of the vested interests. It was respectful and deferential to the Catholic hierarchy, was heedful of the needs of the business community, orthodox in its financial policies, cautious in social questions and emphatic in its efforts to preserve law and order. In short, it was a respectable, middle-of-the-road, middle-class, conservative political party—albeit, a vigorous one.

Fianna Fáil, however, had as yet attained no such respectability, although its participation in the Dáil after 1927 did tend to confer on it an air of legitimacy which it did not have in its first year. Its support was drawn from all sectors, but mainly it would seem from the small farmers, the landless labourers and the industrial workers. As well as drawing much of its support from these less well-off sections of the community, it also found followers among those—and they were numerous—who had been alienated by some aspect or other of the government's policy. Its policies were far more radical than were those of Cumann na nGaedheal. It promised social welfare reforms, protection for Irish industry, the division of the larger farms, increased tillage and a breaking of the constitutional ties which bound the Free State to Britain. It also succeeded in presenting itself as being the more 'Irish' and more nationalistic of the parties. Its propaganda emphasised the Commonwealth role of Cumann na nGaedheal, and the support which that party attracted from former Unionists. It saw itself as the party of the 'plain people of Ireland' (a phrase rarely far from the lips of Fianna Fáil speakers in those days) and the legitimate heir of the Republican tradition.

Cumann na nGaedheal and Fianna Fáil were the two major forces in Irish politics in the 1920s. Although they had sprung from a common source, the issue of the Treaty had separated them and the experience of the Civil War had made this separation irreconcilable. The controversies of the 1920s exacerbated the existing divisions to such an extent that by the end of the decade the differences between the two parties appeared almost fundamental and made any possibility of a rapprochement appear very remote indeed.

Fianna Fáil and Cumann na nGaedheal, though the major and dominant political forces during this decade, were not the only ones. There was also the Labour Party and the I.R.A.

The Labour Party, which was the oldest of the three political parties, had been founded in Clonmel in 1912, and numbered amongst its founder members James Connolly and James Larkin. The outbreak of the Great War in 1914 meant that the party did not have an opportunity to contest a general election until 1918. The party then refrained from participating in that contest so as to give Sinn Féin a clear run and prevent the nationalist vote from being split. The party favoured acceptance of the Treaty and contested the

1923 election, winning fourteen seats. From then until Fianna Fáil's entry into the Dáil in 1927, Labour, under the leadership of Thomas Johnson, formed the official Opposition.[10]

Although Labour had supported Cumann na nGaedheal on the question of the Treaty, it was at variance with that government on most other social and economic issues. The increasingly conservative tone of the government's activities, its obvious understanding with the vested interests and its repressive anti-I.R.A. legislation was to alienate, before the end of the twenties, whatever Labour support it had originally won. After Fianna Fáil's entry to the Dáil in 1927, these two opposition groups—Labour and Fianna Fáil—were to find themselves at one on most major questions and increasingly in alliance against the government. But Labour made little real electoral headway during these years. In fact, it never held more than twenty-two seats in the Dáil and never looked as if it might break the supremacy of the two major parties.

Labour's failure to make an electoral breakthrough is largely, though not solely, a result of historical accident. Labour made its first appearance and bid for support at a time in the country's history when the dominance of constitutional issues virtually excluded all others. With political debate concentrated almost entirely on such issues as Home Rule, the Treaty, the Republic, Document no. 2, the Oath of Allegiance, Dominion status, Labour with its insistence on economic and social issues was to appear almost irrelevant. Then too, Labour suffered from the presence of the I.R.A. which, with its republicanism, radical socialism and revolutionary methods, was to be a magnet attracting many who, under more normal circumstances, might well have joined the Labour Party. There were two further factors. Labour was sectional in outlook and appeal, and never succeeded in broadening its base sufficiently to attract middle-class support. Finally, it was weakened by the conspicuous success of Fianna Fáil in winning to its side many small farmers, labourers, industrial workers, who, had they voted on class lines, might well have voted Labour. Consequently Labour was destined to remain through all these years a 'small party of moderate non-revolutionary men with little of James Connolly's radicalism about them'.[11]

Finally, there remains to be considered the I.R.A. which, as a sizeable, armed, un-uniformed, aggressive body, standing for full-blooded Republicanism, was a significant political force during these years. It sought the establishment of a thirty-two-county republic through force of arms, the elimination of all traces of British influence from the life of the nation and a reorganisation of the social and economic structure of the state. Although most of the leaders of the I.R.A. shared a disposition towards socialism, they never managed to achieve the same degree of unity or clarity on social issues as they did on their Republican objectives. According to one observer of the period, 'many of them had lived on the excitement of being on the run with a gun . . . while others . . . on account of their youthful experiences found it difficult to come to terms with bourgeois society . . . (they) were idealists without sense of law or order.'[12]

Fianna Fáil and the I.R.A. remained on friendly terms during these years. There was no formal link binding the two groups, but the many ties of past comradeship, the common objective of a thirty-two-county republic and a common hostility to the ruling Cumann na nGaedheal party ensured a mutual sympathy, understanding and willingness to co-operate. The I.R.A. regarded Cumann na nGaedheal as traitors who had betrayed the Republic, executed their fellow Irishmen and were now in league with the most conservative, reactionary and anti-national forces in the country. As such, they were absolutely outside the bounds of any toleration and were worthy of all the punishments reserved for traitors.

The I.R.A. in turn were distrusted and feared by the supporters of the government, many of whom saw in the socialist or iconoclastic policies of the I.R.A. a threat to property, law, and the status quo. To such people, the I.R.A. were nothing short of thugs and gun-bullies, through whom the forces of Communism would gain a foot-hold in the country.

It was around these groups that the political life of the Free State revolved during the decade following the Civil War. They were distinct and clearly defined groups whose political debate centred largely on the issues generated by the signing of the Treaty. It was a debate envenomed and inflamed by the memories of that war and its aftermath, and it was carried on in an atmosphere characterised by bitterness and an almost total distrust which made impossible any restoration of normal political relations. All of these groups were to play important roles in the events which led to the emergence, development and decline of the Blueshirt movement in the early years of the 1930s.

2 A New Government and a New Association

The new government

The last Cosgrave administration governed from September 1927 to January 1932. It had been returned at the second 1927 election, just two months after the death of Kevin O'Higgins, and it is now clear that the death of O'Higgins had a powerful psychological effect on the Cabinet, contributing to a hardening of attitudes and a tendency to favour caution and retrenchment. The government's new lack of adventurousness was also influenced by the presence of a strong and uncompromising Dáil opposition, which Fianna Fáil quickly came to be, and by the fact that at no time during these years, did it have an overall majority. It was in the field of external affairs that this government made its most notable advances, with Patrick McGilligan in particular playing a very distinguished part in the Imperial Conferences of 1926, 1928 and 1930. The advances in this area were especially important, as one of the strongest arguments in favour of acceptance of the Treaty had been that it provided the basis for rapid and far-reaching constitutional development. This prediction was largely fulfilled during the 1920s, and culminated in the Statute of Westminster (1931), the effect of which was to confer unlimited legislative power on the Free State government.[1]

In its handling of internal affairs, however, the government had not nearly so much success, and succeeded in antagonising a number of important sectional interests— teachers, police, civil servants and old age pensioners— through threatened pay cuts. Its anti-I.R.A. legislation was regarded as repressive, and its constant harping on the dangers of revolution and socialism, combined with a sometimes excessive pietism, was hardly likely to appeal to the new, younger voters. The charge, made by a subsequent historian, that, during its last administration, the government was 'overconfident of its own competence and reckless in its belief that a Fianna Fáil government would collapse on account of ignorance and inexperience', seems to have had some justification. Certainly, government speakers rarely troubled to conceal the contempt in which they held the ability and qualifications of their opposition counterparts. [2]

The term of office of this government was not due to expire until the latter part of 1932, but in January of that year, Cosgrave dissolved the Dáil and fixed the election date for 16 February. Cosgrave had two main reasons for moving forward the date of the election. He wanted to prevent the election campaign from coinciding with the Eucharestic Congress which was being held in Dublin in June, and he wanted to ensure that the Irish delegates at the Imperial Conference in Ottawa in July would have the confidence of the electorate. [3]

The election campaign, for which all parties had been preparing for some time, was a busy but peaceful one. Heckling at meetings—especially at Cumann na nGaedheal meetings—was frequent, but serious disruptions were rare. There were, in fact, only two major disturbances during the campaign. A Cumann na nGaedheal meeting which General Richard Mulcahy was addressing in O'Connell Street, Dublin, was subjected to sustained heckling and organised attempts were made to wreck the platform. The meeting was broken up and numerous arrests followed the police baton-charges which were needed to clear the crowds. [4]

The second major incident occurred in Sligo-Leitrim, where the Cumann na nGaedheal candidate, J. J. Reynolds, was shot dead. It was quickly established that the shooting was not a political one, but the incident did add to the general tension of the campaign. [5] In general, however, the campaign was conducted in a serious and orderly manner.[6]

Cumann na nGaedheal fought the election mainly on its record. It saw as its major achievements during the previous decade, the restoration of law and order, the suppression of violence, the constitutional development of the state as a co-equal member of the Commonwealth, and such economic measures as the Shannon scheme and the sugar beet factories. It stressed, too, the fact that it had successfully restored normal trading conditions, and that Irish agriculture now had a substantial share of the British market. Its election literature emphasised the extra-constitutional past of Fianna Fáil and its close links with the I.R.A. It warned of the instability which would inevitably follow a Fianna Fáil victory, and of the dangers of Communist infiltration. For example, in one poster, the red flag was placed partly over the tricolour and the legend read: 'We want no Reds here, Keep their colour off Your Flag.' Another poster, bearing the caption 'His Master's Voice', showed de Valera marching forward at the point of a gun-man's pistol. The most spectacular poster of all was a luridly coloured sheet, based on the famous Duffy's Circus, and entitled 'Devvy's Circus'. It featured 'Señor de Valera, World-famous Illusionist, Oath swallower and Escapologist', and much more in a similar vein.[7]

The Fianna Fáil policy was far more detailed and specific, promising changes over a wide area. These proposed changes included the abolition of the Oath of Allegiance, the retention of the Land Annuities, the establishing and fostering of Irish industry, the decentralisation of government, the elimination of large ranches and the division of such lands among small farmers and landless labourers. It promised too, the suspension of the Public Safety legislation and the release of all political prisoners. The election literature of Fianna Fáil highlighted the pensions and gratuities which had been paid to ex-members of the Free State Army by the government, and it alleged that there were strong connections between the government and the ex-Unionist and Freemason groups.[8] The amounts paid in gratuities and service pensions to some of the more prominent ex-members of the army, who now had Cumann na nGaedheal connections, featured in a number of widely distributed election posters.[9] Other posters depicted Cosgrave as taking orders from the ex-Unionists in the Kildare Street Club, and as making servile gestures to that group. The party's campaign was greatly boosted by the memory of the recently introduced budget cuts of Ernest Blythe, which provided Fianna Fáil with a ready-made basis of support amongst teachers, police, civil servants and old-age pensioners. The opportunity was not lost by party speakers.

The I.R.A. did not participate directly in the campaign, but under the slogan 'Get Cosgrave Out', it threw its strength behind the Fianna Fáil effort.[10] This caused no surprise, especially since Fianna Fáil promised that, if elected, it would immediately suspend the Military Tribunal and release all political prisoners.

The election resulted in sweeping gains for Fianna Fáil which increased its 1927 figures by fifteen seats. It would now have seventy-two seats in the new Dáil as against fifty-seven for Cumann na nGaedheal.

The detailed results were:[11]

Party	Seats	Votes	Percentage of total Vote
FIANNA FÁIL	72 (+15)	566,475 (+154,642)	44·6
CUMANN NA NGAEDHEAL	57 (−5)	449,810 (−3,254)	35·3
LABOUR	7 (−6)	98,285 (−7,013)	7·7
FARMERS	3 (−3)	28,972 (−45,751)	3·3
OTHERS	14 (+1)	129,665 (+13,133)	9·1

In winning fifteen new seats, the Fianna Fáil popular vote had risen by over 150,000 votes on the September 1927 figure, but at the same time, the Cumann na nGaedheal popular vote had dropped by only 3,000 votes. Thus it would appear as if Cumann na nGaedheal managed to maintain the bulk of its traditional support and that Fianna Fáil's gains were made largely among those who had not voted in 1927, and amongst the supporters of Labour and Farmers. Fianna Fáil's success in winning to its side the bulk of this new support can be attributed to a number of factors—the party's new respectability brought about by Dáil participation, improved organisational efficiency, a comprehensive and detailed policy, the help of the I.R.A. and finally the tiredness of the electorate after ten years of government by the same party.

The first meeting of the Seventh Dáil took place on 9 March, 1932. The *Irish Times* reporter present described it as 'a drab assembly, a mosaic of blue, black and brown figures blending into a colourless ensemble'. But the *Irish Press* reporter saw the assembly in a different light: 'No doubt where the mastery lies, and it is the mastery of youth over middle age. A curious thing is the youngness of the outgoing Ministry, with behind them a middle-aged, even elderly Cumann na nGaedheal Party, while opposite is a party with hardly a white head.' This first meeting of the new Dáil took place against a background of rumour and speculation concerning the possibility of a *coup d'état*. The possibility of the National Army refusing to serve under its former enemies was widely debated, and on 26 February, *The Irish Press* had spoken of 'a rumour to the effect that two Cumann na nGaedheal ministers and others are to attempt to obstruct the transfer of power to Fianna Fáil'. Although this charge was immediately denounced by Cosgrave as being 'grotesquely untrue',[12] it was later repeated in the Dáil by a Fianna Fáil T.D.[13] And it is easy to see how such rumours could have originated and spread, for the memories of the Civil War were still very vivid; many of the leading officers in both army and police had fought under arms against the new government. And on a more mundane level, the great publicity which Fianna Fáil had given to the gratuities and pensions paid to ex-members of the Free State Army may easily have given the impression that such pensions would be terminated or reduced by the government and that a series of purges was imminent. In the event, however, these rumours proved to be groundless and the worst fears of many of the Fianna Fáil back-benchers who entered the Dáil chamber on that March afternoon, some with revolvers in their pockets, proved without foundation.[14] The loyalty of the army and police force was to be unquestioned, and this de Valera was quick to appreciate.

The election of Eamon de Valera as President of the Executive Council was tense but smooth, with eighty-one votes for and sixty-eight against. His election was supported by the Labour Party and by a number of Independents, including James Dillon, the newly elected Independent T.D. for Donegal and son of John Dillon, the last leader of the Parliamentary Party.[15]

De Valera's Cabinet was more or less along the lines expected, with Seán T. O'Kelly as Vice-President and Minister for Local Government and Public Health. Frank Aiken was Minister for Defence, Dr James Ryan took charge of Agriculture, P. J. Ruttledge was Minister for Lands and Fisheries, Seán MacEntee had Finance, Thomas Derrig was in Education and Seán Lemass, the youngest member of the Cabinet, was Minister for Industry and Commerce. The only real surprise was the appointment of James Geoghegan as Minister for Justice. All the other Cabinet members had been founder members of the party, but Geoghegan had been elected to the Dáil for the first time in 1930 and had previously been a Cumann na nGaedheal supporter. This point was immediately noted by the I.R.A. which disapproved vehemently of his appointment.[16] But de Valera, by appointing to probably the most sensitive of all departments a man who had not taken part in the Civil War and who had not been involved in the controversies of the previous decade, could immediately demonstrate that his government was not about to embark on a series of reprisals and vendettas.

The first months in office of the new government were characterised by the speedy implementation of a wide range of policies and election promises—so speedy indeed that the Cumann na nGaedheal opposition at times feared the imminence of a new revolution.

On 9 March, just a few hours after de Valera had announced the composition of his Cabinet, the newly appointed Ministers for Defence and Justice visited Arbour Hill Barracks, where the political prisoners were being held. The ministers immediately compiled lists of names of those interned and ordered improvements in the food and general amenities. Frank Aiken warmly greeted one of the most prominent of the I.R.A. internees, George Gilmore, and they spent some time in conversation. The minister announced the government's intention to release all political prisoners as soon as possible.[17]

On the following day, twenty prisoners were released, including George Gilmore, his brother Charles, Frank Ryan and Seán Hogan who had been in jail since 1922, when he had been sentenced to life imprisonment for murder. On their release, the prisoners were greeted by a large crowd which included Madame Despard, Madame MacBride and Seán MacBride.[18] Three days later, large meetings were held in Dublin and Ennis to celebrate the release of the prisoners and warnings were issued to Cumann na nGaedheal that the hour of retribution had come. During the following weeks, the government continued to release political prisoners until all ninety-seven had been freed.[19]

On 18 March the Public Safety Act was suspended. This in effect meant that the Military Tribunal was dissolved and that the special powers of arrest and detention given to the police were withdrawn. It also meant the lifting of the ban on a number of organisations including the I.R.A., Saor

Éire and the Communist Party of Ireland. However, the I.R.A. demand that the Public Safety Act be repealed was not acceded to—the Act was merely suspended, giving the government the power to reintroduce it at any time.[20] In April the Minister for Justice announced that the C.I.D. would be reduced in strength and the head of the C.I.D., Colonel David Neligan, would be relieved of his position and sent on compulsory leave of absence. The I.R.A., however, wanted the total disbandment of the C.I.D., and were far from satisfied with a mere reduction made, according to the minister, on the grounds of 'economy'.[21]

De Valera argued that in following these policies, his government was not being dictated to by the I.R.A. His government hoped to get 'willing obedience to the law, instead of trying to secure it by coercive measures'. But he stressed, even at this early stage, that his government would not tolerate the presence in the country of private armies. His party, he said, 'stood for one government and one army'.[22]

One of the Fianna Fáil election promises had been the abolition of the Oath of Allegiance, and on 22 March, the Free State government made clear its position on this point. It stated that the Oath was not mandatory in the Treaty; that the people in the Free State had an absolute right to modify the Constitution as they desired and that there could be no normal relations between the two countries as long as one side insisted on imposing on the other 'a conscience test that had no parallel in treaty relationships between states'.[23] This declaration brought an immediate and intransigent reply from the British government, the Secretary of State for Dominion Affairs, J. H. Thomas, stating that the Oath was an integral part of the Treaty and could not be modified by the Free State government alone.[24]

The British intransigence in no way affected de Valera's position—and on 23 April, the text of a Bill to abolish the Oath of Allegiance was published. The Bill was passed in the Dáil after a number of lengthy and at times, bitter, debates.[25] It was introduced in the Senate on 25 May, but on 8 June was rejected by thirty votes to twenty-two. The Senate passed a much-amended Oath Bill on 28 June but the Dáil disagreed with these amendments on 12 July. The Senate insisted on its amendments. The Dáil refused to agree to them and the Bill was again passed by the Dáil in its original form.[26] This meant that the Bill would not become law for eighteen months, and if the Dáil was to be dissolved before the eighteen months had elapsed, the Bill would automatically lapse. Not surprisingly, this action of the Senate greatly angered the Fianna Fáil leaders and supporters and increased their already considerable dislike of that chamber.

The third major pre-election pledge of Fianna Fáil had concerned the non-payment of the Land Annuities to the British government. The Land Annuities, which dated from the 'Bright Clauses' of the Landlord and Tenant (Ireland) Act of 1870, were annual payments made by Irish farmers in order to repay the sums lent to them for the purchase of their land. The money was collected from the farmers by the Free State government, and as regards the land purchased before the Treaty, was paid over to the British National Debt Commissioners to meet the service of the loans raised for that purpose. The figure involved was somewhat more than £3 million per year, and more than £76 million were still to be paid. This sum de Valera proposed to apply to finance a scheme of de-rating to assist the small and productive farmer. The reason he said he could not remit the payments altogether—as the I.R.A. wanted—was because he still had to collect the annuities on the large amount of land purchased compulsorily since the Treaty under the Act of 1923, for the Free State Exchequer itself had to finance this transaction, which had been carried through by the issue of land stock instead of the payment of cash to landlords. The Land Commissioners could not remit the annuities of the tenants who purchased before the Treaty of 1921, and collect those of the tenants who purchased since the Treaty without causing tremendous confusion.[27]

3

On 1 July, the Free State government defaulted over the half-yearly payment of the £1·5 million due in respect of the annuities. Three days later on 4 July, J. H. Thomas moved a financial resolution in the House of Commons giving power to the Treasury to make orders imposing on any imports from the Free State into the U.K. duties up to a hundred per cent over and above any existing customs duties. This Bill became law on 11 July, and on the following day, the British Treasury made an order imposing a duty of twenty per cent *ad valorem* on live animals, butter, eggs, bacon, cream, pork, poultry, game and other meats of all kinds imported from the Free State.[28] Ten days later, the Free State retaliated by enacting the Emergency Imposition of Duties Bill, and the Free State list of retaliatory taxes included coal, cement, electrical appliances, electrical equipment, sugar, molasses, coal and steel.[29] The economic war had begun.

The speed and decisiveness with which Fianna Fáil had moved to implement its election pledges and the nature of the policies involved had caused considerable unease and apprehension in the Cumann na nGaedheal ranks. As 1932 progressed, the members of that party seemed to become visibly more alarmed at the course events were taking. The release of the I.R.A. prisoners was represented in the Cumann na nGaedheal newspaper, *United Irishman,* as an attempt by the government to intimidate the opposition and to threaten freedom of speech as well as increasing the possibility of Communist infiltration. It was claimed that the government was creating a situation in which armed reprisals would become a commonplace. Cumann na nGaedheal had opposed the attempt to abolish the Oath of Allegiance largely because it saw this as a deliberate and unwarrantable violation of the Treaty. It opposed the government's annuities policy, partly because it felt the agreement to pay the annuities was morally binding and partly too because it saw in the economic war a major threat to the livelihoods of the agricultural community.[30]

A new association: First appearance of the A.C.A.

It was against the background of events leading up to the election of 1932 that a new association made its first appearance, and it began to develop during the period when Fianna Fáil was implementing its new policies.

This new association was known as the Army Comrades Association, and it was officially formed at a meeting in Dublin on 9 February 1932—just a week before the date of the general election. The founding meeting had been preceded by a number of preliminary gatherings, organised mainly by Commandant Ned Cronin. This first meeting of the new association was quiet, and attracted very little attention, and the objectives of the association, issued after the meeting, were completely uncontroversial.

These objectives were:
1. To uphold the state.
2. To honour Irish Volunteers who died during the Anglo-Irish struggle, and eventually to raise a national memorial to them.

As its name suggested, the association was designed for old army comrades, and membership was to be confined to ex-members of the National Army, and to those members of the 'B' reserve and pre-truce volunteers who had aided the army at its inception but were unable to join up. The organisation declared itself to be non-political and non-sectarian, and pledged itself to guard the interests of its members, especially those who were in need.[31]

The first president of the Army Comrades Association, elected at the inaugural meeting, was Colonel Austin Brennan, a Clareman, who had had a distinguished record during the Anglo-Irish War, and whose brother was currently Chief of Staff of the National Army. The vice-president was Fr M. Drea, a Kilkenny priest, who had been a chaplain to the army. The secretary and driving force behind the founding of the new organisation was Commandant Cronin, from north Cork. Cronin had been very active during the Anglo-Irish War and during the Civil War. He was regarded by both friends and enemies as a man of tremendous personal courage and energy. He had, apparently, long felt the need for an organisation to look after the interests of ex-members of the army and to honour the memory of dead members. With that object in mind he had organised a number of meetings of ex-officers in late 1931. It was at these informal and unpublicised meetings that the decision to go ahead with the formation of an army comrades' association was taken.[32]

The first meeting of the A.C.A. in February 1932 attracted very little attention. Perhaps this was due to the fact that it occurred just a week from general election day, or because the event seemed of such little significance. The only newspaper which reported the meeting was the *Irish Independent,* and even here the story only merited an obscure paragraph.

This is somewhat surprising in view of the fact that there had been an organisation of officers and ex-officers of the National Army in the late 1920s—the National Defence Association—and this association had had a rather controversial and well publicised—if brief—period of existence. The National Defence Association had been formed at a meeting on 28 August 1929, and, unlike the A.C.A., included serving as well as former officers. Its main stated objectives had been 'the development of a higher standard of service among officers of the Reserve; the cultivation on the part of the public of an appreciation of the problems of national defence and the promotion of the welfare and comfort of the officers and their families'. The new organisation began with the approval of the Minister for Defence, Desmond Fitz-Gerald.

The National Defence Association had only been in existence a year, when the minister withdrew his approval. As a result, all serving and regular officers were forced to sever their connections with the association. The withdrawal of approval had occurred—partly, at any rate—because the executive of the association had expressed itself very dissatisfied with the administration of the defence forces. The executive made a number of serious allegations, which, if correct, would have amounted to a serious indictment of the way in which the army was being run. It alleged, for example, that there was no proper training in the army; that army conditions were worse than in any branch of the public administration; that there was no security of continued employment; that there was no prospect of provision for the future; that members were so unsettled and disturbed by erratic, and often biased methods of control, that the contentment and unity so essential in all armies had been rendered impossible. The executive also alleged that there had been cases of definite victimisation of officers, that the legal remedies provided for the investigation of grievances on the part of personnel had been ignored, and that flagrantly illegal attempts had been made to interfere with the impartiality of officers serving on court martial and bound by oath to administer justice.

The allegations had been made in a letter published in the *Daily Mail* on 14 November 1930 and signed by General Seán MacEoin, Colonel T. E. Day (retired), Colonel T. Fitzpatrick and Major H. E. McCorley (retired) on behalf of the executive committee. It was claimed that the association included amongst its members three T.D.s, the Commissioner of the police force (Eoin O'Duffy), many police officers, eighty-nine per cent of the serving army officers and seventy-nine per cent of the retired officers. Shortly after the compilation of this list of grievances, ministerial approval was withdrawn, and all serving officers had to resign from membership. Not long after this, the association went out of existence. Colonel Fitzpatrick claimed that the association had been suppressed by the government. He alleged that reserve officers like himself had their commissions withdrawn and that the organ of the association, *An tOglach,* had been taken over by the government and let die. And the main reason for all these actions, he claimed, was that the association had been critical in pointing out conditions in the army.[33]

Although less than fifteen months elapsed between the

dissolution of the National Defence Association and the formation of the Army Comrades Association, there does not appear to have been any connection between the two organisations. The Army Comrades was made up entirely of ex-members of the army, and had no formal links at all with the army authorities. Nor did it intend to comment upon conditions in the army. Its stated aims were rather those of a benevolent association, and it was open to all ex-members, not just officers as had been the National Defence Association.[34]

The new Army Comrades Association took no part whatsoever in the 1932 election, and no recorded reference to the formation of the association was made by any of the political parties. However, the work of setting up branches throughout the country went ahead, quietly but none the less with considerable success. The formation of these new branches merited very little attention in the press, apart from an occasional paragraph in local newspapers. A private A.C.A. convention was held in Wynn's Hotel, Dublin on St Patrick's Day, just five weeks after the inauguration of the association, and it was announced at this meeting that there were now eighty-seven branches in existence in twenty-four of the twenty-six counties. This convention was presided over by Colonel T. F. O'Higgins, in place of Colonel Brennan, who was suffering ill-health at the time. The meeting condemned the withdrawal by the government of the preferential treatment hitherto given to ex-soldiers in the awarding of public positions and contracts.[35]

Like the founding meeting, this one received very little attention in any of the newspapers, and the association was not as yet seen in any controversial light. Indeed, the generally unobtrusive and non-party political behaviour of the A.C.A. at this time can be seen from a study of *An Phoblacht* and *The Irish Press* of this period. *An Phoblacht,* as the official organ of the I.R.A., and *The Irish Press,* as the Fianna Fáil newspaper, were both hostile to Cumann na nGaedheal and carefully watched the activities of that party and its leaders.

No reference was made by either paper to the A.C.A. during this time (February–July, 1932), and indeed, had there been any suspicion of connivance between the A.C.A. and Cumann na nGaedheal, or had the Fianna Fáil or I.R.A. leaders seen sinister or dangerous portents in the existence of the A.C.A., then almost certainly their fears or suspicions would have been publicised by one or other of these papers.

This quiet and unobtrusive phase in the life of the A.C.A. was to last from its foundation in February to its reorganisation under new leadership in August 1932. But quiet as this phase was, it was also a time of steady and sustained growth for this as yet little-known and uncontroversial association.

3   The Blue Shirt Appears

The decision to change

During the first six months of its life, the activities of the Army Comrades Association had been quiet and uncontroversial. The effective leadership of the association had fallen to Dr T. F. O'Higgins, T.D., and at a special meeting of the A.C.A. executive on 11 August 1932, he was elected to the presidency of the association, in place of Colonel Brennan, who resigned because of ill-health. Colonel O'Higgins was a brother of Kevin O'Higgins and was at this time Cumann na nGaedheal T.D. for Laois-Offaly. He had been a member of Sinn Féin from 1917 and had been imprisoned both in Mountjoy and in Ballykinlar. He had joined the Free State Army in 1922, and in 1924 had become Director of Medical Services. He had resigned his commission in February 1929, and during the following months had been elected to the Dáil.[1]

The election of Dr O'Higgins to the leadership was to mark an important change in the role and policy of the A.C.A. For a start, the fact that the new leader of the A.C.A. was not alone a Cumann na nGaedheal T.D., but a member of one of the most important Cumann na nGaedheal families in the country and on very close terms with the Cumann na nGaedheal leadership, meant that henceforth it would not be so easy for the A.C.A. to claim with conviction that it was completely non-party. In addition, the membership of the A.C.A.—drawn from ex-members of the National Army—was likely to have an overwhelmingly large proportion of Cumann na nGaedheal supporters. Thus the accession of O'Higgins to the leadership was bound to attract the attention of the other parties.

Of even greater importance was the fact that the change of leadership coincided with a major change in policy. Immediately after the meeting on 11 August, Dr O'Higgins issued a statement which indicated the extent of these changes. He began by pledging the support of his association to 'the lawfully constituted government of the state' and declared their total opposition to Communism. He went on:

As an organisation we do not desire to meddle in politics, but we must be permitted to say that we regard as charged with extremely dangerous potential the new fashion of branding as traitors certain public men with whom we happen to have had the privilege of being associated in defence of the state. Should an Irishman come to harm as a result of 'traitor-pointing' the consequences may be a deplorable condition of reprisal and counter-reprisal which would bring discredit on our race.

Henceforth his association intended to protect the right of free speech for all:

We shall deem it our bounden duty to resist any counter-attempts to interfere with free speech or the free expression of opposition.

He instanced two members of the A.C.A. who had been attacked recently by 'I.R.A. or Communists or free-lances', and declared:

We will stand by our comrades . . . and aid the government in the vindication of the law.

He further attacked the government's attitude to the I.R.A., especially on the question of holding arms.[2]

He then went on to announce that his association had decided to add a volunteer division to its organisation:

We are now ready to enrol as volunteers all who feel the need for the existence of a powerful, steadying, moderate body of opinion in the country.[3]

No further details were given at this stage other than an

announcement by Dr O'Higgins that the A.C.A. would be willing to federate with any existing bodies

who consider the time is ripe for the creation of a composite body, with the object of neutralising the influence of those hidden forces of disorder which are operating in our country, and may grow into a ruthless tyranny if not checked in time.[4]

This announcement by Dr O'Higgins that the A.C.A. was to set up a volunteer force was unexpected. None of the newspapers had any idea that changes were imminent, nor had there been any public discussion on the matter. But the new announcement did create considerable interest and, during the next few days, there were many enquiries to A.C.A. headquarters from prospective members of the 'volunteer force'. In the next week, Dr O'Higgins elaborated on the change in policy and on the reasons behind it. He appealed to old comrades to join the association, telling them that at the present time 'the press was being throttled, and the courts were being intimidated'. By joining the new A.C.A., they could ensure that there would be 'no intimidation by the gun'.[5] He described, too, how the association had grown since its foundation. Although originally a small association, when the 'present government removed the preference shown to ex-soldiers on work being done out of public funds there was a considerable growth in strength'. But he continued to emphasise that the association was a peaceable one and that its main objectives were the protection of freedom of speech and the curbing of Communism. His organisation was not armed, nor could the members drill so long as drilling remained illegal.[6]

This new departure drew a quick reaction from President de Valera. He rejected completely the claim that there was a threat to free speech or that the opposition was being threatened. He was emphatic that there was no disorder in the country. Nor was there any Communism. The new force was 'unwanted and unnecessary'.[7]

The Irish Press, which reflected the official Fianna Fáil line, made its first editorial reference to the A.C.A. on 31 August. It accused Blythe and Mulcahy, whom it regarded as the instigators of the new body, of a 'reckless eagerness to re-awaken the passions of the Civil War'. It professed to see the A.C.A. as 'one of the most cynical things that has happened in Irish politics for a generation'.

Even more hostile was the reaction of the I.R.A. Up to now the I.R.A. newspaper, *An Phoblacht,* had not regarded the A.C.A. as a serious or significant political force, but it immediately saw the new O'Higgins-led body in a very different and sinister light. On 20 August in its first reference to the A.C.A., it described it as 'the new Fascist force'. It dismissed out of hand the A.C.A. claim to be a non-political body, insisting that the 'inspiration and leadership springs right out of the Cumann na nGaedheal Party'. It rephrased the objectives of the A.C.A. under the following headings:

(i) To promote clashes with Republicans and by thus creating confusion in the public mind, pave the way for an imperialist military dictatorship;

(ii) to uphold the British-imposed Treaty and Constitution and to frustrate the people's desire to end these;

(iii) to attempt to force Fianna Fáil to attack Republican organisations;

(iv) to enthrone blatant Fascist and economic and social reaction, and

(v) to safeguard the privileges—grants of land, army reserve pay—which the comrades were given as a reward for their services to imperialism.

Each week from 20 August onward, the paper carried strong attacks on the existence of the A.C.A., usually referring to it as the 'Pensioners', or the 'White Army', and most frequently describing it as a 'Hitlerite' force prepared to carry out a *coup d'état.*

From this point on, the A.C.A. was to grow rapidly in numbers and in political importance, and by the end of 1932

had firmly established itself as a major political force. Before
examining this rapid development, it is necessary to discuss
in some detail the factors behind the change in policy.

There appear to have been three principal reasons for it.
First there was the growing conviction among Cumann na
nGaedheal supporters that the I.R.A. and Fianna Fáil supporters were out to deprive Cumann na nGaedheal speakers
of the rights of free speech and assembly, and that this was
being done with the connivance of the government. Secondly,
there was a feeling that the forces of Communism were
gaining ground and were becoming a real menace. Thirdly,
there was the more mundane fact that the preference hitherto
given to ex-army men in the awarding of public posts no
longer existed and that now fears of possible victimisation
existed among Cumann na nGaedheal supporters. A more
detailed examination of each of these factors is necessary.

Fianna Fáil's election victory had been followed by a series
of meetings throughout the country, and at many of these
meetings, not surprisingly, exuberant speeches were made
and an aggressive attitude to Cumann na nGaedheal was
frequently in evidence. This aggressive note intensified with
the release of I.R.A. political prisoners, and at many of the
numerous country-wide meetings held to welcome home the
released prisoners, the government and people were exhorted
to deal strongly with 'the Cosgravite traitors'. There was also
a renewal of I.R.A. drilling throughout the country and a
new recruitment campaign was announced. The tone of the
I.R.A. weekly newspaper, *An Phoblacht,* grew more stridently
hostile and frequent calls were made for the suppression of
'Free State traitors' and for an end to their freedom of
speech. 'No free speech for traitors' was a slogan on many
I.R.A. lips at this time. An editorial on 12 March had referred to the Cosgrave government as 'the murderers of our
comrades'. On 19 March, Peadar O'Donnell, addressing
30,000 people in College Green at a meeting to welcome
released prisoners, declared he was 'glad the murder-
government was put out of power, but these men must be

put finally out of public life, they must never be allowed to come on a public platform'.[8] On 2 April, the I.R.A. Chief-of-Staff, Maurice Twomey, told the 10,000 gathered at the Easter Commemoration ceremony in Glasnevin Cemetery that henceforth 'their energies must be directed to exposing those who assisted English policy in Ireland'.[9]

The tone of these and numerous other such prouncements, coupled with the perceptible growth in I.R.A. enthusiasm and activity, was undoubtedly causing a sense of unease amongst Cumann na nGaedheal supporters. Ernest Blythe, General Mulcahy and Dr O'Higgins were foremost among those condemning the new developments. In May, for example, Blythe claimed the government was tolerating the I.R.A. because 'they wanted a machine for terrorising the voters at the coming election'.[10] The Cumann na nGaedheal newspaper *United Irishman* carried weekly denunciations of the growing menace of the I.R.A. An editorial on 23 July, typical of many such, expressed 'alarm at the growing strength of the I.R.A., which the government policy is permitting to become something like a real army. We confess we cannot understand why the government is afraid to tackle this mixed-grill of gangsters, neurotics and half-baked Communists'.

But the leaders of the A.C.A. claimed emphatically that their fears were based on something more solid than mere threats or inflammatory speeches. According to Dr O'Higgins, violence and intimidation had been a feature of Free State life since the advent of Fianna Fáil to power. In his first statements, O'Higgins attacked 'the hidden forces of disorder which were operating in the country' and had claimed that 'the press was being throttled and the courts intimidated'. And on 23 August, he published a list of acts of violence which were, he claimed, instrumental in convincing the A.C.A. executive that members and supporters of the previous government were in need of protection.[11]

The twelve incidents listed by O'Higgins occurred during the months of July and August 1932 and were as follows:

6 July: G. Dempsey, a member of the I.R.A., charged with possession of arms. Has since been released from custody without serving the sentence imposed on him by the court.

22 July: Australian flag removed from a house in Lansdowne Road.

7 July: Union Jack flagstaff cut down and flag removed at Dun Laoghaire.

13 July: Shots fired at a farmer in Co. Clare.

14 July: A 'hold-up' in Clontarf, where the masked raider was beaten off with bottles.

20 July: Thirty-five men turned up at Kinnity, armed with sticks, to prevent an eviction.

22 July: Revolver shots fired at a G.N.R. carriage.

25 July: Armed attack on a farmer's house in Fenagh, Co. Leitrim, by people who call themselves Republican police.

3 August: An attack by members of the I.R.A. on ex-Captain Gavin of Belcarragh, Co. Mayo. The raiders were beaten off and one member of the I.R.A. was wounded.

17 August: A number of men effected the reinstatement of a man evicted under a court order at Carrick-on-Shannon.

18 August: Shots fired at the house of W. Shaughnessy of Loughrea.

20 August: A Kilmainham family were turned out by I.R.A. men.

As far as the A.C.A. was concerned, the alleged threat to freedom of speech and freedom of assembly was the immediate and main reason for the decision to extend the association's activities. On the whole question of the existence and extent of this threat, however, there is a great deal of confusion and diametrically opposed viewpoints. The government spokesmen claimed that the country had never been more peaceful and that there was very little violence from March to August 1932. As far as newspaper reports and court prosecutions are concerned, this claim would seem to be substantially correct. The two most serious incidents were the breaking up of a Cumann na nGaedheal meeting in Cork in April and the preventing of Cosgrave and McGilligan from speaking,[12] and an attack on Bandon police station in March.[13] In many ways, the list supplied by O'Higgins seems to confirm rather than negate this view, as many of the incidents cited by him are comparatively minor and insignificant. On the other hand there is the equally important fact that a firm and unshakeable conviction existed among many Cumann na nGaedheal leaders and supporters that the I.R.A.—with the government's connivance—was about to unleash a campaign of terror and retribution. These fears found weekly expression in the columns of the *United Irishman* and were mentioned with increasing frequency in many Cumann na nGaedheal speeches. Survivors of the period, both prominent and obscure, are adamant in the belief that these fears had a solid basis in fact.[14] Certainly, given the history and memories of the previous decade, it is easy to see how such fears could be so widespread and deep-rooted and how they could be fanned by some of the articles and speeches of their political opponents.

An interesting comment on this question can be found in the December 1932 issue of *The Round Table*. The Irish correspondent of this periodical was John Horgan, a Cork solicitor, who had been an unsuccessful Cumann na nGaedheal candidate in the 1932 election. He was undoubtedly conservative in his views, but was regarded as an observer of integrity. He described the background to the A.C.A. decision thus:

Emboldened by immunity from prosecution, their [I.R.A.] followers throughout the country embarked during the summer on a definite campaign of petty outrages, such as attacking lonely houses, cattle driving, and calculated interference with the right of free speech designed to intimidate anyone who wished to criticise the policy of the present government, and eventually to prevent a free election.

And on the formation of the A.C.A.:

There can be no question that some such disciplined organisation was essential, unless we were prepared to face chaos and outrage during the coming winter.[15]

Thus it seems fair to say that there was a widely-held sense of fear among many supporters of Cumann na nGaedheal during mid-1932, and this sense of fear—whether it was justified or fanciful and exaggerated—was an important fact in determining the A.C.A. decision to enter on a new phase. It is clear that in the existence of these fears can be found one of the most fundamental explanations for the development of the A.C.A. along the lines it took.

A second reason given by O'Higgins for the decision to reorganise the A.C.A., was the danger of Communist infiltration. As 1932 progressed, it became increasingly common for Cumann na nGaedheal speakers to see Communism as a real and immediate threat to the country and to see in the I.R.A. a Communist or quasi-Communist body. This editorial in the *United Irishman* of 15 October clearly expresses this view:

The I.R.A. whilst being the main body is but one of the conglomeration of revolutionary bodies whose programmes are those outlined by the Third International, and whose activities, though falling in different spheres, are directed and controlled by the same leaders . . . There is no doubt that these leaders are in touch with the International Communist organisation, and that their object is to impress on us here a Soviet Regime, with all power and complete control of all activity in the hands of the few whom the upheaval would throw on top.

This obsessive fear of Communism was in no way unique to Ireland at this time—it was a common feature of political life in all contemporary European countries. In Ireland, the frequent and vigorous ecclesiastical condemnations of Communism; the constant admonitions about the need for vigilant alertness in the face of Communist infiltration; the very comprehensive and often undiscriminating application of the term 'communist', all combined against a background of unrest, uncertainty and suspicion to create a climate where anti-Communist scares became a potent political factor.

It is easy to see also how the I.R.A. could so easily be the focus for this fear of Communism. The policy of Saor Éire, a political wing of the I.R.A., had been condemned by the bishops in 1929;[16] some leading members of the I.R.A. such as Peadar O'Donnell and George Gilmore, were known to have strong left-wing views;[17] the general predilection of the I.R.A. in favour of violence rather than constitutionalism was easily seen as an attempt to foment the conditions necessary to bring about the Revolution.

The actuality of the Communist danger is another question. That the scares existed and that the I.R.A. was often identified with Communism in the eyes of its opponents is fairly clear. There is, however, no evidence to suggest that the Communist movement was widely organised or indeed had any foothold in the country. While many members of the I.R.A. may have held left-wing ideas, and while some may have been Communists, there is absolutely no evidence to suggest that the I.R.A. was in any way a Communist-front organisation or that the majority of its members had Communist leanings. In the 1932 election, the total Communist vote had not been greater than 5,000.[18]

The third main need for the A.C.A. as put forward by O'Higgins, was, in fact, a continuation of its original purpose —to protect the interests of ex-members of the National Army. Under the Cosgrave regime, it had been usual practice to give preference to ex-army men in the allocating of state and Local Authority contracts and in the filling of positions in the public service. The advent of the new government meant that this position no longer prevailed and when General Seán MacEoin tabled a question on this subject in the Dáil in April, he was told by the Minister for Industry and Commerce, Seán Lemass, that 'the men concerned will have equal opportunity with all others of securing employment in the categories mentioned'.[19]

4

Many Cumann na nGaedheal supporters now felt that there was discrimination in the awarding of many public posts, and the *United Irishman* began to cite, almost weekly, numerous allegations of corruption, favouritism and victimisation at local level.[20] Also of some importance in this respect was the pre-election publicity given by Fianna Fáil to the pensions and gratuities which had been awarded by the Cosgrave government.[21] The effect of this publicity was probably to cause many of the recipients to fear that under Fianna Fáil their pensions would be discontinued. These fears proved to be unfounded, but their existence was undoubtedly of importance in influencing the new development of the A.C.A.

The factors most responsible for influencing this change in A.C.A. policy would seem to have been fear and distrust. The fear was for the most part potential rather than actual—fear of violence, intimidation and suppression of free speech at the hands of the I.R.A., fear of a Communist infiltration spearheaded by the I.R.A. and fear of victimisation in public appointments at the hands of the Fianna Fáil government. Allied to this fear was an overwhelming sense of distrust—a distrust which was the product of the Civil War and a decade of bitter recriminations—in the democratic intentions of their Fianna Fáil opponents.

A worsening situation

In announcing the change of leadership and the decision to reorganise, Dr O'Higgins had intimated that henceforth members of the A.C.A. would provide protection for speakers at public meetings and would act as stewards and bodyguards for those whose meetings were in danger of disruption from hostile elements. This service was offered to all parties, and within a few weeks of the announcement—weeks which saw a big increase in A.C.A. membership—members of the association were busily engaged in this type of activity.

On Sunday, 4 September, members of the A.C.A. acted as stewards and provided a guard of honour at a Cumann na nGaedheal meeting which W. T. Cosgrave was addressing in Trim, Co. Meath. During the course of the meeting, A.C.A. members were involved in clashes and scuffles with some hostile members of the audience. On the same day, at a Cumann na nGaedheal meeting in Waterford, Patrick McGilligan was shouted down and a very stormy meeting had to be abandoned because of the threats and hostility of a large section of the audience.[22]

Three days later, similar scenes were repeated at an A.C.A. meeting in Sligo and eventually the platform was stormed and the tricolour was hauled down.[23] On 2 October, a Cumann na nGaedheal meeting at Paulstown, Co. Kilkenny, which was to have been addressed by Desmond FitzGerald, was disrupted and had to be abandoned.

The Paulstown meeting did not attract nation-wide attention, nor had it any wide significance. But as an example of the type of disruption now becoming more common at political meetings and of the temper of these meetings, this account of the meeting taken from the local paper, *The Kilkenny People* of 8 October, 1932, offers a valuable illustration:

The meeting was timed to take place at seven o'clock and it was arranged that the speeches would be delivered from the village pump platform which faces the parish church and Mr James Brophy, Co.Co. was to have been chairman. The main speakers were to have been Mr Desmond FitzGerald T.D., ex-Minister, and Mr D. Gorey, ex-T.D.

Mr Gorey motored into the village about a quarter of an hour before the scheduled time of the meeting, but Mr FitzGerald did not put in an appearance.

Immediately the devotions were over the crowd, numbering two to three hundred people, congregated around the pump, on the platform of which a table was placed for reporters. As soon as Mr Brophy appeared on the platform a number of young men took up positions around him. Mr Brophy at once pushed a young man off the platform, whereupon he was set upon, and he too was pushed off and roughly handled. Mr Gorey rushed to Mr Brophy's assistance asking the attackers 'not to strike an old man'.

There were shouts of 'Up de Valera'; 'We don't want the agents of England here'; 'Where are the Army Comrades now?'

Mr Gorey ascended the platform and he too came in for similar treatment. Blows were freely exchanged and angry political arguments took place between Mr Brophy, Mr Gorey and the 'opposition'. Mr Gorey was described as a 'Black and Tan officer', and there was a fire of questions hurled at him such as 'Who are the cowardly curs behind the hedge?'

Mr Brophy was subjected to questionings by a prominent local Fianna Fáil supporter as to local burnings. When Mr Brophy made reference to 'American robbers' there was a rush towards him and he was subjected to more rough handling.

Mr Gorey in the mean-time was in hand-grips with several young men and defended himself as best he could. An egg was fired at him and streamed down his back.

A local Civic Guard was in the centre of the warring activities, but his efforts to restore order were unavailing. During the disturbances Mr Martin Medlar, a well-known Fianna Fáil supporter, mounted the platform and proposed 'a vote of confidence in the present Government'. His remarks were greeted with loud cheers and cries of 'Up de Valera'.

The Rev. R. O'Brien P.P. with his curate Rev. Fr Griffin came from the church and passed through the crowd doing their best to restore quietness. Their presence seemed to be having the desired effect, but when Mr Brophy went towards the school-house, apparently with a view to holding a meeting there, a number of young men rushed towards him and he was again struck, his walking stick being broken in halves. During the ensuing scuffle another Mr James Brophy, from the village of Paulstown was knocked down and badly kicked on the ground.

When matters eased off a motor car containing three or four men drew up in the village and was surrounded by a crowd apparently under the impression that it contained Mr Desmond FitzGerald, but the ex-Minister was not there. Matters soon afterwards quietened down and Mr Gorey and Mr Brophy left the village amidst a salvo of party cries.

As the meeting had been disrupted before it could begin, it was reconvened a fortnight later. There was a large force of police present at this second meeting, and it was stewarded by over 200 members of the A.C.A. from Kilkenny, Carlow, Dublin and Tipperary. This meeting also attracted a number of British pressmen apparently hoping for a repeat of the incidents of a fortnight earlier. This time, however, the meeting passed without incident and all speakers were heard without interruption.[24]

On 9 October there occurred what were probably the most serious disturbances to date. Shortly before a Cumann na mGaedheal meeting in Kilmallock, Co. Limerick, was due to start, a crowd of about three hundred young men gathered in a different part of the town and, led by a group carrying banners, formed up four deep and marched in the direction of the Cumann na nGaedheal meeting, shouting anti-Cumann na nGaedheal slogans. The dozen police present moved into line across the road to meet them. When it looked as if this police cordon would be broken, about fifty members of the A.C.A. under Commandant Cronin rushed to the Guards' assistance. However, the crowd broke through this cordon and soon there was general turmoil. In the pitched battle which followed, broken poles were used as weapons in addition to sticks, hurleys and stones. Then suddenly, two shots rang out as Commandant Cronin fired over the heads of the crowd. The shots had the effect of causing many of those involved to run for shelter. Thus the first stage of the Kilmallock riots ended. All this time the opening speaker, Mr G. Bennett, had been making his speech.

Later during the meeting, further scuffles broke out and many shop windows were shattered by flying stones. After a while, comparative quiet was again restored with the 'opposition' grouped at one end of the street, the cordon of police a few yards away and the A.C.A. halfway between the police and the meeting. As Michael Hayes, T.D., the former Ceann Comhairle, began to speak, a renewed spate of stone-throwing began. A large jagged flint narrowly missed his head but struck one of General Mulcahy's body-guards full in the face. By this stage, many of those at the meeting were bleeding or swathed in bandages.

The next speaker was General Mulcahy, and as he rose
to speak, the disorder intensified. The General, according to
the *Limerick Leader* reporter, 'not satisfied with speaking from
the floor of the lorry, chose the higher elevation of the driver's
canopy whereon he stood silhoutted against the sky and
completely ignoring his opponents'.

Shortly after this, a rival meeting was begun fifty yards
from where Mulcahy was speaking. The main speaker at this
meeting was the Chairman of the East Limerick executive
of Fianna Fáil, Mr Michael Hayes.

The Cumann na nGaedheal meeting ended at half-past
four in the afternoon, and at five fifteen, the battle broke
out again and lasted for over an hour. The fighting was even
more fierce this time, with hurleys, sticks and stones being
freely used. Although it subsided round about half-past six,
the lorry load of A.C.A. members from Limerick were unable
to leave the town until a military escort—the members of
which were armed with rifles—arrived at nine o'clock. The
departing A.C.A. lorry was followed for about two miles out
of the town by a hooting and jeering crowd.[25]

While the Kilmallock incidents were the most serious in
which the A.C.A. were involved during 1932, the association
was involved in further incidents before the close of the year.
An A.C.A. meeting in Ennis on 21 October was broken up
when the platform was attacked and taken over by Republican supporters. The meeting was then addressed by Seán
Hogan who had recently been released from Portlaoise
prison.[26] On 6 November, a Cumann na nGaedheal meeting
being addressed by W. T. Cosgrave in Cork city, was completely wrecked amidst frequent and bitter clashes between
I.R.A., Fianna Fáil and A.C.A. supporters. As Cosgrave left
the meeting, his car was attacked and heavily stoned.[27]

This increase in physical violence was, not surprisingly,
accompanied by a greater bitterness in the speeches of many
of the leading politicians on all sides and by a more rancorous
tone in the partisan newspapers. As an example of this new
level of personal bitterness, the speech of Seán MacEntee at

Mallow on 2 October is noteworthy. After warning members of the A.C.A. that their pensions and whatever public positions they held would be forfeited if they remained in the association, he ranked W. T. Cosgrave with the classic traitors of Irish history—with Sadlier and Keogh, Carey, Nagle, McNally, Pitt and Castlereagh. He declared: 'We will have his name spat upon.'[28]

As the year drew to its close, the Army Comrades had their biggest meeting to date. On 4 December over six hundred members congregated in Carrick-on-Suir where their leader, Dr O'Higgins, was to address them. The *Irish Times* reporter present described the scene: 'Shortly after mid-day each detachment fell in under its leader, every man wearing the three-foil badge of the association on a white ribbon in his button-hole. Headed by a banner they marched in military formation, strong, along the main road to meet the cars bringing the speakers.'[29] Already it could be seen that members were wearing a distinctive badge. The army influence was apparent also in the way the Comrades were organised in detachments and marched in military formation. And at this meeting, O'Higgins again outlined the reasons for the existence of the association. He declared:

Our association was not brought into being for display or excitement, but because we saw that what we held dear was being trampled in the mud. During the summer everyone saw that democracy was in danger from the gun-man. Courts were brought into disrespect and became buildings in which witnesses perjured themselves. . . . If the country supported the A.C.A. movement order and stability would be restored, and this would lead to prosperity for all, and the fulfilment of the first objectives of the association—to find employment for ex-members of the National Army.[30]

During the last four months of 1932, under O'Higgins' leadership, the A.C.A. grew at a spectacular rate. From being a semi-benevolent association, inauspiciously inaugurated, it had blossomed into a major political force. By the end of the year, its leader was claiming a membership of

30,000. It was also incurring more and more the wrath and bitter hostility of Fianna Fáil and the I.R.A.

This new development in the A.C.A. coincided with increased activity on the part of the I.R.A. and with an increase in incidents of violence. Whether the new disquiet was a direct consequence of the new role of the A.C.A., or whether matters would have been very much worse had it not been for its presence, it is not possible to say. All that can be said with certainty is that as 1932 came to an end, the temper of political life became sharper, violence increased and the possibility of civil strife was more real than at any time since 1927. Certainly a note of semi-hysteria was in the air, as can be seen from this description of the contemporary scene in a *United Irishman* editorial of 10 December:

It has become all too apparent that Mr de Valera is leading the country straight into Bolshevik servitude. We do not say that he had set out with the object of creating a communist state . . . but whatever his intention may have been, or may now be, he is proceeding along the Bolshevik path almost as precisely as if he was getting daily orders from Moscow. His government is unmistakably out to demoralise the police force, and render them incapable of dealing with armed terrorists. His financial policy is leading inevitably to despoliatory taxation, which, rounded off with a dose of inflation, may be trusted to dispose of our Irish Kulaks.

The spread of the A.C.A. had probably been the most spectacular political development of late 1932, but it had not been the only one. The question of the Oath of Allegiance was still unresolved, but in October de Valera had the Governor-General, James McNeill, dismissed and replaced him with Domhnall Ó Buachalla. It was inevitable that there would be a clash between the Fianna Fáil government and the Governor-General, who was the King's representative in Ireland as well as being Head of State. Instead of abolishing the office altogether, as many of his followers would have wished, de Valera instructed Ó Buachalla to make the Governor-Generalship as unobtrusive as possible. Thus the new Governor-General, or *Seanscal* as he was officially called, took office at an annual salary reduced from £10,000 to £2,000, resided in a suburban house and not in the Vice-Regal Lodge, and took no part in any public functions. It was in 1936, after the abdication of King Edward, that the office of Governor-General was formally abolished by Mr de Valera's government.[31]

The economic war was prosecuted vigorously by both governments. The trade figures for August 1932 give an indication of the immediate effects on Irish exports in the first full month of the conflict:

Imports were down by £774,022 on the August 1931 figures. Exports were down by £1,890,351.

The adverse balance for the month was £1,433,204 as against £316,875 for August 1931.

The cattle trade suffered a loss of £901,616 for the month. Two-thirds of the market for bacons and hams was lost. Four-fifths of the market for poultry and half the butter market disappeared.[32]

Reports soon began to circulate that many farmers faced with a slump in prices and with the loss of their export markets, were refusing—or neglecting—to pay their land annuities.

In September, partly as a direct consequence of the worsening agricultural situation, a new political party was founded. It was made up of a number of Independent and Farmers T.D.s in the Dáil, brought together by Frank MacDermot and James Dillon. MacDermot, a member of an old Roscommon family, had seen active service in the First World War and had later stood unsuccessfully as a Nationalist candidate in Belfast. He was elected to the Dáil for the first time in 1932, and before long, the futility of being an Independent convinced him of the need to form a new party. Under the joint leadership of James Dillon and himself, the new National Centre Party was launched in September 1932. Its policies sought an immediate end to the economic war, the eradication of Civil War bitterness and what it termed 'a more realistic' approach to Northern Ireland. The party could be expected to gain considerable farming support, as well as making a strong appeal to the remaining supporters of the Parliamentary Party, and it was more likely to cut across Cumann na nGaedheal rather than Fianna Fáil support.[33]

The 1933 election

When the Dáil recessed for the Christmas vacation in mid-December, Mr de Valera had given no indication that he was contemplating a dissolution and new election. The matter had not been discussed nor even mentioned in conjecture by any of the political correspondents, and consequently it came as a general surprise when, on 2 January 1933, Mr de Valera announced that the Seventh Dáil was being dissolved and that there would be a general election on 24 January.[34]

This sudden decision came as a surprise even to some of his own ministers.[35] However, it was quickly seen that there were a number of very compelling reasons behind it. First of all, he felt that his position in the negotiations with the British government would be greatly strengthened if his policies and government received popular endorsement at home. Secondly, he did not have an overall majority in the 1932 Dáil, but was dependent on the support of Labour. There were indications of restiveness on the part of the Labour Party, which was not fully happy with some aspects of his policy, and had called for more courageous leadership from the government.[36] Thus he could not fully count on Labour support on all issues and felt that his freedom of manoeuvre was somewhat circumscribed. Thirdly, there were indications that an attempt was being made to unite the various anti-Fianna Fáil opposition groups. In December, the Lord Mayor of Dublin, Alderman Alfred Byrne, T.D., who was a pro-Cumann na nGaedheal Independent T.D., had been attempting to bring the main opposition groups together to form a united front.[37] These moves had been tentative and had excited little enthusiasm, but by calling a sudden election, de Valera very effectively forestalled them. Finally, there were four by-elections pending, and a defeat in any one of these could be interpreted as a setback for his government.

By dissolving the Dáil on 2 January, only three weeks were available for campaigning—three weeks moreover at the very height of winter. In addition, the fact that the last election was only nine months past, meant that all parties, and especially the smaller ones, would find their resources severely strained. But in spite of these limitations, the prediction of the *Irish Times* political correspondent that the campaign was 'likely to be one of the fiercest and most fiercely contested in the history of the state' was to be largely justified.[38]

Fianna Fáil's election policy was on lines very similar to the policy of the previous year. The policy promised internal political peace based on the abolition of the Oath, the retention of the Land Annuities and their reduction by half. Tillage was to be greatly increased and there would be further protection for Irish industries. Later in the campaign, de Valera announced that if Fianna Fáil won, he would abolish 'the Senate as at present constituted' and substantially reduce the number of seats in the Dáil. The party nominated in all 103 candidates, just one less than at the previous election.[39]

Cumann na nGaedheal's policy was little different to that presented in 1932, except that it promised to end the economic war in three days, reduce the annuities by half, and suspend payment of them for two years. The party also promised that the tariff structure would not be altered without careful investigation. The party put forward eighty-five candidates, eighteen fewer than Fianna Fáil and sixteen fewer than in 1932.[40]

Labour, worse hit financially than either of the major parties, put forward only nineteen candidates, twelve fewer

than in 1932.[41] The Centre Party had twenty-six candidates
in twenty-one constituencies. Six of these candidates were
outgoing T.D.s.[42]

The position of the I.R.A. was not as clear as it had been
in 1932, and at first it refused to come out clearly on either
side. An editorial in *An Phoblacht* on 7 January accused
Fianna Fáil of 'professing republican and even revolutionary
aims and yet doing little to give effect to them':

> In contrast to its professions are its practices: for instance the
> jailing of Republicans because they hold arms for the defence of
> Ireland, or because they refuse to recognise the legality of British-
> created writs in Ireland. . . . The coercive legislation of the
> imperialist regime has not been repealed. . . . The C.I.D. and
> military forces which enforced coercion during the previous
> regime have not been disbanded. . . . No practical steps have been
> taken towards breaking the connection with the British Empire.

A week later, however, the Republicans had decided on
their election strategy, and this was outlined in a *Manifesto
to the Irish People*, published by the General Convention of
Oglaigh na hÉireann—the I.R.A. The manifesto urged 'our
members and the mass of nationalist opinion that looks to
us for leadership, to work and vote against the Cosgrave
candidates and their so-called Independent allies. In practice
this means that the Fianna Fáil government should be assisted into office again'. But this support was by no means
unqualified:

> We do not commit ourselves in any way to acceptance of the
> policy of the Fianna Fáil Party. Reviewing the record of that
> party during its term of office as the Twenty-Six-County Govern-
> ment we see evidence of its weakness in face of Cumann na
> nGaedheal, and its inability or unwillingness to achieve Re-
> publican aims, and we note with dismay its attempt to stabilise
> and build up an economic system which, for all that it alleviates
> unemployment at the moment, will perpetuate the evils of social
> injustice. We call on the people to return that government, but
> at the same time to see that the youth of the country are left
> free to arm and train, and that soldiers of the I.R.A. now in

prison be released forthwith.. . . . And we appeal to the Irish people, once the election is over, to rally for a free United Irish Republic, wherein the great common people will be enthroned, and the Irish Republican Army will be their servants.[43]

The official attitude of the A.C.A. to the election was outlined in a directive issued on 6 January following a meeting of the association's executive. This directive laid down that during the coming campaign, the A.C.A. would be strictly neutral as far as parties were concerned. But the association would strive to implement its main policy which was to ensure free speech and to prevent intimidation. Members of the association would attend meetings of any party to which they were asked to afford protection.[44]

When the list of candidates standing in the election was published, however, it quickly became evident that the non-partisanship of the A.C.A. was open to serious question. At least five people prominently associated with the A.C.A. were standing as Cumann na nGaedheal candidates—Dr O'Higgins in Laois-Offaly, Ernest Blythe in Monaghan, General Mulcahy in Dublin City North, Commandant Cronin in East Cork and Colonel Jerry Ryan in Tipperary.

The campaign began immediately upon de Valera's announcement of the dissolution and 3 January was a day of intense electioneering activity. The same hectic pace prevailed throughout the entire campaign and the violence which characterised the closing months of 1932 was much in evidence. On 6 January, there were continuous clashes between members of the A.C.A. and opponents during a meeting which was being addressed by O'Higgins at Portarlington. It is interesting to note a description of this meeting in *The Irish Times* of 7 January, which shows the readiness of both sets of supporters for combat:

When it was seen that the interruptions would continue, about forty members of the A.C.A. moved towards the young men who were making the row. Dr O'Higgins asked his men to stand where they were, and then, addressing the interrupters, said, 'You men know, as I know, that the men behind me are the best, and, if it comes to a fight, the toughest element in the country. We stand for fair play for all parties; but if only one party is to have fair play in this election, we are going to see that all parties are put on level terms. It is very little satisfaction to us to be put in a position to defend Cumann na nGaedheal meetings, while other parties can hold their meetings in perfect peace. I want to say now that if Cumann na nGaedheal is prevented from holding meetings in any town, or anywhere in the Free State, we are going to secure that no other party will be allowed to hold a meeting here either.'

Two days later, what were probably the most serious incidents of the campaign occurred in Dublin at a meeting being addressed by General Mulcahy. The meeting was taking place in O'Connell Street and, according to the reporters present, a section of the crowd made 'determined efforts to cause disturbances'. The meeting was completely wrecked and over fifty people were injured in the police baton-charges and during the clashes between members of the A.C.A. and their opponents. On the same day, there were frequent disturbances at a Cumann na nGaedheal meeting in Cliffoney, Co. Sligo, and that night, attempts were made to wreck a Cumann na nGaedheal meeting in Rathmines. A.C.A. members were present at both meetings.[45]

The intensity of the violence at this early stage—the campaign was just three days old—suggested that matters could very easily get out of hand, and on the day following the O'Connell Street riots, de Valera summoned the Commissioner of the Police, General Eoin O'Duffy. He told O'Duffy that, as Commissioner, he was directly responsible to him for the maintenance of good order during the campaign, and that the entire police force and, if necessary, the army, were at his disposal. There were further consultations on the following day and then a strictly-worded notice was issued to the newspapers condemning the incidents of the previous few days and warning that the entire resources of the state were at the disposal of the Commissioner for the maintenance of order, and that he was determined to see that order and freedom of expression were preserved.[46]

In spite of this warning and the increased police activity which followed it, there were further incidents during the campaign—none of which, however, were as serious as those which took place in O'Connell Street. On 11 January attempts were made to wreck a meeting which was being addressed by General Seán MacEoin in Longford.[47] On 16 January a meeting of the National Centre Party at which Frank MacDermot was speaking, was broken up at Arigna.[48] Then in Tralee on 22 January, there were serious disturbances at a Cumann na nGaedheal meeting at which W. T. Cosgrave was speaking. Clashes between Army Comrades and their opponents were frequent and there were several baton-charges by the police. In all, over fifty people were reported injured in the affair. On the same day, there were less serious disturbances at Cumann na nGaedheal meetings in Dublin, Newcastlewest and Listowel.[49]

Members of the A.C.A. played a very prominent part in the election campaign and acted as stewards and bodyguards at Cumann na nGaedheal and Centre Party meetings. For this, they were warmly thanked by these parties. Frank MacDermot was to claim later that he 'doubted very much whether there could have been anything like freedom of speech had it not been for the A.C.A.'[50] This view was stressed in each issue of the *United Irishman*.[51] But as far as Fianna Fáil and the I.R.A. were concerned, the presence of the A.C.A. was blatantly provocative and one of the chief causes of many of the disturbances. *An Phoblacht* alleged that members of the A.C.A. were acting aggressively. De Valera claimed that the activities of the A.C.A. during the campiagn were a constant danger to public peace and added considerably to the difficulties of the police in protecting order.[52]

The A.C.A. was also to be the object of another controversy during the campaign. After returning from the Imperial Conference in Ottawa, Seán T. O'Kelly had alleged that the British government favoured the A.C.A. and saw in it the best means of defeating de Valera's policy and even of creating civil war.[53] This statement received wide publicity, and was repeated by Mr de Valera, who was even more specific:

When a certain organisation was forming here Mr J. H. Thomas in Ottawa told Mr Seán T. O'Kelly 'we need not have any question of settling with you because you will have another civil war in Ireland in another few months'.[54]

Thomas denied this statement, or that he had referred to the A.C.A. or to the possibility of civil war when discussing Anglo-Irish relations with Irish ministers in Ottawa.[55]

Against this background of bitterness and distrust, the election took place. *The Irish Times,* the voice of Irish Unionism, had thrown its support fully behind Cosgrave, urging its readers to 'fix their minds on their responsibility to their country, to their Empire and to their own responsibility',[56] and to vote Cumann na nGaedheal. This endorsement, however, was not to prove enough, and the result of the election vindicated fully de Valera's political judgement in calling the snap election. His party was returned with an overall majority—the first time any party had achieved this since the foundation of the state. The result was as follows:[57]

Party	Seats	Votes	Percentage of Total Vote
Fianna Fáil	77 (+5)	691,758 (+124,000)	49·7
Cumann na nGaedheal	48 (−9)	419,498 (−40,000)	30·5
Labour	8 (+1)	79,210 (−19,000)	5·7
Centre Party	11 —	126,906 —	9·1
Others	9 (−5)	68,954 (−60,711)	5·0

Thus, for the second time in under a year, de Valera had defeated Cosgrave at the polls, and this time, the defeat was decisive and overwhelming. Fianna Fáil got the biggest vote received by any party in the history of the Free State and now, with seventy-seven seats, was no longer dependent on Labour for its overall majority. De Valera could regard the result as a popular vindication of his major policies and feel that his position, both in his negotiations with Britain and in domestic affairs, was greatly strengthened.

For Cumann na nGaedheal, the result was little short of disastrous. The feeling within the party that a Fianna Fáil government could not last longer than a year, and would inevitably disintegrate through incompetence and inexperience, was rudely shattered, and Fianna Fáil was now securely lodged in power. The opposition party's popular support had declined further and with a loss of another five seats it was now fourteen short of its pre-1932 position. The party was damaged too by the emergence of the new Centre Party, which had won from it some important rural seats. Finally, one of the party's most prominent front-benchers, Ernest Blythe, lost his seat in Monaghan.

When the Dáil reassembled on 8 February, de Valera was re-elected President of the Executive Council by eighty-two votes to fifty-four. With one important exception, his Cabinet was the same as in 1932. The Minister for Justice, James Geoghegan, whose appointment and performance had been strongly condemned by the I.R.A. during 1932, was not re-appointed. His place was taken by the former Minister for Lands and Fisheries, P. J. Ruttledge, with Senator Joseph Connolly moving to that department, and Gerald Boland becoming Minister for Posts and Telegraphs.[58]

*   *   *

As has already been mentioned, the activities of the A.C.A. during the election campaign had incurred the displeasure of Fianna Fáil and the I.R.A. There were some, too, within

5

the A.C.A. itself, who felt that the association was losing sight of its original objective. At a meeting of the A.C.A. executive on 10 February, a motion was put forward in the name of Commandant Frank Bolster which, if passed, would have made the organisation completely non-political. The motion was defeated and Commandant Bolster resigned from the A.C.A. After resigning, he claimed that at the recent election, contrary to the original intention of the association, the A.C.A. had been identified with one particular political party. He was of the opinion that in all its actions during the campaign, the A.C.A. was strictly a political association in every sense of the word. He claimed that the physical and moral support of the leaders and members of the association was given exclusively for the benefit of a certain political party. He said also that three of the leading members of the A.C.A. executive had gone forward as candidates of that party during the election.[59] This criticism by Bolster attracted very little attention, and the resignation six days later of the chairman of the Mallow branch of the A.C.A., Lieutenant J. J. O'Driscoll, received even less notice. O'Driscoll resigned because, he claimed, 'the organisation was not non-political'.[60]

These resignations had little noticeable effect on the A.C.A. and aroused no recorded comment. On 14 February a meeting was held in Dublin which was to mark a further stage in the development of the association. The first stage had lasted from the time of its foundation in early 1932 until August of that year, during which time it was, or certainly appeared to be, a non-political, benevolent association of ex-comrades. The second stage began with the accession of O'Higgins to the leadership in August 1932, followed by the emergence of the A.C.A. as a major force in political affairs. And now at this meeting of the association's national executive on 14 February, it was decided to further extend the scope of activities and methods of operation of the association.

It was stressed in the statement issued after this meeting that the fundamental principles of the A.C.A. would remain unaltered—opposition to Communism, the safeguarding of ex-servicemen's interests, and the protection of public meetings where necessary in order to preserve freedom of speech and assembly. Now, however, in order to help it carry out these objectives more efficiently, a 'distinctive badge or uniform' would be adopted and parades and route marches would be held on suitable occasions.[61]

No reason was given for this decision to adopt a badge or uniform other than that it would help the members to carry out their aims more efficiently. Nor was it announced immediately what form this 'distinctive badge or uniform' would take. Up to now, there had been no official emblem but many members had taken to wearing an emblem on a three-foil badge, as at the Carrick-on-Suir meeting. The question of a badge or uniform was next discussed at a meeting of the national executive on 24 March.[62] It appears that the idea of adopting a distinctive shirt as the uniform of the movement was suggested by Commandant Cronin and found general favour with the members of the executive. O'Higgins suggested that the colour be grey, but after some discussion, Blythe's proposal that the colour be blue was adopted.[63] After the meeting, it was officially announced that henceforth, the distinctive dress of the movement was to be a blue shirt with shoulder straps and black buttons. Members would also be expected to wear a black beret.[64]

No reason was given for this decision to adopt a shirt. One of those who approved of the idea and was at the meeting when the decision was taken, claims that there were two main factors which influenced the executive. First it was hoped that the provision of a common uniform would increase the bonds of comradeship among the members. The second reason was more practical: by providing a distinctive uniform, it would be possible to prevent a recurrence of the incidents at Trim the previous year when two groups of Army Comrades from different areas had each mistaken the other for the opposition and had become engaged in combat. The wearing of a uniform would prevent the possibility of such a future clash and aid general efficiency at meetings.[65] The question immediately arises as to what extent this decision to adopt the blue shirt was due to the influence or example of continental Fascist movements. By 1933, the major Fascist movements, especially Mussolini's, were well known in Ireland—certainly they were well known to those who were politically aware. There was no 'shirt' tradition in Irish politics or in Irish tradition and it would be asking altogether too much to expect that this particular development, at this particular point in time, was not in some way, connected with the presence of shirted movements in Europe. Indeed it is hardly possible that there can be any doubt on this point—that the shape and form the Army Comrades now took was a result of continental developments, and that these influenced them.

The A.C.A. leaders however, were quick to deny any such influence, and from the very start, the *United Irishman* insisted that the shirt was being adopted to promote comradeship, obliterate class distinctions and as an aid to efficiency in the work being carried out.[66] The opponents of the A.C.A. however, were immediately to detect sinister implications in this new development. It was suggested that the decision had been precipitated by Cumann na nGaedheal's two electoral defeats; that the decision was born out of a despair of democratic processes and was a prelude to an all-out assault on the institutions of democracy. These allegations in turn were stoutly denied by the A.C.A. leaders who claimed this new move was an attempt to prop up the democratic structure against attacks from the left.

It is difficult from this point in time, and with scanty documentation, to uncover the real motives behind the decision. It is possible that the motives of the members of the executive were mixed and may have been in some cases not altogether clear. But it is possible that some members of the A.C.A. executive saw in a Fascist-type movement the only hope of ousting Fianna Fáil or else regarded it as a means of national regeneration. Fascism, after all, at this stage had few of the opprobrious connotations it was later to aquire. Mussolini, Dollfuss and Salazar were all respected leaders of Catholic countries—countries, moreover, which had had historic ties with Ireland. It would be surprising if this train of thought was not important in influencing to some extent the adoption of the blue shirt. But it must also be recognised that the decision may have appealed to others for the reasons officially given—increasing comradeship and aiding the efficient protection of speakers at public meetings.

In any event, the blue shirt made its first public appearance at the Kilkenny County convention of the A.C.A. on 8 April 1933—just two weeks after the national executive had made its decision.[67] A week later, Ernest Blythe was photographed wearing a blue shirt at an A.C.A. 'at home'.[68] The immediate reaction to these new developments was very varied. The Cumann na nGaedheal newspaper, *United Irishman,* was most enthusiastic and began to devote more and more space to the activities of the Army Comrades. On 11 March, it could claim that the A.C.A. was becoming 'a civilian corps d'élite'. The article continued: 'Scarcely a trace of the original benevolent society of ex-Army men remains. However, the best of all the original members are still in it . . . and there are very many younger recruits. Great responsibility rests on them for bringing the nation in safety through the dangers that threaten it from the left and the right.' Then in late March, the paper began to provide a weekly column of notes and comments on A.C.A. activities written by 'Onlooker'. (It was later alleged that 'Onlooker' was in fact Ernest Blythe.) In May an article appeared which chided some Cumann na nGaedheal members 'who are chary about giving real encouragement to the militant body of which Dr O'Higgins is head'. The writer saw three possible reasons for this 'attitude of reserve' and they were: distrust of the A.C.A. because members of other parties were included in its ranks, jealousy that it might some day rival Cumann na nGaedheal, and fear that some hot-headed comrades might get out of hand and cause trouble. The article went on to discount these fears:

We can only say that in our opinion there is no justification for any member of Cumann na nGaedheal failing to give his full support to the A.C.A., and to join it if he is young enough and otherwise free. The A.C.A. has vital national work to do and needs the support of men of goodwill of all parties in order that it may do it efficiently. It will not injure any constitutional political party, and it has already developed a spirit of discipline sufficiently strong to ensure that none of its members will overstep the bounds of order and good sense.[69]

But a new and more militant note was also discernible and especially in the writings of 'Onlooker'. For example: 'Everything points to the probability that within the next year or so, democracy will be preserved in the Free State only by the strong hands and stout sticks of the citizens enrolled in the A.C.A.'[70] And later in the same article: '. . . established to meet a dastardly attack, it (A.C.A.) relies not on persuasion but on combat. It is organised for combat and it wants members who will not shrink from combat if the sight of preparedness fails to frighten off attack.'[71] In a further article he urged A.C.A. members to arm with truncheons when entering a hostile area, 'but never to give unnecessary offence or provocation'.[72] A month later, a new line of thought appeared which was shortly to be repeated in more forceful terms. 'Onlooker' claimed that younger members of the A.C.A. 'think that all parliaments gabble too much, and they are not at all sure that the national will can be properly ascertained by merely counting heads'.[73]

Side by side with this type of article, there was the growth and spread of the wearing of the blue shirt, and soon it was a common sight in all parts of the country. 'Onlooker' called for new and militant songs for the association and urged members to use the new Blueshirt salute. On 20 May, he told his *United Irishman* readers that 'personally, I intend to salute by raising my right hand full length above the shoulder, with the palm to the front'. Before long, the use of this salute too had become a commonplace.

Although the A.C.A. leaders had disclaimed any continental influence in these new developments, there were other politicians who thought differently. De Valera warned the A.C.A. that any attempt to follow continental patterns would be unsuccessful.[74] *An Phoblacht,* which up to now had been referring to the A.C.A. as the 'pensioners' or as the 'White Army', likened the Blueshirts to the Hitlerite Brownshirts and accused the A.C.A. of being 'an armed organisation to provoke civil war in Ireland, and with England's help prevent loyal Irishmen from using England's difficulties to Ireland's advantage'.[75] It saw the A.C.A. as 'a pro-Treaty, a pro-British organisation which aims at the restoration by force of the Cosgrave regime', and went on: 'Toleration of it is therefore unthinkable. Every man should have the right to arm for freedom. No man should have the right to arm in defence of England's interests here.'[76]

Perhaps of greater significance were the observations of the leader of the Centre Party, Frank MacDermot, between whose party and the Blueshirts existed none of the traditional hostility which informed the relationships between pro- and anti-Treaty forces. According to MacDermot:

The A.C.A. came into existence for the express object of defending liberty for the individual, not suppressing it, and for securing freedom of speech, and on the whole I think it has done a useful and perhaps absolutely indispensable service. I doubt very much whether there could have been anything like freedom of speech at the last general election had it not been for the existence of that body.

Notwithstanding that, I am frankly going to say that I do not like its existence in principle, because I do not like the existence of any political army in principle and I am exceedingly nervous that developments may occur here such as occurred in Germany where you had a number of political armies that in the course of time, especially after they started wearing uniforms, were breaking each other's heads and committing the most appalling outrages on inoffensive citizens. The A.C.A. in its present form came into existence as a result of the I.R.A., just as the southern Volunteers, before the European War, came into existence as a result of the Ulster Volunteers. One violence produces another. One licence produces another.[77]

Side by side with the growth in strength and political importance of the A.C.A., or the Blueshirts as they were now more frequently called, a number of other important political developments occurred during the second quarter of 1933. First and most important was the growing rift which was now an open split between the erstwhile allies Fianna Fáil and the I.R.A. The I.R.A. was critical of Fianna Fáil's failure to realise a thirty-two-county republic. It was impatient with Fianna Fáil's insistence on constitutional methods and seemed to feel that the government should organise an armed invasion of the North or at least not interfere with the I.R.A.'s plans in this respect. It had long been critical of Fianna Fáil's reluctance to dismiss those public officials who had incurred Republican wrath for their activities during the decade of Cosgrave rule.[78] Then, too, the I.R.A. had come into conflict with the government when it had begun to prosecute its own economic war with the initiation of the 'Boycott Bass' campaign—a campaign whereby those publicans who refused to comply with the I.R.A. demand that no Bass products be sold, were intimidated and had their stocks smashed.[79] But the last straw had undoubtedly been the decision of the government to set up a new volunteer reserve in the army. The I.R.A. was clear that this volunteer force was intended to act as a counter attraction to the I.R.A. and siphon off many possible recruits.[80] Finally, the I.R.A. charged that 'under Fianna Fáil administration the coercive legislation of the Imperial regime has not been repealed. On the contrary it has been used to jail Republicans in Dublin, Clare and Kerry.'[81] So for all these reasons, relations between the I.R.A. and Fianna Fáil declined steadily during the early months of 1933 and by mid-1933 the I.R.A. was openly hostile to the government party.

Another important occurrence was the amazing and somewhat inexplicably hysterical wave of anti-Communist feeling which seemed to grip Dublin during March. On 26 March, speakers at a meeting of 'Irish Unemployed Workers', which was being held in O'Connell Street, had their meeting wrecked and were chased along O'Connell Street by an angry crowd.[82] Two days later, there was a demonstration outside Connolly Hall, the head-quarters of the Revolutionary Workers Group. The crowd sang 'Faith of Our Fathers' as they besieged the hall. Later that night two men 'stated to be Communists' were attacked by a section of the crowd and after a chase, narrowly escaped being thrown into the Liffey.[83] On the following night, there was another attack on the hall and this time there was prolonged street fighting during which thirty-three people were injured. The newspaper accounts state that the crowd sang hymns and Irish national songs as they attacked the hall. There were further demonstrations on subsequent nights when the hall was under heavy police protection.[84]

It is difficult to pin-point the source of this violent wave of anti-Communism, and there is probably no single explanation. Warnings about the dangers of Communism were frequent. Bishops' pastorals rarely appeared without carrying such admonitions. The Bishop of Galway especially was constantly adverting to this theme. He had described the I.R.A. and Saor Éire leaders as Communists 'and murderers'.[85] The *United Irishman* carried weekly warnings on the spread of Communism, pointing out the alleged link between the I.R.A. and international Communism and accusing the government of 'Kerensky-type softness' in its dealings with the I.R.A. This type of anti-Communist phenomenon, however, was not unusual in many European countries at the time.

De Valera condemned the witch-hunt. He said in the Dáil that according to his information, the Communist movement in the Free State had failed to obtain any serious measure of support, and that it was in fact on the wane. He said that his government did not propose to adopt repressive measures which he felt would have the effect of securing for the movement a sympathy which up to then no section of the community had given it.[86]

*   *   *

O'Higgins had become leader of the A.C.A. in August of 1932, and as has been seen, his accession ot the leadership was to mark a fundamental change in the character and activities of the association. The changes begun in August continued during the eleven months of his leadership, during which time the membership of the association increased dramatically, the blue shirt was adopted as its common uniform and the wearing of the shirt spread rapidly. By April 1933, there was little resemblance between the then A.C.A. and the association which had been founded in Dublin just fourteen months earlier. It must be stressed too that during all this time, in spite of official protestations that the A.C.A. was non-political, it was almost generally regarded as being on very close terms with Cumann na nGaedheal, and as sharing many of that party's ideals.

This development of the A.C.A. had taken place against an exciting and very unsettled background of bitter speeches, frequently disrupted public meetings, occasional and sometimes hysterical bouts of anti-Communism and the ever present threat of violence. It was a period which had seen the emphatic confirmation of Fianna Fáil in power and the second electoral defeat in under a year for Cumann na nGaedheal. It had seen too an intensification of the economic war and the waging of a private economic war by the I.R.A. The economic war was causing a crisis for those engaged in agriculture—no alternative markets had been found and farmers now had considerable surpluses of unsaleable produce.

All these factors contributed to the increasing tension and growing restlessness which characterised Irish politics in early 1933. The atmosphere was clouded by an almost universal feeling of distrust and mutual suspicion. It was a situation in which anything could happen, and a renewal of the Civil War was prophesied by more than one observer. With two private armies, arms easily procured and a surfeit of bellicose sentiments, it is not surprising that many were apprehensive on this score. But to some the most ominous note of all was one struck by some among the A.C.A. who were professing to a declining faith in the efficacy of parliamentary government and were beginning to cast their thoughts to other, as yet unspecified, methods of government.

It was against such a background that the A.C.A. was to change its leadership once more, and to enter upon a new, more turbulent and more unpredictable stage in the unfolding drama that was Irish political life in 1933.

4 General O'Duffy Takes Over

BEFORE discussing the development of the Army Comrades during the second half of 1933, it is necessary to return first to the early months of that year when an event occurred which was to have a profound, if delayed, impact on the future fortunes and direction of the association.

On 22 February, two weeks after de Valera's re-election as President of the Executive Council, he summoned the Commissioner of the Civic Guard, General Eoin O'Duffy to his office and, in the presence of the new Minister for Justice, Patrick Ruttledge, informed him that he was being relieved of his duties as Chief of police. O'Duffy was informed that the decision was a Cabinet one and therefore could not be changed. He was told, however, that the government was anxious that he continue in the public service, and he was offered an alternative position with the same salary as he currently had. O'Duffy refused this offer and a meeting of the Executive Council was called to discuss the refusal. After this meeting de Valera again summoned O'Duffy and again pressed him to accept the offered position. O'Duffy again refused.

De Valera then named as O'Duffy's successor Colonel Eamon Broy, the Chief of the detective division. Broy's appointment was to cause a certain amount of surprise within the police force, as it was made over the heads of at least two officers of superior rank—Deputy Commissioner Coogan and Assistant Commissioner Walsh.[1]

O'Duffy's sudden and abrupt dismissal caused considerable controversy and speculation. *An Phoblacht*, which had been campaigning for this dismissal for over a year, welcomed it but criticised the government for having waited so long.[2] *The Irish Times,* on the other hand, was highly critical and called for a full explanation from de Valera saying: 'If a public servant is liable to lose his office at the desire of a minority, it is time that President de Valera should abandon his pretence of democracy.'[3] In the Dáil, the matter was raised by a number of opposition deputies, who were severely critical of the government on this matter.[4]

Pressed to explain the reasons for the sudden dismissal, de Valera was at first reluctant to divulge any detailed information and confined himself to saying that O'Duffy had been removed from office 'because in the opinion of the Executive Council a change of Commissioner was desirable in the public interest'.[5] The matter was debated fully in the Dáil on 14 March, when Cosgrave moved a motion strongly disapproving of the action of the government. This time de Valera was more explicit:

Mr de Valera: 'It is because we realise that the ultimate responsibility for peace and order depends on us that we are going to see to it that those who will have the immediate responsibility will be people in whom we have full confidence. Let us note that, without any of the bunkum—full confidence. Deputy Cosgrave asked me was there any characteristic in the quality of the new occupant of the office that the old occupant did not have. I say yes, one, that he was not the chief of police for ten years under the last administration.'
Mr Rice: 'Now we know it.'
Mr de Valera: 'Yes, certainly, now you know it. During those ten years every act of indiscipline was condoned.... We want a chief of police of whom no section of the community can say that that man is deliberately and politically opposed to us, and is likely to be biased in his attitude because of past political affiliations.'[6]

De Valera made the official position even more clear during the course of this heated debate when he said that: 'The principle on which the government had acted was that ultimate responsibility for peace and order rested upon the

Executive Council, and that what responsibility they should delegate would rest upon people in whom they had full confidence.'[7]

This view or explanation was not accepted by all and a number of allegations were made that de Valera was acting under pressure from the Republicans and from his own back-benches. The *United Irishman* was quite emphatic that the decision to replace O'Duffy came as a result of pressure from these groups.[8] This was also the view of many of the opposition speakers in the Dáil. Cosgrave alleged that the 'O'Duffy must go' movement was started by Communist-I.R.A. extremists.[9] This is also the view which Donal O'Sullivan takes in his book *The Irish Free State and its Senate*.[10] Captain Walsh, who was O'Duffy's private secretary at this time, claims in his unpublished biography of O'Duffy that the decision to relieve O'Duffy of his duties was taken at a special meeting of the Fianna Fáil Party on 21 February and that de Valera had bowed to this pressure.[11]

It does look as if there was considerable pressure on de Valera from these sources asking for O'Duffy's removal. According to Walsh, the first demands were made at a secret session of the Fianna Fáil Ard-Fheis in 1932. *An Phoblacht* had long been carrying on an anti-O'Duffy vendetta. Under the sobriquet 'Yo-Yo' Duffy, almost weekly attacks were made on his record during the Cosgrave regime and on his handling of affairs since 1932. His handling of the general election of 1933 had been strongly criticised, and this extract from *An Phoblacht* of 21 January gives an indication of the I.R.A. attitude:

Yo-Yo Duffy, the notorious Chief of Police, was in charge of arrangements to secure free speech for traitors. As a result traitors were allowed to talk, while citizens who cried 'Up the Republic' were arrested.

The front-page headlines in the paper on 4 February and 18 February had called for O'Duffy's dismissal.

However, there is no evidence to show to what extent, if

at all, de Valera was influenced in his decision by this sort
of thing, and, on balance, it is very possible that the explanation given under pressure in the Dáil is the most accurate,
that is, that he did not have full confidence in O'Duffy.
Certainly O'Duffy was not removed for inefficiency. The
Minister for Justice had earlier written to O'Duffy to con-
gratulate him on the manner in which the two biggest events
since Fianna Fáil had come to power—the Eucharistic
Congress and the 1933 election—had been handled by the
police.[12] Nor were there any allegations of corruption nor
any question of any charges being preferred against O'Duffy.
In fact, de Valera had appealed to him to stay on in the
public service, and later that year, at the Fianna Fáil Ard-
Fheis, he defended the award of a pension to O'Duffy, saying
that 'although we had doubts, there was no evidence to say
definitely that General O'Duffy was not acting honourably
and honestly in his position'.[13]

Nevertheless, there were some strong and convincing
reasons why de Valera did not want O'Duffy as Commissioner in 1933, and an examination of O'Duffy's personality
and record offers some clues.

O'Duffy had been a strong and very independent Commissioner of police. He had a flair for publicity and had
frequently been in the headlines in the 1920s. He was extremely well known throughout the country. He was a
leading member of the National Athletic and Cycling Association and managed the highly successful Irish team at
the 1932 Olympic Games. He was also a prominent member
of the Gaelic Athletic Association and had been Treasurer
of the Ulster Council. He had been a successful, if flamboyant, commander during the War of Independence and
had ended up as deputy Chief of Staff and a close confidant
of General Michael Collins. He was appointed Commissioner
of police in 1922 and had held the position of Chief of Staff
of the army for a period after the 1924 mutiny. In addition
he had received great national prominence during the
Tailteann Games of the mid-1920s and more recently during

the Eucharistic Congress of 1932. As a result, he was very widely known and seemed to be in a position of considerable independent strength.[14]

His tenure under the Cosgrave regime had been character-ised by this flair for self-publicity and by a streak of inde-pendence unusual in a public official. Indeed, according to one member of the Cosgrave government, O'Duffy felt that the government should not control the police.[15] In 1929, he had publicly challenged an order of the Executive Council. The government had decided as part of an economy measure to close down twenty-nine Garda stations, to abandon the proposal to open five new stations and to reduce by one guard the personnel of each of 500 barracks. O'Duffy had strongly disapproved of this Cabinet decision and had made his views known to the newspapers.[16] In 1932, he had publicly disagreed with the government's proposal to reduce the salaries of the Civic Guard.[17] It was later alleged in the Dáil by a Fianna Fáil T.D., Seán Moylan, that there had been a serious disagreement between O'Duffy and Kevin O'Higgins over police discipline in 1927.[18] Ernest Blythe who was Minister for Finance in the Cosgrave government, is on record as saying that O'Duffy had been somewhat in-subordinate on a number of occasions and that had Cumann na nGaedheal won the 1932 election, O'Duffy would have been transferred to some other position.[19]

In the light of this background, de Valera's contention is more easily understood. The immediate reason for his de-cision at that particular time is not quite so clear, but two suggestions have been made. One is that O'Duffy had been furnishing the Executive Council with exaggerated reports on the size and strength of the Communist movement in the country, and that these reports had eventually exhausted the patience of some members of the Cabinet. The other sug-gestion is that he had failed to discipline some members of the police force who, in the opinion of the Executive Council, had been guilty of insubordination.[20]

Whatever the immediate reason—if, indeed, there was an

Commandant E. Cronin addressing a meeting at
Charleville, Co. Cork, April 1934

The salute being given at the same meeting

Blueshirts at Inchicore, Dublin

General Richard Mulcahy, T.D., speaking at Skibbereen, Co. Cork, January 1934

immediate reason at all—it is easy to see why de Valera acted the way he did. De Valera knew of O'Duffy's past, of his record under the Cumann na nGaedheal government, of his strong, independent and sometimes unpredictable personality and of his great unpopularity with the rank-and-file members of Fianna Fáil. These factors taken on their own could have been sufficient to explain the stand taken by de Valera, but in addition there were other extraneous but highly relevant factors—there was the growing unrest throughout the country, the increasingly militant attitudes of both the I.R.A. and the A.C.A., the widespread drilling and finally the example of the recent coups and revolutions on the continent of Europe. Bearing these considerations in mind as well as the personality of the man involved, it is easy to see why de Valera wanted to have a police chief in whom he could have 'full confidence' and it is easy to see also how O'Duffy might not have been that man.

O'Duffy's dismissal had caused a great deal of controversy and his cause was championed in the Dáil by both Cumann na nGaedheal and the Centre Party as well as by such newspapers as *The Irish Times,* the *Irish Independent* and of course, the *United Irishman.* To these groups the dismissal was seen as an act of blatant political victimisation and an indication of the influence of the I.R.A. and left-wing followers on the de Valera government. O'Duffy himself did not enter into the controversy except by a statement which he issued on 15 March in which he attacked de Valera's statement and claimed that he had acted impartially at all times. He announced also that he had no definite plans for the future and that he would not make any decision until he returned from a holiday.[21] Shortly after this he set off from Dublin on a continental cruise and did not return until 15 May.[22]

*   *   *

According to Captain Walsh, who was O'Duffy's private secretary at the time, O'Duffy was visited three days after

6

his return by a former Cumann na nGaedheal minister, who urged him to enter politics. O'Duffy was interested but took no definite decision at this stage. From now on, according to Walsh, there was a constant stream of callers to O'Duffy's house 'begging him to take control of the A.C.A.' and it appears also that very many of the sympathetic letters which O'Duffy had received after his dismissal had suggested to him that he undoubtedly had a brilliant political career ahead of him if he so chose.[23] This pressure on O'Duffy was to continue for some time and it appears that foremost among those who wanted O'Duffy to enter politics were Ernest Blythe and Professor Michael Tierney.[24] It can easily be seen why some of the A.C.A. leaders should have been so anxious to have O'Duffy in their movement. First of all there was the position of O'Higgins who had some strong personal reasons for wanting to relinquish the leadership. O'Higgins was at one and the same time County Medical Officer for Meath, T.D. for Laois-Offaly and leader of the Army Comrades. In addition he had a big family, and the strain of all these simultaneous duties was beginning to prove extremely demanding; indeed it appears that there was some family pressure on him to relinquish his leadership of the Army Comrades.[25] Secondly, O'Duffy did appear to have many positive advantages which increased his attraction as a potential leader. His somewhat spectacular career during the War of Independence and his closeness to Michael Collins were well known. He had supervised the organisation of the police force and apparently done so with considerable success. He was a well-known national figure in both athletic and G.A.A. affairs. He had a reputation as a vigorous and competent organiser with limitless energy. He had suffered victimisation at the hands of Fianna Fáil, and the fact that he held no other full-time position meant that he would be able to devote himself unreservedly to the affairs of the Army Comrades. Thus, with this background and with such qualifications, it is easy to see why he could have appeared as the ideal choice to lead the Army Comrades.

There was a further quality which 'Onlooker' professed to see in O'Duffy which added to his attraction—in fact, according to 'Onlooker' it was an advantage possessed by no other possible head of the organisation:

He had had no association with any existing political party, or with any particular type of politico-economic policy, and therefore would be acceptable as a leader to men of widely different schools of political thought.

He will be able to demonstrate that the A.C.A. is an entirely independent and autonomous national organisation. He will be able to formulate policy without being embarrassed by the record of past deliberations and decisions which would not suit present conditions.[26]

It was obvious, however, that this hope of 'Onlooker' was unrealistic. As a Civil War figure, and as Chief of police for ten years under the Cosgrave regime, it was clear that O'Duffy would be unacceptable as a political leader to the great majority, if not to all, of the I.R.A. and Fianna Fáil supporters.

As far as O'Duffy himself was concerned, the offer of the leadership of the Army Comrades must have appeared an attractive proposition. He was an ex-member of the army and had in fact been active in the earlier National Defence Association. More than that, he was a public figure who now had no public position. He was a man who loved organising and revelled in publicity. His instinct for action and the pressure of his friends and associates had whetted his appetite for politics. To such a man in such a position the offer of the leadership of a growing, vigorous and autonomous organisation must have appeared both flattering and attractive.

There were some preliminary negotiations in June, and finally a meeting was arranged between O'Higgins and O'Duffy. This secret meeting took place in County Meath in early July.[27] It is not clear what agreement was reached at this session, but shortly afterwards, a circular was sent out to all A.C.A. district officers calling a special convention for

Thursday 20 July 'when business of the utmost importance will be decided'. The circular declared that the business would 'include the consideration of such vital questions as changes in name and constitution, direction and administration of the A.C.A. and the uniform to be worn by officers'.[28]

This decision to call a special convention, or rather the extent of the changes which were to be effected at the convention, seems to indicate one of two possibilities—either that O'Duffy intended taking over in more than name, that he intended imposing important structural changes on the association or else that the A.C.A. leaders, having persuaded O'Duffy to accept, now had new and extensive plans for the remodelling of the organisation and intended using the change of leadership as a suitable occasion for their implementation.

The announcement from the A.C.A. that a special conference was pending and that far-reaching changes in the association were likely, gave rise to some speculation in the newspapers and O'Duffy's name was mentioned as the possible new leader.[29] In the Dáil at this time, de Valera had indicated that his government was strongly opposed to the way in which the A.C.A. was developing and would take serious steps against it. On 14 July, speaking on the Vote for his own Department, he had warned that while he did not believe that at the present time conflict was likely, 'we are not going to permit people to parade in uniform. That is definite. When it comes to that stage, we believe it has come to a dangerous stage, and it is the duty of the government to step in.' He went on to say that his government 'would use all the forces at its command to prevent it'.[30]

Later in the same debate, having accused the A.C.A. of being primarily responsible for the disturbances during the election, he said: 'We have not been unmindful of the developments on the continent and elsewhere, and we have not lost sight of the fact that apparently certain people in the country are organising themselves with a certain model in front of them.'[31]

*   *   *

The special A.C.A. meeting was held in the Hibernian Hotel in Dublin on 20 July, and the large number of delegates present were told by O'Higgins that he was about to resign. He was resigning, he said, because the burden of leadership had become too heavy on his shoulders. He outlined for the delegates the reasons for the existence of the association and lauded its role in 'preventing the spread of Communism, in protecting life, property, free speech and democracy in the country'. He told the delegates also that there was nothing secret or sinister about their organisation—it was an open and frank organisation, and this openness and frankness was proclaimed first by their badges and now by their shirts.

He told them also that while considering the question of resigning he had been looking around for a possible successor. Then 'Providence and President de Valera made General O'Duffy available'. He knew straight away that O'Duffy's great qualities—his fearlessness, his impartiality and his equal administration of the law—would make him the ideal man to head the A.C.A. O'Higgins then proposed that O'Duffy be elected in his place and this was seconded by another original member of the A.C.A., Colonel Jerry Ryan. O'Duffy was then unanimously elected.[32]

O'Duffy now made his acceptance speech, in which he emphasised two main points. He stressed that he was not the nominee of any particular party and that the autonomy and independence of the movement would be zealously protected under his leadership. Secondly, he saw the association playing a new and more prominent role in the political life of the Free State from then on. He ended on the quasi-messianic note which was to become a feature of his subsequent speeches: 'It is because I see in the members of your association the class of members which can be moulded into a great national organisation which can, and please God will, raise the youth of this country above the bitterness of mere party politics that I have answered the call.' Straightaway, he announced major immediate changes in the association. Its name was to be changed. It would no longer

be the Army Comrades Association—from now on it would
be the National Guard. Like the A.C.A., the National Guard
would be strictly non-party. It would not be subject or
subsidiary to any other organisation. Its membership would
be restricted to citizens of Irish birth or parentage who professed the Christian faith. Members of secret societies would
not be eligible for membership.[33]

None of these major changes were debated at the meeting.
They were announced by the new leader and accepted without any obvious dissent. Shortly afterwards, the new constitution of the National Guard was published and it
underscored the radical changes which had occurred in the
structure and objectives of the association.

The constitution defined the objectives of the National
Guard as follows:

To promote the re-union of Ireland.

To oppose Communism and alien control and influence in
national affairs and to uphold Christian principles in every sphere
of public activity.

To promote and maintain social order.

To make organised and disciplined voluntary public service a
permanent and accepted feature of our political life and to lead
the youth of Ireland in a movement of constructive national
action.

To promote the formation of co-ordinated national organisations
of employers and employed, which, with the aid of judicial
tribunals, will effectively prevent strikes and lock-outs and har-
moniously compose industrial differences.

To co-operate with the official agencies of the state for the solution
of such pressing social problems as the provision of useful and
economic public employment for those whom public enterprise
cannot absorb.

To secure the creation of a representative national statutory
organisation of farmers, with rights and status sufficient to secure
the safeguarding of agricultural interests, in all revisions of
agricultural and political policy.

To expose and prevent corruption and victimisation in national
and local administration.

To awaken throughout the country a spirit of combination, discipline, zeal and patriotic realism which will put the state in a position to serve the people efficiently in the economic and social spheres.[34]

The constitution is interesting both for what it omits and for what it includes. The original objective of the founders of the A.C.A. had been to safeguard the interests of ex-soldiers. Under O'Higgins this aim had been subordinated, but was nevertheless regarded as of prime importance. Now in the new organisation it was not even mentioned, and in fact no reference whatsoever is made to ex-soldiers.

The most interesting part of the new constitution was that outlining proposals for harmonising industrial relations and for the creation of a representative national statutory organisation of farmers. These proposals mark the first tentative introduction of corporate ideas into Irish politics and certainly the first espousal of these ideas by an Irish political movement. Before very long these ideas were to become an integral part of Blueshirt policy, but at this point they made their first appearance almost surreptitiously and certainly without any public debate or elaboration. It was not made clear who was mainly responsible for the introduction of these ideas—whether the initiative came from intellectuals such as Michael Tierney or James Hogan, from earlier A.C.A. members such as Cronin and Blythe or whether O'Duffy himself introduced them as a condition of accepting the leadership.

Another interesting feature of the new constitution was the matter of eligibility for membership. The original A.C.A. confined membership to ex-members of the National Army. This was gradually extended and under O'Higgins, membership was open to all men of good will. Now, however, membership was open to 'all citizens of Irish birth or parentage who profess the Christian faith'. The question immediately arises about this proviso: was it merely pious window-dressing or was it an attempt to exclude Jewish citizens from joining? As the only persons excluded under this heading would be Jews and atheists, and as these made up a minute segment of the population, the justification for the proviso is hard to find. If it was anti-Semitic in intent, this was the only time such a phenomenon was to appear during the life of the Blueshirts. There was no history of anti-Semitism in the movement nor were there any subsequent manifestations. The most likely explanation of the proviso is that it was occasioned by pietistic zeal.

So in July 1933, almost four months to the day after his resignation as Commissioner of police, General Eoin O'Duffy took over leadership of a large and active political force—a force dedicated by its constitution to constructive national action and committed to seeking considerable changes in the political and economic structure of the country. It was a political force which eschewed political activity in the narrow party sense. It was a force dedicated to the political virtues of combination, discipline, zeal and patriotic realism, and which placed great emphasis on the contribution of youth. Its leader, though a national figure, was as yet untried in the art of political generalship. It was a force whose very existence excited the greatest hostility and foreboding in those who were already its enemies.

The advent of O'Duffy to the leadership of the National Guard was to promise a continuation of the excitement and drama which was now so much a part of the Free State's political life. It was also to add a new, unpredictable, unprecedented and potentially explosive factor to an already over-charged situation. Only the most rash would have attempted to predict the outcome of the next few months.

5   The National Guard

O'Duffy came to the leadership of the National Guard with a reputation as a vigorous and experienced organiser and he lost little time in applying this vigour to the affairs of the National Guard. The speed at which events were to move during these first weeks of his leadership was to make them amongst the most exciting and explosive since the end of the Civil War.

In his first statement as leader, O'Duffy attempted to clarify any doubts about the methods and objectives of the organisation:

The National Guard recognises the courts, the police, the civil service and the army as the fundamental institutions of the state. While I am in charge I will ensure that the organisation will keep within the law and that illegalities will not be tolerated. Physical drill will be practised only as a means of promoting good health, character and discipline. With the same object a distinctive dress will be worn. The National Guard being a non-military or civil organisation there will be no military equipment of any kind. Blue is adopted as the organisation's colour for flags, shirts, ties, badges etc. just as sports clubs adopt a distinctive blazer or jersey. Any organisation may adopt a special colour without infringing the law. There would be no secrecy about the personnel, methods, or objects of the National Guard.

He added that the National Guard would be highly disciplined and stood for unconditional opposition to Communism.[1]

The first reaction at government level to the National Guard came not from the Free State government, but from the government of Northern Ireland which on 22 July issued an order under the Civil Authorities (Special Powers) Act banning the National Guard in Northern Ireland.[2] The primary reason for this ban was that one of the main objectives of the National Guard was the abolition of the border. O'Duffy was not at all perturbed by the decision, and announced that the National Guard already had a membership of 25,000.[3]

Three days later O'Duffy announced that membership had reached the 30,000 mark and that he was about to leave Dublin on an extensive three-week reorganisational tour throughout the country. Before leaving, he gave a press interview, in the course of which he was asked whether the National Guard was a Fascist organisation. He said it was not, nor was it intended to be. But, he added, if there was any good point in the Fascist, or any other organisation they were prepared to adopt it. He announced also that preparations were in progress for the annual commemorative parade to Leinster Lawn in honour of Arthur Griffith, Michael Collins and Kevin O'Higgins on 13 August and that he would be back in Dublin to lead the parade.[4] Leinster Lawn is at the front of Leinster House, and it had been the custom during the Cosgrave regime to hold an annual commemorative ceremony. The ceremony had not been held in 1932, but as one of the original objectives of the A.C.A. had been to honour dead members of the army, it was not surprising that O'Duffy should seek to revive this ceremony.

He also set about organising a newspaper for the National Guard and on 5 August, the first issue of *The Blueshirt* appeared. 'Onlooker', who up to now had been writing on A.C.A. affairs for the *United Irishman*, transferred to this new paper. In the first issue, he echoed the opinions O'Duffy had expressed on Fascism on 25 July. He said that the National Guard was not a Fascist organisation, it was 'purely a product of Irish needs and conditions' and 'anything it may have borrowed from abroad was incidental and subsidiary'. He later emphatically denied that the National

Guard was in any way Nazi or anti-Semitic—'It is a Christian organisation, but not anti-Semitic.'[5]

The first official reaction to the new developments in the National Guard came the following week-end, 29–30 July, when detectives and police visited a number of houses in Dublin and other parts of the Free State demanding the surrender of firearms which were being held under licence and under official permit. Amongst those who were asked to surrender their guns were leading members of Cumann na nGaedheal, including Patrick McGilligan, Gearoid O'Sullivan, and Ernest Blythe. Blythe refused to surrender his gun, saying that he had no intention of making himself a defenceless target at the behest of Mr de Valera or any of his colleagues.[6]

O'Duffy meanwhile continued to make his arrangements for the forthcoming parade. He announced on 30 July that he expected that there would be at least 20,000 people taking part. He attacked the manner in which the collection of guns was being carried out and declared that the purpose behind the collection was to 'create an atmosphere to justify interference, official or unofficial, with the National Guard, a body of unarmed men, enrolled in a non-military organisation, which is gradually securing the confidence of the people in its policy.' He went on to say that his organisation was non-political, unarmed and totally opposed to any form of dictatorship.[7]

On the following day, 31 July, he announced a surprising change in the plans for the proposed parade. Instead of having 20,000 marching they had decided that 'because of the economic conditions prevailing they could now only accept a small representation from each county, say 3,000–4,000 in all'. He went on to deal with the rumours which had been freely circulating during the previous few days:

It has been canvassed in government circles that we intend seizing the seat of government and the military barracks in Dublin on that occasion. No serious-minded person will believe this. In a previous interview I asked for the co-operation of government and state services to make the ceremony worthy of the occasion. Instead, scares are deliberately being created. The sorely tried people of this country have had enough of scares already and the purpose of the National Guard is to allay any fears for the future in this respect.

He said also that he had no intention of giving up his gun and explained why:

. . . the person in the position of Chief of police during the past eleven years, when banks, business houses and private individuals were held up by armed men and robbed, and under whose direction the criminals were arrested and punished, could hardly be regarded by the police as one whose life was not in danger of attack. . . . While I was Commissioner of the Guards, and since I was removed from office, I was accompanied by an armed member of the Garda for the reasons given above. Today this member has been taken from me. I have made representations in the matter, and I have had no reply. Under the circumstances and in justice to myself I am not going to give up my gun. [8]

The collection of firearms continued on 1 August, and once again, Ernest Blythe refused to give up his arms. [9] On the same day, the Dáil met and the matter was raised. De Valera defended the collection: The arms were collected, he said, so that 'they would not be used improperly'. His government was determined not to allow private armies in the country, or parades in public in uniform and they would not allow guns be carried in public places. He later elaborated further on the need for the government's drastic action:

There is a situation in this country at the present time which everybody who is not blind recognises, in which we have two forces, one going to arm against the other; two forces each of which would be used as an excuse for the increase and growth of the other. The government would not be worthy of the confidence placed in it by the people if it permitted any such thing as that to go ahead. We are hoping to see that people who have arms that we can get, will not retain them in these circumstances. [10]

Later, he accused 'the gentlemen opposite' of 'having started an organisation the very purpose of which is quite clear'. He then accused O'Duffy of wanting to subvert the Constitution and of aiming at a dictatorship. He also attacked the idea of uniformed parades in public, which could, he felt, lead to civil war. It was because of this very dangerous situation that his government was determined not to allow people to have private armies in the country.[11]

He was accused of victimisation by the opposition, in that he had picked out only one group in the arms confiscation drive, and had apparently ignored the I.R.A. De Valera replied by saying that he had hoped that with the removal of the Oath of Allegiance the need for armed action had been removed. But in any case, he went on, there was a great difference between the I.R.A. and the National Guard. 'The National Guard', he said, 'is not a body which has any roots in the past, not a body which can be said to have a national objective such as the I.R.A. can be said to have.'[12]

O'Duffy's earlier condemnation of the raids was strongly repeated in the Dáil by members of the Opposition in a very bitter debate. Cosgrave accused the government of deliberately fostering sensation to divert attention from the economic position of the state.[13] Patrick Hogan said that de Valera wanted to outlaw the National Guard 'because he was justifying his own criminal past'. Later he claimed that the purpose of the raids was to persuade people that the National Guard was an organisation similar to the I.R.A.[14]

Despite these criticisms, the collection of firearms continued on 2 August and this time O'Duffy's two revolvers were confiscated.[15] On the following day government pressure on O'Duffy continued when the Dáil debated a Bill to give him a pension. An amendment, put forward by Fianna Fáil, which gave the government the power to suspend the pension at any time it liked without giving any reason, was passed by fifty-two votes to thirty-three.[16]

On 4 August the seriousness with which the government

was treating the Blueshirts became very clear when it was seen that there was a dramatic increase in the number of police on duty at Government Buildings. Many of the police were armed with revolvers and a large quantity of beds was delivered to the buildings to accommodate this increase in numbers.[17] By 6 August there were 300 police on duty at Government Buildings, operating for the most part in pairs, and carrying heavy revolvers in holsters at their belts. There were strong rumours too, that a new auxiliary police force was about to be created and that recruits were flocking into Dublin from all parts of the country.[18]

On 8 August wild scenes took place in the city centre during a National Guard dance in the Metropole Hotel. Those arriving at the dance—many of the men wearing blue shirts—were booed and heckled by the large crowd which had gathered in O'Connell Street. There were some scuffles and attacks, followed by a series of police baton-charges. The car in which W. T. Cosgrave was travelling was assailed with flying stones, sticks and hurleys, and the occupants had to receive protection from police and Blueshirts.[19]

It was against this highly-charged and very tense background that O'Duffy chose to outline publicly for the first time his ideas on the question of parliamentary democracy. In a statement which he issued to the press on 8 August, he spoke of the great enthusiasm for the National Guard which he had encountered in the south and south-west. He said, moreover, that there was also great support for the idea 'that party politics had served their period of usefulness and the sooner a change was effected the better.' He went on to say that he had explained on his tour that he thought it would take at least twelve months hard work to wean people from the present system, but in all cases he had received the same reply: 'We are ready now.' He said he was very pleased that his 'desire to keep the National Guard independent of all political parties is already shared by all the members. They are determined on this.. . .' He ended his statement by declaring that he had 'a sacred duty' to perform—to lead the

National Guard on the occasion of the parade—'and from this duty I will not flinch—come what may'.[20]

Some explanation for the arms raids of the previous week and for the increased police activity around Government Buildings was provided in the Dáil on 9 August by the Minister for Justice, P. J. Ruttledge. He alleged that the A.C.A. had been a heavily armed organisation and, to prove his case, he quoted from a report which he alleged had been submitted by O'Duffy in September 1932 when he was still Commissioner of police. According to this report:

The organisation has the support of members of the late government, the most active being General Mulcahy. Mr Blythe supports the organisation through the medium of the *United Irishman*. The majority of Cumann na nGaedheal T.D.s and ex-army officers throughout the Saorstat are also organising.

There is no doubt that a considerable number of ex-army officers are in possession of revolvers, and even rifles, held surreptitiously, as souvenirs of the pre-Truce period. Further, many ex-National Army men, when leaving the army in 1923–25 brought arms with them.

I have however been informed, as already reported to the Minister, that certain members of the organisation hold extreme views and would be prepared to urge the use of force in pursuit of their policy . . .

Should the movement at any time desire to adopt other than constitutional methods, it can, without doubt, lay hands on a sufficient quantity of arms and ammunition to render it a very formidable insurrectionary force, and a source of extreme danger to the peace and stability of the country.[21]

And to make his charge even more clear, Ruttledge went on to quote an extract from the *United Irishman* of 15 July 1933:

There are indubitably good reasons for the world-wide tendency at present apparent to supersede, modify or side-step the old parliamentary system. The days of its usefulness are gone.[22]

In spite of the charges being levelled by Ruttledge—in fact on the day following Ruttledge's accusations—O'Duffy announced that final plans for Sunday's parade were in hand. On the same day, almost as if he were oblivious to the charges that he sought to subvert the system of parliamentary democracy and to the implications of these charges, O'Duffy unveiled an elaborate version of his plans for 'remodelling' the Free State parliament.

Under O'Duffy's scheme, parliament would consist of representatives of professional and vocational groups such as farmers, teachers, engineers and those engaged in labour. He would not dispense with the present system altogether, but, instead of election by constituencies, he would substitute election by professional and vocational groups. In an organisation extending from the parish to the central council, each profession or vocation would select its representatives who should be the best men that it could produce. No legislation affecting any trade or profession would be introduced without the sanction of the group directly concerned. He felt that 'it would take two or three years to educate the people and win them away from the old political shibboleths' which had brought so much bitterness into the politics of the present day. He hoped to have some thousands of young men to provide education and set an example. When he was asked if his plan was not the same as the Fascists had tried in Italy, he replied: 'Yes, but it is the only part of our movement which is Fascist.' Again he attacked the party system: 'The present parliamentary system is English.' The system he championed was closer to the old Irish parliamentary methods of government.... People in the country were sick of the existing party system and they had told him so. He added that the National Guard was going from strength to strength. Party politics were, he said, barred within the organisation and any overtures which had been made to them by Cumann na nGaedheal or the Centre Party had been rejected.[23]

O'Duffy had made this statement and announced the final plans for the parade on Thursday 10 August. Special trains were arranged from various parts of the country to bring

General Eoin O'Duffy takes the salute at the Blueshirt Congress, August 1934

Blueshirts arriving at the Mansion House, Dublin, for the 1934 Congress

*Mrs E. O'Neill takes the salute at Kinsale,
Co. Cork, December 1933*

*Mr James Dillon, T.D., speaking at Cork,
October 1933*

Blueshirts to Dublin, the proposed route was outlined and route officials were appointed. Clearly O'Duffy intended to go ahead with his 'sacred duty' of leading the parade and saw no reason to alter his plans. But it was equally clear that the government was seeking an early showdown with the National Guard—hence the arms confiscations, Ruttledge's Dáil allegations, de Valera's warnings and the references to European movements. As the week advanced and tension increased, there was speculation that the parade might be banned altogether.[24] It was felt that if the government took seriously its own allegations that the National Guard was heavily armed, was out to subvert the Constitution and was consciously modelling itself on European Fascist movements, and if it felt that there was a possibility of O'Duffy's attempting a *coup d'état* or seeking to emulate Mussolini's famous March on Rome, then undoubtedly the parade would be banned. And so it was.

Early on Saturday morning, a proclamation was issued by the government banning the parade. This was done under Article 2A of the Constitution—the article which had been suspended—but not repealed—by Fianna Fáil in 1932. It was perhaps ironical that this power was now to be used, not against the I.R.A., but against supporters of the former government. The reasons for the ban were set out in the proclamation:

In the opinion of the government the purposes and methods of the organisation are clearly opposed to the liberties of the citizens of the Saorstat, and to the interests of peace and order. It is the avowed aim of the association to destroy the existing parliamentary institutions, and the military character of its organisation and the symbols it has adopted are evidence that its leaders are prepared, in favourable circumstances, to resort to violent means to attain this end. In spite of repeated public warnings they have persisted in ordering their followers to wear uniforms at the proposed parade. A parade in such circumstances, by such an association would be calculated to lead to grave disorder, and to have lasting reactions unfavourable to the public peace.

7

The proclamation also dealt with the government's decision to reintroduce Article 2A of the Constitution:

In doing so it has in mind not merely the proposed parade of uniformed men, but the fact that considerable quantities of fire-arms are held by members of this and other organisations in the Saorstat. In such a situation, clashes which might not otherwise be regarded as serious would lead here, as they have led in other countries, to conditions bordering on anarchy, and favourable to the designs of opponents of democratic rule, and of the enemies of our country. The government is determined not to permit such a situation to develop and will not hesitate to use its powers to the full to prevent it, and to take all necessary measure against persons guilty of acts or statements calculated to promote these designs.[25]

The action of the government in banning the parade placed O'Duffy in a very awkward position. He had already declared, on more than one occasion, that the National Guard would operate strictly within the law. But he had also proclaimed publicly that he had a sacred duty to lead the parade and that 'from this duty he would not flinch come what may'.[26] Thus if he held the parade, his organisation would be in direct conflict with the law, and if he called it off, he would inevitably lose face. It was a dilemma much as faced O'Connell before the Clontarf meeting. And like O'Connell he chose to call the meeting off. His decision may have been occasioned by a loss of nerve, or perhaps, as he said himself in a statement issued on Saturday afternoon: 'We do not want, on an occasion like this—a solemn and dignified occasion—to have anything in the nature of a public disturbance, which would dishonour our glorious dead.'[27] He was determined that in spite of the ban they would honour their dead. He issued instructions that on the following Sunday—20 August—a church parade of the National Guard was to be held in every district in Ireland, and where possible, members should attend a Solemn Memorial Mass.[28]

Although O'Duffy had called off the parade, it was

obvious that the government were taking no chances, and armed police from all parts of the country were drafted into Dublin for the week-end of 13 August. Government Buildings were held in a state of virtual siege and the surrounding streets were closed to members of the public, while an armoured car and lorries of armed police toured the city and suburbs all day. There was also a strong force of police gathered around the cemetery at Glasnevin where O'Duffy had intended laying a wreath and delivering an oration at the graves of Collins, Griffith and O'Higgins.

The day, however, passed quietly with only a few minor incidents, the most serious of which occurred in O'Connell Street at noon when two men wearing blue shirts were set upon by a crowd and roughly handled.[29]

The banning of the parade was the first crisis which O'Duffy had to face as Blueshirt leader, and indeed the whole incident raises some interesting questions which are not easily answered—Was O'Duffy planning a coup? Did the Government have good reason to fear such a coup? Why was the parade banned?

There is no evidence that O'Duffy was planning or contemplating a coup. He had specifically stated that those taking part would be unarmed and all his utterances had stressed the peaceful—almost pilgrimage-like—nature of the occasion. The commemorative ceremony had, after all, been an annual affair under the Cosgrave government and it was understandable that O'Duffy should want to revive it. Part of his intention in reviving it may have included a desire to demonstrate the strength and spectacular growth of the Blueshirt movement, and what better way to do this than by a massive parade through the centre of Dublin. The effects of this would be calculated to impress upon the government the size and strength of the movement and at the same time serve to attract many new members of the movement. A parade of this nature would certainly appeal to O'Duffy's sense of drama.

As far as the government was concerned, the decision to

ban the parade is easily understandable and appears to have had substantial justification. It is possible that it had information that some elements in the Blueshirts were advocating extreme tactics. This is possible, but even if it did not, there was every possibility that a big Blueshirt parade would lead to a serious breach of the peace. The I.R.A., for example, was likely to react violently, as might supporters of the government. In such an eventuality, the forces at the disposal of the government might not prove adequate to prevent serious disorder. In addition, there was the question of the army. It had been resolutely loyal to the new government in 1932. Was there the same certainty now, especially with so many former members in the Blueshirts? If, in the event of a confrontation, a direct appeal was made by old comrades, was there a possibility of a split in the army? Perhaps the likelihood of this happening was small, but few things were certain in the Ireland of 1933. As far as the government was concerned, the holding of this parade could conceivably result in an attempted coup; it was almost certain to involve bloodshed and violence and might even precipitate conditions of civil strife. The risks were too great. The parade was banned.

There is one further point. From a tactical point of view, the government's decision was a shrewd one. By forcing a show-down with the Blueshirts before that movement had time to fully consolidate its strength, it effectively wrested the initiative from it, forced it on the defensive and placed O'Duffy in a highly invidious position. The government too could show strength and resolution.

After this initial set-back to his plans, O'Duffy was to receive further reverses. His intention that the National Guard would hold church parades on Sunday 20th was frustrated when 'his attention was drawn by a high ecclesiastical authority to the fact that such parades were contrary to the Statutes of Maynooth'. He therefore called off these parades but announced that in their place a National Guard parade would be held in each district on Sunday 20 August.[30]

This change in plan was announced on 15 August, and three days later Ruttledge stated that in the event of such parades being held, the government would have no alternative but to enforce the provisions of the Constitution (Amendment No. 17) Act of 1931, and proclaim any bodies or organisations attempting to hold such parades.[31]

O'Duffy and many opposition leaders had attacked the banning of the first parade, but this time O'Duffy did not comment on Ruttledge's statement. On Sunday 20 August the planned National Guard parades were held in many centres throughout the country. Most of these parades were peaceful though there were skirmishes in Limerick, Cork and Waterford.[32]

The government's campaign against the National Guard continued. On the same day as the parades were being held, de Valera was speaking at a public meeting, where he repeated Ruttledge's warning that the National Guard would be proclaimed an illegal organisation if the parades were held, and members openly professing to belong to it would be subjected to the penalties provided under the Public Safety Acts. He went on to give his own interpretation of the latest developments in that association: he said that 'they knew that when people were reading the English newspaper versions of happenings on the Continent, that some nincompoop would think he had some divine commission to become a dictator; but when that gentleman tried to organise ex-soldiers, to give them uniforms, then the government thought it was time to call a halt. . . .' He added that although he spoke of General O'Duffy, he believed he was 'only the catspaw in the whole thing'.[33]

On the day following the illegal parades (21 August), Ruttledge alleged that the National Guard was engaged in gun-running activities on a substantial scale. Later the same day, a lengthy meeting of the Executive Council was held at which the whole position of the National Guard was discussed. After the meeting, an order was issued proclaiming the National Guard and announcing that the Military

Tribunal would be re-constituted with the same personnel
as under the Cosgrave regime.[34]

On the night following the banning of the National Guard,
O'Duffy held an uninterrupted meeting at Cootehill, Co.
Cavan. A large force of police was present but did not intervene.[35] On the following night O'Duffy travelled with Blythe
and Mulcahy to Waterford, where they were scheduled to
address a National Guard meeting. This time O'Duffy was
informed by the police on his arrival that the meeting was
banned and could not take place. A considerable crowd had
gathered for the meeting, but the police order was obeyed
and it did not take place.[36] The same pattern was repeated in
Fermoy on the following night—25 August. Again a large
crowd had gathered and again the organisers were told by
the police that the meeting was banned, just a short time
before it was due to start. As in Waterford, there were no
incidents.[37]

This was on Friday, and on the same day the government
announced that the meeting arranged by O'Duffy for Beal-
na-blath on the coming Sunday had been proclaimed.[38]
O'Duffy, however, ignored this ban and after a hectic and
ingenious car-chase which extended over half of County
Cork, he succeeded in outwitting the police and addressed
a meeting in Bandon. This was Sunday 27 August.[39]

Needless to say, the government measures against the
National Guard had been strongly criticised by the *United
Irishman*. The banning had come about, it said, because the
government 'was insane with panic' and because de Valera
was 'out to smash and intimidate his opponents, and set up
a dictatorship'. It continued: 'The banning of the National
Guard is a clear threat to the liberties of the people and to
the constitutional stability of the State . . . a menace to every
party outside Fianna Fáil.' It went on to say that in spite
of the differences of opinion between the various opposition
groups—Cumann na nGaedheal, Centre Party and National
Guard—and in spite of O'Duffy's ideas on constitutional
reform, 'it was now the duty of all to stand wholeheartedly

behind General O'Duffy's organisation when it is being wrongfully attacked and persecuted. It is necessary that citizens of all shades of political opinion who value personal liberty and impartial administration should speak with one voice against abuse of authority.'[40]

It quickly became obvious that the banning of the National Guard would serve, as nothing had before, to draw the various anti-Fianna Fáil forces closer together. Before discussing the immediate implications of the banning, however, it is necessary to revert to some other political developments which were taking place at a slower pace and without much public knowledge during the summer months of 1933. Beginning in June, a series of meetings had been inaugurated with the object of bringing Cumann na nGaedheal and the Centre Party together as a united opposition party. The first meeting had taken place between Cosgrave, Patrick Hogan, MacDermot and Dillon under the chairmanship of T. W. Westrop-Bennett, the Chairman of the Senate. Not much progress was made at this meeting but in the early weeks of August there had been larger meetings of both parties. Among those present at the later meetings had been O'Higgins and Blythe, both of whom were also prominent in the National Guard.[41]

It appears that these discussions had been progressing reasonably smoothly and on 9 August the political correspondent of *The Irish Times* could say that the amalgamation of these parties was only a short time away. However, it is interesting to note at this stage that O'Duffy stated emphatically (10 August) that any overtures which had been made to him by the Cumann na nGaedheal or Centre Parties had been rejected.[42]

The banning of the National Guard meant that circumstances were now dramatically altered. Opposition unity was now made to seem a much more urgent and pressing necessity. O'Duffy's position was very different now also. His organisation was isolated and outside the law, and unless some new and strong allies could be found, its future looked bleak.

At the banned National Guard meeting in Waterford on 24 August, a deputation had arrived to meet O'Duffy from the Centre Party and Cumann na nGaedheal. It is not clear whether or not this was an official delegation, but the probability is that it was an unofficial one. It appears that the possibility of forming a united opposition party was discussed and that the delegation urged O'Duffy to bring the National Guard into this new party and to accept its leadership.[43] O'Duffy gave no immediate decision, but on 28 August, the day after his Bandon meeting, he cut short his southern tour and returned to Dublin. There he called a meeting of the national executive of the National Guard, at which it was agreed to go ahead with plans for a merger, on the understanding that the National Guard would be continued as a separate body in the new organisation.[44]

During the next few days there were further meetings between the representatives of the three groups. After some preliminary discussions, a set of outline proposals were put forward by the Centre Party to serve as the agreed basis for discussion during the consultations. These proposals were:

  (i) The party was to be known as the United Ireland Party.
  (ii) O'Duffy was to be the leader.
  (iii) Cosgrave was to lead the party in the Dáil.
  (iv) The executive committee was to consist of twelve members to be nominated by O'Duffy, Cosgrave and MacDermot.[45]

These proposals were discussed privately by each party and then jointly, though without any final decision being reached. The executives of each of the three parties then held a further private meeting at which the merger proposals were ratified. This was during the last days of August and in early September. Then on 8 September, O'Duffy addressed special conventions of both Cumann na nGaedheal and the Centre Party, and on the same day the new party was formally launched. It was to be known as the United Ireland Party or Fine Gael.[46]

The first officers of the new party were announced that day. O'Duffy was named as president and there were six vice-presidents. Three of the vice-presidents—Cosgrave, Dillon and MacDermot—were predictable choices and it was expected that, as leaders of the merging parties, they would hold such positions. But the remaining three vice-presidents were all surprising choices. There was Peter Nugent who was nominated by MacDermot, Professor James Hogan, Professor of History at University College, Cork and a brother of Patrick Hogan, and Professor Michael Tierney, Professor of Greek at University College, Dublin, a former Cumann na nGaedheal T.D. None of these three were members of the Dáil. Incidentally, it seems that the choice of the name 'Fine Gael' was suggested by Professor Tierney. It appears that the Centre Party was keen on the name 'United Ireland Party', but both Cumann na nGaedheal and National Guard members favoured an Irish name. The title 'Fine Gael' had originated at the Irish Race Convention in Paris in 1923. As a compromise, the full title of the new party was 'United Ireland Party—Fine Gael'.[47] Fine Gael was a far less cumbersome title than Cumann na nGaedheal and soon displaced 'United Ireland' as the generally accepted name for the new party.

Under the proposals submitted by the Centre Party in the earlier negotiations, it was suggested that there should be twelve members on the national executive of the new party, made up of four members nominated by each of the three merging groups. However, by the time agreement had been reached on the composition of the executive, it had eighteen members—six from each group. O'Duffy's six nominees were T. F. O'Higgins, T.D., Commandant E. Cronin, Colonel Jerry Ryan, Captain Padraig Quinn, Seán Ruane and Charles Conroy; B.L. Cosgrave nominated as his representatives General R. Mulcahy, T.D., Ernest Blythe, John Marcus O'Sullivan, T.D., Dan Morrissey, T.D., J. Fitzgerald-Kenney, T.D., and J. A. Costello, T.D. The Centre Party representatives were F. B. Barton, P. Baxter, E. J. Cussen, Robert

Hogan, E. Curran, T.D. and E. R. Richards-Orpen.[48]

It can at once be seen that the very size of the new national executive was going to mean that it would be an unwieldy body. In all, it had twenty-five members—a president, six vice-presidents and eighteen nominated members. It is also very interesting to note that a majority of those nominated had little or no political experience. Two of the vice-presidents—Hogan and Nugent—had never been members of the Dáil. Most of those nominated to the executive by O'Duffy had little real political experience—coming mainly from military backgrounds. None of MacDermot's nominees were what could be termed nationally-known figures and only one was a member of the Dáil. Cosgrave was in a difficult position and had to exclude from his nominees some former Cabinet ministers such as McGilligan, Desmond FitzGerald and Patrick Hogan. Indeed, the most striking feature of the new executive was the fact that so many of the members were so little known throughout the country and had such little political experience. The leader of the party did not hold a seat in the Dáil and fourteen of the other twenty-four members of the executive were also non-T.D.s.

A week after the foundation of the party it was announced that the National Guard was to be re-formed as a new organisation within the Fine Gael Party. Its name would be changed to the Young Ireland Association; its members would continue to wear blue shirts, and its director-general would be O'Duffy.[49]

Before going on to discuss the development of Fine Gael and the Young Ireland Association under the leadership of O'Duffy, it is necessary first to attempt to examine in some detail the factors which led to the formation of this new movement.

There is first of all the extraordinary change of mind of O'Duffy on the question of political parties—a change which seems to have occurred some time between the banning of the National Guard on 22 August and the formation of Fine Gael three weeks later. From the moment he had taken over the National Guard, O'Duffy had insisted that it was and would remain an independent and non-political organisation. On 8 August, he had declared that political parties had outlived their period of usefulness, and that it was the desire of the great majority of the members of the National Guard that it remain independent of all political organisations. On 10 August, furthermore, he had championed a system of vocational representation for the Irish parliament.

O'Duffy's volte-face, however, is, especially after the banning of the National Guard, easily understandable. A number of compelling reasons can be suggested to explain his decision. First and most immediately, there had been the banning of the National Guard, which, in the words of the *United Irishman* 'provided the last argument required to convince intelligent men of all schools of political thought that they were up against an unscrupulous government capable of going to any extremes to crush them in detail, if they did not stand together.'[50] Had O'Duffy continued on his own, he would have found himself in an extremely isolated position, and without legal recognition.

Secondly, and this was recognised by all parties, there was a large element of unreality in O'Duffy's claim that the National Guard was completely independent of all political parties. It is easy to see how this could have been so. In the first instance, the National Guard had developed from the Army Comrades Association which, in its original form, was composed of ex-members of the National Army. Most of these had either fought against the Republicans in the Civil War or felt that their pensions and gratuities were in danger from a Fianna Fáil government. It is very probable, too, that the bulk of these members were supporters of Cumann na nGaedheal. Also, of course, many of O'Duffy's chief lieutenants in the National Guard were prominent members of Cumann na nGaedheal. These included O'Higgins, Blythe and Mulcahy. There were many other T.D.s too who had been associated either with the A.C.A. or with the National Guard. Among these were Gearoid O'Sullivan,

T.D., Patrick Hogan, T.D., Dr O'Reilly, T.D., Seán Broderick, T.D., General Seán MacEoin, T.D., O. G. Esmonde, T.D. and Seamus Burke, T.D.[51] It is difficult to see how an organisation which had such names amongst its most prominent supporters hoped to persuade its opponents that it was completely independent of all political parties. Also of course it was only at Cumann na nGaedheal and Centre Party meetings that the Blueshirts were providing protection. There was no question of the Blueshirts being asked to participate at Fianna Fáil or Labour Party meetings.

Thus, while in its formal structure and in its constitution the National Guard was a completely independent and autonomous organisation, and while O'Duffy and other members may have wished it to be so, there can be no doubt that in the popular mind and the eyes of their friends as well as their opponents, there was a very real and close connection between the National Guard and Cumann na nGaedheal. A realisation of this may have made it easier for O'Duffy to contemplate a merger with Cumann na nGaedheal.

A third factor which probably influenced O'Duffy was the fact that he was under pressure from some of his aides to accept. It was felt by some, including Blythe and Michael Tierney, that O'Duffy might provide the vigorous type of leadership which the conditions of the time seemed to demand and which Cosgrave, who had lost two elections in a row, was unlikely to provide. This pressure was probably strengthened by the fact that the Centre Party seemed reluctant to have Cosgrave as leader, but would agree to merge under O'Duffy.[52]

Finally, and not least important, there was the appeal to O'Duffy's vanity and ambition. After all, he had been in active politics a mere eight weeks, and already he was being offered the leadership of a united opposition party—the second biggest in the state and one which would possibly provide the next government. Such an offer would have been difficult to refuse.

Taking all these factors—the banning of the National

Guard, the close ties already existing between the National Guard and Cumann na nGaedheal, the pressure from his colleagues and his own ambition—into account, it is easier to see why O'Duffy accepted the leadership, and his volte-face on the question of political parties seems more explicable.

It finally remains to consider the attitude of the other two parties to the merger. Cosgrave's position was un-doubtedly a difficult one. Having founded the Cumann na nGaedheal Party and having led a Cumann na nGaedheal government for ten years, he was now being asked to merge his party into a new organisation in which he would hold a secondary position, and in which the leadership would go to a man with no political experience, coming from an as yet untried political movement. It is clear that Cosgrave was not especially enthusiastic about the whole idea and it seems that his reservations were shared by some of his front-bench colleagues—most of all by Patrick Hogan.[53] However, Cosgrave's decision to work for the merger seems to have been influenced by two main considerations. Firstly there was his belief that opposition unity was essential at all costs —a belief that Fianna Fáil was out to smash all opposition and unless the various groups came together they might all perish. But neither the Centre Party nor the National Guard was anxious to have Cosgrave as their leader, and in order to bring about opposition unity, it was necessary for Cosgrave to forgo the leadership. This he was prepared to accept. Secondly, there seems to have been a group within Cumann na nGaedheal which was anxious to replace Cosgrave as leader. The feeling among these was that under his leader-ship the party had lost two elections within a year and seemed to be making little progress. It was felt that a more vigorous and extrovert type of leadership such as O'Duffy was likely to provide, was necessary to counter de Valera.

These were the factors which most influenced Cosgrave in agreeing to accept a subordinate role. It was wholly in keep-ing with his character that he was prepared to sacrifice his personal position in the interests of unity. It does appear however, that he was never very enthusiastic about the prospect of O'Duffy taking over the party, but he did give his full support and loyalty. Had Cosgrave refused to step down, the merger would not have taken place, and it was probably the realisation of this fact which most influenced his final decision.

As far as the Centre Party was concerned, it was anxious for opposition unity, but was unwilling to be swallowed by Cumann na nGaedheal. MacDermot had been worried by some of O'Duffy's undemocratic pronouncements, and it appears that one of the conditions of O'Duffy's being accepted as leader was that he abandon these ideas. This settled, the party seemed to welcome the merger.[54] With O'Duffy as leader, and with the participation of the National Guard, the appearance of being absorbed in Cumann na nGaedheal vanished, and the fact that each of the three leaders could nominate an equal number of members to the party executive seemed to put the Centre Party on an equal footing with Cumann na nGaedheal and to give it a degree of influence not proportionate to its numbers.

In the weeks which followed O'Duffy's entry into politics, events moved with an almost stunning rapidity. The National Guard had a legal existence of just over a month, and an independent existence of seven weeks, at the end of which time O'Duffy found himself at the head of a new and powerful political party. Indeed, the formation of this party—and certainly the manner in which it was formed—owed much to the government's decision to ban the National Guard. It began to look as if the government had seriously miscalculated by its decision to ban the Blueshirts, for instead of weakening O'Duffy, he now emerged at the head of a united opposition party, and instead of crushing his movement, it now had a new and strengthened position as part of a much larger organisation. The initiative now lay with O'Duffy.

6   Fine Gael under O'Duffy

THE new Fine Gael Party began vigorously. Within a month of its foundation, it had issued its policy statement, had begun to establish branches on a nation-wide basis, was rallying its support through a series of country-wide meetings and recruiting, and its harrying of the government in the Dáil reached a new intensity. Seán Lemass had been quick to refer to the new party as the 'Cripple Alliance',[1] but this description hardly tallied with the strenuous and extensive activity which marked the first weeks of the new party's existence.

The policy document of the new party was far more wide-ranging than anything which had hitherto been presented by either Cumann na nGaedheal or the Centre Party, and it marked the introduction of a number of ideas new to Irish politics. In common with the other parties, Fine Gael sought the ending of Partition but advocated—as Cumann na nGaedheal has always done—reunification 'as a free and equal member of the British Commonwealth of Nations'. It affirmed its total allegiance to the democratic system of government and declared its unrelenting opposition both to all forms of Communism and to any 'self-declared army or dictatorship'. The party would seek to abolish Proportional Representation and would work for reforms in the local government structure. The influence of the American 'New Deal' can be seen in some of the party's plans for dealing with the unemployment problem, especially where it advocated the setting up of a reconstruction corps for able-bodied unemployed. But most interesting of all were the plans to establish industrial and agricultural corporations with full statutory powers.[2]

Perhaps the most intriguing feature of the new policy is to be found in what it omitted. No trace is to be found of the plans which O'Duffy had been developing on the remodelling of the Free State parliament, and no mention is made of O'Duffy's previous statement, that he would be willing to adopt certain Fascist characteristics if they proved suitable to the Irish situation. It appears that the jettisoning by O'Duffy of this aspect of the National Guard policy was one of the conditions demanded by both the Cumann na nGaedheal and Centre Party leaders in return for accepting O'Duffy as leader of Fine Gael.[3] Nevertheless, the inclusion of provisions dealing with the setting up of economic and agricultural corporations—previously advocated only by the National Guard—indicates that O'Duffy was by no means abandoning all the ideas which the National Guard had been pioneering, and it marks the first advocacy by an Irish political party of a nascent corporatism.

O'Duffy had come to the new party with a reputation for considerable organisational ability, based largely on the part he had played in setting up the Garda Siochana in the 1920s and in helping to organise the 1932 Eucharistic Congress in Dublin. Not surprisingly then, O'Duffy took charge of the organisational drive which Fine Gael launched at its inception. And it quickly became apparent that this drive would be nothing if not vigorous. By the end of November he claimed that the new party had over 700 branches, and at the Fine Gael Ard-Fheis in February 1934, this number had risen to 1,038.[4] It is not possible to say with accuracy to what extent these were new branches or merely old Cumann na nGaedheal or Centre Party ones under a new name, but it does seem that Fine Gael was determined to establish its grass-roots organisation on a much more extensive and formal basis than had been the case with Cumann na nGaedheal. The party also arranged a series of meetings throughout the country, an activity in which all leading members of the party participated. O'Duffy himself had spoken in twenty-three of the twenty-six counties by March 1934, often addressing two or more meetings in the same day. His general strategy was to spend three or four days in a particular county or area, addressing meetings and seeing to matters of organisation. Local Blueshirts invariably turned up in large numbers at O'Duffy's meetings, and on many occasions bus-loads of Blueshirts from other areas were drafted in. Invariably too the Blueshirts provided O'Duffy with a guard of honour, and the Blueshirt salute—with up-raised hand—was becoming more and more a feature of these rallies. Not surprisingly attempts were made to disrupt many of these meetings, and clashes between Blueshirts and opponents were a frequent occurrence.[5]

The Fine Gael Party in the Dáil was led by Cosgrave, and his front bench included representatives of all three groups. It consisted of MacDermot, Dillon, J. M. O'Sullivan, Costello, Mulcahy, O'Higgins and McGilligan. The alloca-tion of front bench places obviously posed a problem, in that the amalgamation of three parties meant that some former Cumann na nGaedheal ministers had to be relegated to the back benches. Thus four ex-ministers found themselves on the back benches—Desmond FitzGerald, Fitzgerald-Kenney, Fionan Lynch and Patrick Hogan.[6] Hogan was almost uni-versally regarded as one of the most able of the Cumann na nGaedheal ministers and his relegation to the back benches seems to have been his own choosing—partly be-cause he was attempting to build up his solicitor's practice in County Galway, which he had had to neglect during his time in office, and partly too because he made it clear that he had little confidence in the new arrangement and in particular in O'Duffy as a leader. From now until his death in 1936, he was to become increasingly detached from public affairs. Of the other front bench members, MacDermot and Dillon obviously had to be included and it would seem that O'Higgins and Mulcahy owed their places primarily to their membership of the National Guard.

8

The practice of members of the Dáil wearing blue shirts was begun on 27 September by Sidney Minch, the Fine Gael T.D. for Kildare, and the following day a dozen T.D.s —including O'Higgins and FitzGerald—appeared in the Dáil attired in their blue shirts.[7] This practice was strongly condemned by Fianna Fáil and later in the year admission to the Senate visitors' gallery was refused to people wearing blue shirts.[8]

The foundation of the new party, with its stated and de-clared avowal of adherence to democratic principles, in no way mollified the approach of the still suspicious government. Two days after the foundation of Fine Gael, de Valera made it clear that he did not believe that the National Guard, merely by amalgamating with the other groups, had aban-doned the aims for which it had been banned. He would not be satisfied until all traces of Blueshirtism had disap-peared, because as long as they remained, the purpose for which they had been founded—the violent subversion of democratic government—had not been given up.[9] Thus on Friday 15 September, the premises of the National Guard at 5 Parnell Square were raided by the police; documents were seized and doors were locked and sealed.[10] On 3 November Fine Gael appealed to the Military Tribunal for permission to re-open these premises, and stated that they would produce documents to show that their organisation was a political one only. After a hearing which lasted three days, this appeal was refused and the premises remained closed. The Tribunal did not give any reasons for its de-cision.[11]

The banning of the National Guard and the closing of its offices had taken place during the Dáil recess, and when the Dáil met on 28 September, the opposition tabled a motion of censure on the government. Although the motion was defeated by eighty votes to sixty-five, the debate is of interest in that it demonstrated once again the total hostility between the two sides and showed how incompatible was the view which each side had concerning the origins and *raison d'être* of Blueshirtism. The government line was clear. The National Guard, declared Lemass, had set out to overthrow democratic institutions in the state and for this it was banned.[12] Ruttledge, quoting from departmental files, accused the National Guard of being a heavily armed organisation.[13] De Valera reiterated these charges and went on to describe the Blueshirts as Fascists. He accused O'Duffy of using the symbols of Fascism to attract young people into his organisation and declared that O'Duffy wanted one-party government and was preparing to achieve this by force. He dismissed out of hand the suggestion that there was any need for a private army to protect the opposition politicians. He went on: 'We cannot make people popular. We are doing our best to prevent people interfering with those who are unpopular, and we did give our opponents full protection.' He ended up by warning: 'We are dealing with people who were involved in a Civil War on a previous occasion, and who are going about trying to initiate another civil war.'[14]

The government line was supported by the Labour speakers, and the party leader, William Norton, defended the government's ban on the National Guard which, he said, had been aiming at 'that system of political dictatorship that had disgraced the pages of recent political history in other countries.'[15]

Not surprisingly, the Fine Gael view was diametrically opposed to all this—the Blueshirt movement was in no way anti-democratic or subversive, it was not a Fascist movement. It was entirely peaceable and was brought into existence— in fact, came into existence—through the wilful and provocative failure of the government to provide adequate protection for its opponents from the gangsterism of I.R.A. and Fianna Fáil supporters, and because of the government's blindness to the increasing danger of Communism. A number of speakers described in detail meetings of theirs which had either been broken up by their Fianna Fáil/I.R.A. opponents, or which would have been broken up had it not been for the presence of Blueshirts. According to John A. Costello:

There arose in this country a spontaneous movement to protect the rights and liberties of the people. That particular movement, spontaneous as it was, was not in any way organised, engineered or fostered by any particular party, or by any politicians. The A.C.A. came spontaneously into being because the government whose duty it was to safeguard the rights of its citizens were neglectful of their duty, because they thought it was in their own interests that they should overlook the hooliganism that was going on in every part of the country.[16]

And if the Labour leader had supported the Fianna Fáil position, the Independent Labour member for Cork city, R. S. Anthony, declared that 'the A.C.A. was established at a time when it was almost impossible, and certainly dangerous, to advocate any policy that contravened in any way the policy of the present executive.'[17]

The debate demonstrated very clearly—if such demonstration was really necessary—the impossibility of finding any agreement between the two groups. The government attitude plainly indicated that further steps would be taken to curb or remove the Blueshirts, and it was equally clear that every such act would further confirm the Blueshirts in their belief that they were up against a ruthless and vindictive government.

The closing of the National Guard office and the Dáil debate were followed by a period of uneasy calm, during which time each side continued to repeat the, by now familiar, accusations. Then on 30 November, in a series of police raids in Dublin, Kilkenny, Gowran, Mallow, Bantry, Macroom, Cashel and Waterford, the houses of some prominent members of Fine Gael were raided and searched for arms and ammunition. In Dublin the houses raided included those of O'Duffy and Blythe, and also the Fine Gael offices at 23 St Stephens Green, where almost everything on the premises was taken away on a lorry.[18] The raids were justified by the Minister for Justice on the following day in the Dáil. He claimed that the police authorities were convinced that 'there were reasonable grounds for suspecting that there were on the said premises treasonable or seditious documents, and firearms and ammunition'.[19] On the afternoon following these raids, Ruttledge told the Dáil of what had been found. The documents which he read to the Dáil included letters from Commandant Cronin, the Secretary of the Young Ireland Association, a circular from the Young Ireland Association headquarters, and letters from prominent Blueshirts in various parts of the country.

A directive from Cronin to National Guard branches, dated 22 August, instructed that if the association were banned, the work of the organisation would continue, and made some practical suggestions:

(*a*) A small number of active officers in each district shall evade Arrest and devote themselves to intensive organisation.

(*b*) Blue shirts are to be worn and meetings and parades to be held as usual, and while nothing must be done to court the arrest of members or any clash with the state forces, the organisation must not be allowed to be driven underground or to become furtive.

(*c*) Volunteers, if arrested, would declare their membership of the National Guard, recognise the Military Tribunal but give no information to the Tribunal and if convicted refuse to pay fines or go bail.

A further letter from Cronin to National Guard secretaries told them of the foundation of the new party (Fine Gael), but then went on: 'The vital work on which the National Guard has been engaged must go on without slacking or interruption. Volunteers, while playing a leading part in the new body must also do their own work zealously and conscientiously under their own officers and their own headquarters.'

Ruttledge went on to quote from other documents in support of his point that the National Guard and the Young Ireland Association were in fact the same organisation. He also suggested that there were splits within Fine Gael and alleged that certain elements in the National Guard were using Fine Gael as a cloak for their subversive intentions.

He quoted from a circular Cronin had issued on 13 September, which stated that 'the National Guard may be referred to in future as the Young Ireland Association' and from a circular marked 'confidential' and with the same date, which urged National Guard members to seek key positions in the new party saying 'the National Guard must be the predominant factor in all such committees of the new party'. A circular from National Guard headquarters, dated 14 September, declared that it should be the aim of the National Guard 'to get all the representation possible on each executive set up by the United Ireland Party, so as to be in a better position to promote the growth and influence of the National Guard'. A further directive on 4 October, again signed by Cronin, made the same point.

Ruttledge claimed that the raids which had been carried out demonstrated that leading members of the Blueshirt movement were armed, and he went on to quote from a letter from a Kildare Blueshirt, Mylie Magee of Ballymore Eustace, which Ruttledge alleged had been found in the raids. The letter included the passage 'We are very short of guns. I am on the track of two Colts ·45. I don't know if I will be successful or not.' A letter found in the house of one Eugene O'Riordan, of Glanmire, and sent from the Cork City headquarters of the National Guard on 23 September, included instructions for appointing a local intelligence officer and intimated that the intelligence system was to be 'of a militant nature'.

In addition to alleging that the Young Ireland Association was no more than the banned National Guard under a different name, and that it was arming and attempting to take over Fine Gael for its own ends, Ruttledge went on to suggest that the United Ireland Party was not quite so united as its name would suggest. In particular, he quoted a letter from a Commandant McManus. Part of the correspondence read by Ruttledge included the passage:

Further than this it has become more and more clear as we progress that we have a bigger destiny yet to fill. To put it bluntly

Cumann na nGaedheal (Cosgrave's party) is finished. The Centre Party is gone to pieces too. Frank MacDermot has turned out to be a political opportunist of the worst kind; working for place and pulling strings with de Valera behind the scenes.[20]

The raids and the reckless accusations being hurled by all groups were taking place against a background of ever increasing violence. These incidents included a growing number of raids by I.R.A. members on those public houses which continued to stock 'Bass' ale in defiance of the I.R.A.'s ban on its sale. These raids frequently resulted in the wrecking of pubs, the destruction of the offending stock and the intimidation of the publican.[21] Later in September there were a number of street clashes between police and I.R.A. in Dublin, and in the same month a Blueshirt captain was shot at and seriously wounded in Dingle.[22] On 24 September, there was prolonged street fighting, both before and after a Fine Gael meeting in Limerick. Numerous police baton-charges failed to restore order at this meeting, and attempts were made to burn a lorry and three cars belonging to Fine Gael supporters. Over thirty people were treated in hospital for injuries, and on the same day a party of Blueshirts in Kilrush was attacked by a very hostile crowd. Shots were fired, and order was not restored until two lorries of military arrived.[23] A week later at a Fine Gael meeting in Cork, military intervention was again necessary to restore order.[24] On 6 October the worst disturbances to date took place at a meeting addressed by O'Duffy in Tralee. The meeting was completely wrecked and O'Duffy received a nasty head wound when struck with a hammer on the way to the meeting. Later, over a hundred Fine Gael delegates were besieged in a hall by a stone-throwing crowd outside. The 200 police present were unable to deal with the crowd, and it was not until soldiers, dressed in battle-kit, arrived from Cork after nine o'clock, that peace was restored. A Mills bomb was thrown through the sky-light over the stage, but it did not explode as it was caught in the wire netting. O'Duffy's car was burned by the crowd, and he and Cronin had to be escorted to the county border by a large police escort. The following day an unexploded bomb was found at the rear of the hall.[25] De Valera later condemned the Tralee incidents, saying that he 'could only call them outrages and crimes'.[26] The military was again called in to restore order at an O'Duffy meeting in Kilkenny on 22 October. At this meeting, O'Duffy accused every member of the crowd who interrupted of being a Communist. He said Communism was strongest in Kilkenny, outside of Dublin; he knew that they had 300 rifles at their disposal and that there was a 'Communist anti-God cell' in nearby Castlecomer. He added that he had the names of those involved.[27] A week later, on 29 October, two locally prominent Blueshirts from Bandon were taken from their homes in the middle of the night and brutally beaten. One of them—Hugh O'Reilly—died two months later as a result of his injuries.[28] He was the first martyr of the new movement.

These were the more serious incidents to occur at this time, but by no means the only ones. Besides such incidents, a new form of activity was beginning which was to escalate dramatically in the coming months—the forcible resistance of farmers to the payment of rates. In September five farmers from County Waterford were arrested and held in custody for over a month before being charged with activities against the payment of rates. After a five-day trial before the Military Tribunal, they were found 'not guilty' on all counts and released.[29]

The increasing violence would seem to have been largely attributable to three main reasons: the first of these has already been touched upon—the growing rift between the government and the I.R.A., which was involving that organisation more and more in clashes with the law. The I.R.A.'s own economic war—especially the 'Bass' campaign —was bound to lead to arrests and brushes with the police. The open I.R.A. drilling could not go on forever. The re-introduction of the Military Tribunal was deeply resented, as were the government measures giving pensions to Civil

War veterans and setting up a Volunteer Reserve. Thus by the end of 1933, the restraints on I.R.A. activity were disappearing and *An Phoblacht* was referring to the Fianna Fáil government as 'a bunch of hypocrites, unfit to govern the country'.[30] This growing antipathy to Fianna Fáil did not alter the I.R.A.'s attitude of hostility to Fine Gael—it was convinced that 'while Duffy is brawling through the country, the inner circle of Blueshirt fascists are planning for the destruction of a system which no longer serves their ends'.[31]

A second factor contributing to the growing unrest was the economic war. The effect on exports was catastrophic—dropping from £36 million in 1931 to £19 million in 1933. The slump was most keenly felt in the livestock trade, where exports dropped from £18 million in 1931 to £7 million in 1933.[32] This drop in exports resulted in a huge glut of unsaleable cattle, as the livestock population remained virtually constant during these years. Despite government assurances, no new markets were found and the home market was not geared to absorb even a small proportion of the surplus. As a result of this decline in exports, many farmers were either unable to pay their rates or else felt justified in withholding them as a protest against the economic war. Thus at the end of the financial year 1933–34, over thirty-six per cent of the entire rate warrant was still outstanding. The position was worst in south Tipperary where over fifty-five per cent was outstanding and in seven other counties—Kilkenny, Waterford, Clare, Limerick, Carlow, Wexford and Westmeath—the figure was well over forty per cent.[33] Unrest and violence associated with the non-payment of rates were to play an increasingly important part in the politics of the Free State as 1933 came to a close.

A further reason for the increase in violence has been mentioned already—the total distrust of each side for the other in a tension-filled and poisonously bitter environment, at a time when all the pent-up and malignant emotions of the Civil War decade were fast coming to a head. Perhaps never before, and certainly never since, has Irish politics been so thoroughly a politics of hatred, as it was at this time.

With the founding of Fine Gael, the lull in Blueshirt activity which had followed the banning of the National Guard was replaced by a spate of parades and meetings. But it was soon obvious that the Blueshirts, under the name of the Young Ireland Association, were to be no less free from the attentions of the government than had been the Blueshirts under the name of the National Guard. While it might be claimed that the National Guard had changed in more than name—it was now part of a constitutional political party and its leaders had abandoned their nascent Fascism— it was clear that as far as the government was concerned, the new association and the old were essentially the same. The documents captured in the raid of 30 November were conclusive proof from the government's point of view that the banned National Guard had not been disbanded, but merely continued under a different name. The government continued to warn Fine Gael that the Blueshirts were both subversive and superfluous and made it very clear that the entrance of the Blueshirts into constitutional politics had not changed the government's attitude towards them.

Despite both this and the growing violence in the country, however, the curt announcement by the government on 8 December that the Young Ireland Association (also known as the Blueshirts) was henceforth an illegal association, came as a shock, although *The Irish Press* had hinted at the possibility of such a ban.[34] *The Irish Times* 'failed to see in what respect the Young Ireland Association had broken the law' and accused the government of acting 'as ruthlessly as the Nazi government in Germany, when it thinks it is being opposed by a powerful opponent'.[35] It is interesting that this time the government felt there was no need to elaborate on the reasons for the banning of the Blueshirts.

This was the second time in a matter of months that an organisation led by O'Duffy had been banned. This time, the attitude of the banned was more defiant. O'Duffy was beginning an organisational tour of County Donegal when the announcement was made and, speaking in Glenties, he declared:

We are a legal body. The dress we wear is legal. I am Director-General of an organisation which has a membership of sixty-two thousand and until I am arrested I am going to continue in that capacity.[36]

The first reaction of Blythe and O'Higgins on the same day was to state emphatically, 'banned or not, the organisation will continue'. The official Fine Gael statement described the banning as 'a monstrous and illegal act of political persecution without any shadow of moral justification'. The statement went on:

It is almost incredible that a government could be so blinded by hatred of their political opponents as to ban a body whose every activity is open to the fullest investigation, and every objective of which is honest and good, while it allows two Communist headquarters to remain open in Dublin, and every variety of Communist activity to be carried on throughout the country.

There is nothing illegal about the Blueshirts and no ban or ordinance can make it illegal to wear one.[37]

O'Duffy's organisational tour of Donegal continued in spite of the ban—thus making it clear to the government that he had no intention of capitulating. On the day following the imposition of the ban, he arrived in Ballyshannon, and, attired in his blue shirt uniform, addressed a large meeting. The police present did not intervene. However, Cronin who was speaking at Bundoran the same day, also attired in a blue shirt, was arrested and brought to Arbour Hill barracks in Dublin, to await trial by the Military Tribunal. On the same day, the Dublin offices of the Young Ireland Association at 23 St Stephen's Green and 62 Dawson Street were visited by the police and closed. Also in Dublin that day, business houses were visited by members of the police and the managers were warned that they were neither to manufacture nor to sell blue shirts.[38]

The following day was a Sunday, and the main centres

of Blueshirt activity were Donegal and Clare. Shots were fired at Cosgrave's car after a very stormy meeting in Annagry, Co. Donegal. All of the nine Blueshirt meetings in County Clare were stormy, the most turbulent being at Lisdoonvarna where the meeting was totally wrecked and attempts were made to pull General Mulcahy from the platform. In Tipperary town a Blueshirt meeting scheduled to take place was banned by the police, and that night a number of men who wore blue shirts at a Fine Gael dance in Clonakilty were arrested.[39]

O'Duffy remained in Donegal on 11 December, and despite the fact that a large number of extra police were drafted into the county and a number of prominent Blueshirts questioned, O'Duffy was not approached by the police. That evening he left for Dublin where an emergency meeting of the Fine Gael national executive had been called. O'Duffy presided over two meetings which were held on 12 and 14 December.[40] It was clear from the initial statements made by the Fine Gael leaders following the banning of the Young Ireland Association, that as far as they were concerned, the association would continue in existence. It seems that there was no question whatsoever of obeying the government's ruling and the meetings were largely taken up with the question of how to keep the movement in existence and at the same time retain a semblance of legality. The statement issued after the second meeting on 14 December soon made clear the tactics to be adopted. The statement announced that the national executive of Fine Gael had decided to dissolve the Young Ireland Association. It would form a new organisation, the League of Youth. A writ would be served on the High Court to establish the legality of this new organisation. The statement went on to say that the new organisation would be a disciplined, unarmed organisation. It would be an integral part of Fine Gael and subject to the control of the national executive, but it would have its own central council and officers. All its members would also be members of Fine Gael and it would work in close harmony with the national executive. The first director-general of the new association would be O'Duffy.[41]

It was very obvious that the disbanding of the Young Ireland Association and its replacement with the League of Youth was nothing more than a change of name, and that just as the National Guard had continued as the Young Ireland Association, so would the Young Ireland Association continue as the League of Youth. That the Fine Gael executive should adopt the O'Connellite tactic of dexterous name-changing was not in the least surprising. The leaders had declared that their association was democratic and constitutional and regarded the banning as a gross instance of political persecution. They saw no good reason why they should disband at the whim of a hostile government, and leave themselves completely defenceless in the face of aggressive mobs and the forces of Communism. Thus the change in name was merely a tactical move to permit the continuance of the Blueshirts, and the decision to apply to the High Court for a writ declaring the legality of the new association was an attempt to wrest the initiative from the government and to establish the new movement on an impregnable legal basis.

It is unlikely that the government expected the Blueshirts to go quietly out of existence at its behest. It may have hoped to weaken it by undermining the basis of its legality. Whatever the government's intention, it quickly became obvious that the Blueshirts were going to remain in existence and that the next round was going to be fought, partly at least, in the courts.

The League of Youth and the
Uniforms Bill

THE formation of the new League of Youth had been
announced on 14 December 1933, and it soon became apparent that the banning of the Young Ireland Association
was not going to interfere with the campaign of meetings
and reorganisation which had been going on since the
founding of Fine Gael three months earlier. O'Duffy quickly
announced that the meeting arranged for Westport on the
following Sunday would go ahead as planned.[1]

No government statement was made following the re-
organisation of the Blueshirts as the League of Youth, but
when O'Duffy arrived at Westport he was met on the out-
skirts of the town by a group of police, told that he would
not be allowed to address the meeting, and warned not to
enter the town. Some confusion followed the serving of this
notice and, accompanied by a group of young Blueshirts,
O'Duffy made a dash across the fields towards the town.
This group broke up into three or four sub-groups and
O'Duffy eluded his chasers.

Meanwhile in the town a double cordon of police surrounded the platform and two lorries of military in war
equipment were stationed outside the police barracks. Other
groups of police turned away all those who were wearing
blue shirts. In O'Duffy's absence, the main speaker was
Fitzgerald-Kenney and he approached the platform at the
head of a procession of over sixty horsemen. The meeting
started and after about half an hour, O'Duffy slipped in to
the edge of the crowd, where he was at once hemmed in by
police. A scuffle followed and he was rescued by a group of

his supporters and borne shoulder-high to the platform, where he began to speak. He had not completed his first sentence when he was arrested by the police superintendent, who climbed on to the platform after him. Surrounded by a large force of police, O'Duffy was brought to the police barracks and lodged under heavy guard. The meeting meanwhile continued amid scenes of utter pandemonium. A shower of bottles and stones descended on the platform and the remaining speakers were unheard above the deafening noise. Before the meeting ended, two prominent supporters of O'Duffy—John L. O'Sullivan and John Kilcoyne—were arrested for wearing blue shirts and lodged in custody with their leader.

O'Duffy was held under armed guard in Westport on the night of the meeting but when the news of his arrest reached Dublin, hurried consultations were held and at ten thirty that evening O'Duffy's lawyers, Patrick McGilligan, John A. Costello and Vincent Rice, made an application at the home of Mr Justice Johnson for an order of *habeas corpus* to deliver up O'Duffy and the two other Blueshirts—Kilcoyne and O'Sullivan. They were given permission to apply to the Supreme Court for a writ.[2]

O'Duffy, still heavily guarded, was moved from Westport to Arbour Hill barracks on the day following his arrest. O'Sullivan was removed with him but Kilcoyne was released.[3] O'Duffy's application opened in the Supreme Court on 20 December and on that same day all copies of *United Ireland* and *An Phoblacht* were seized and confiscated by the police.[4]

The O'Duffy case lasted for two days and the appeal was made on three grounds:—(1) the applicants were being unlawfully detained; (2) they were unlawfully arrested without warrant and were being detained without lawful justification or excuse; and (3) they were being detained for an offence unknown to the law—the wearing of a blue shirt. On the second day of the hearing, Mr Justice O'Byrne ordered the immediate release of O'Duffy and O'Sullivan, declaring that

he was satisfied that they had been arrested for no reason
mentioned under Section 13 of Article 2A of the Constitution.
He also allowed O'Duffy costs. The decision was greeted
with jubilation by Fine Gael leaders, who interpreted it as
a major setback and embarrassment for the government.
Nor were the Fine Gael leaders the only ones to be jubilant,
for immediately on O'Duffy's release the Bishop of Achonry,
Dr Morrisroe, sent him a telegram saying: 'Congratulations
on victory of justice over shameless partisanship and con-
temptible tyranny.'[5]

The legal battles were only beginning, however. Cronin
had been in custody since his arrest in Bundoran on 9
December, and on 21 December he appeared before the
Military Tribunal charged with sedition. The charge alleged
that Cronin had accused the police of 'planting' the ammunition found on the National Guard premises. The trial continued until 29 December when Cronin was found 'not
guilty' on the sedition charge, but guilty of being a member
of an illegal organisation. He was sentenced to three months
imprisonment, not to be enforced if he entered recognisances
to keep the peace. Cronin, however, choosing to adhere to
the instructions which had been issued under his name
during the last days of the National Guard, refused to enter
recognisances and instead elected to go to jail.[6]

O'Duffy's release was to mark the beginning and not the
end of his legal adventures for, two days after his release,
he was summoned to answer five charges before the Military
Tribunal. He was charged with (1) being a member of an
illegal organisation—the Blueshirts; (2) being a member of
the National Guard; (3) urging people to join the Blueshirts;
(4) incitement to murder the President of the Executive
Council, in a speech at Ballyshannon on 9 December; and
(5) accusing the government of the assassination of Michael
Collins and Kevin O'Higgins. The date of the hearing was
fixed for 2 January 1934. O'Duffy's lawyers waited until the
day before the trial was due to commence and then made
an *ex parte* application to Mr Justice O'Byrne asking for a

conditional order of prohibition giving the Military Tribunal
ten days in which to show cause why it should hear the
charges. O'Duffy's application was made on the grounds
that the Military Tribunal had no jurisdiction to hear the
charges and that the first two charges, relating to membership of illegal organisations, did not name any offence or
crime known to the law. Writs to this effect were served on
the Registrar of the Military Tribunal, the Chief State
Solicitor and the Solicitor for the Attorney General.

On the following day, the Military Tribunal, on application from the Attorney-General, decided that the O'Duffy
case should stand over until further notice. The reason given
for this decision by the President of the Military Tribunal
was that it was wished to avoid a clash between the military
and civil courts. He asserted that under Article 2A of the
Constitution the Tribunal had absolute jurisdiction to try
O'Duffy on all the charges preferred against him, and that
the Military Tribunal was not inferior to any court in the
Saorstát.[7]

The High Court action to test the order prohibiting the
Military Tribunal from hearing the charges against O'Duffy
began on 24 January 1934 and continued until 1 February
when the court reserved its judgement. Judgement was
given on 21 March and it was to the effect that the Tribunal
could not try O'Duffy on three of the charges—those dealing
with incitement to kill the President, and with sedition, but
that it could try him on the charges of membership of illegal
organisations.[8]

These court cases were taking place at a time of intense
political activity and continuing violence. The disturbed
conditions that had characterised the latter part of 1933
continued despite the strong warning handed out by de
Valera in Tralee, shortly after O'Duffy's wrecked meeting
there. De Valera had described the occurrences in Kerry
as 'outrages and crimes' and declared that the government
was determined to 'protect its authority and enforce it
against anybody'.[9] These and other warnings by the Minister

9

for Justice were, apparently, little heeded and the first days of 1934 saw the death of the second Blueshirt to be murdered. On 4 January a County Cork vintner with known Blueshirt sympathies died from injuries he had received when he had been beaten up on Christmas day. His death followed close upon Hugh O'Reilly's on 30 December.[10]

Meetings that O'Duffy addressed during January in Wexford, Fethard, Athlone and Skibbereen were marked by incidents of violence. At Wexford a crowd of stone-throwing youths were baton-charged by the police. At Fethard, all roads leading to the town were blocked with stones and tree trunks before O'Duffy was due to arrive, and the meeting that followed was marked by heckling and fist-fights. There were further baton charges at the Athlone meeting, while in Skibbereen a group of armed men arrived in the town before the meeting was due to start and ordered the Blueshirts and Fine Gael supporters who were guarding the platform to put up their hands. Shots were fired over their heads and an attempt was made to burn the platform. However, the meeting went ahead later in the day, in spite of this, and in spite of the fact that all roads leading to the town were blocked. The meeting, in fact, opened with a huge display of Blueshirt strength—O'Duffy, wearing a blue shirt, marched behind more than sixty mounted Blueshirts, at the head of a procession over half a mile long.[11]

On 11 February Cosgrave spoke at Dundalk. The meeting itself was stormy, and the police baton-charged on a number of occasions in efforts to restore order. However, the real trouble came after the meeting. A bomb was thrown into the house of a man called McGreevy, whose son had been a state witness in a Military Tribunal case the previous week. Two boys and an elderly woman were seriously injured, and the woman died a month later from the injuries. The same day there had been serious trouble in Drogheda when a group of Blueshirts, who were going to the railway station on their way to the Dundalk meeting, were attacked by a hostile crowd. Order was not restored until the military had been called out. There was further trouble when the Blue-shirts returned that night and were again set upon. This time the police used tear gas, and an armoured car patrolled the town until the early hours.[12] On 15 February *United Ireland* was again seized by the police and banned.[13] Towards the end of February, three Limerick Blueshirts were sent to prison for being in possession of arms, and before the month had ended, O'Duffy addressed further turbulent and dis-rupted meetings at Balbriggan and Galway.[14]

The violence in the countryside found an echo in the Dáil chamber. The stormy scenes which marked the first day of the new session on 31 January were to set the tone for the rest of the year. The *Irish Times* parliamentary correspondent observed that 'for sheer vitriolic ill-feeling on both sides of the House nothing before has been seen in the Dáil to compare with the savage exchanges that took place yester-day'.[15] The question of the murder of the Cork Blueshirt was raised by Dr O'Higgins at Question Time and sparked off one of the bitterest-ever exchanges in the history of the Dáil. At times nearly half the members were on their feet shouting angry comments and personal abuse across the floor of the House. Epithets such as 'murderer' and 'traitor' were used with abandon. O'Higgins accused the Fianna Fáil members of laughing at the murder, while MacEntee retorted that 'any deputy with the name of O'Higgins had no right to talk about murder in this House'.[16] The *Irish Independent* political correspondent described the scenes as 'the most bitter that I have experienced in our Legislature—and I have known it since its inception'.[17] Later in the session, Seán Lemass remarked that 'the bitterness created by the Civil War has been more intensive during the past six months than it was in 1924'.[18]

The accusations and counter-accusations continued to be hurled recklessly across the chamber with each side accusing the other of setting out to establish a dictatorship. On 4 February de Valera referred to O'Duffy as 'the man who wanted to start a dictatorship by means of a *coup d'état*'.[19]

Fine Gael speakers continued to deny these allegations, and James Dillon challenged de Valera to prove them in court, saying, 'The government has searched the records of the League of Youth; it has searched the houses of the League of Youth; it has read its rules and its correspondence, but it has never been able to prove one single breach of the law by the League of Youth. . . . It is because the government cannot blacken their character, or find anything that will injure their reputation in the eyes of the Irish people that they started their cheap fraudulent charges which they dare not make directly, but which they make in a back-hand way.'[20]

In addition to the charges of dictatorship which the Fianna Fáil speakers were making, it was also being suggested with increasing frequency that serious strains were being felt within the Fine Gael leadership. Lemass described the position thus: 'On the first day Deputy Cosgrave will make a speech saying that the Bill was the worst ever introduced by the government. On the second day General O'Duffy will make a speech saying it is a good Bill, and will criticise the government for not having introduced it earlier. On the third day Frank MacDermot will make a speech trying to prove that there is no difference between Deputy Cosgrave and General O'Duffy'.[21] It was also alleged that O'Duffy's speeches were now being censored by the other leaders, because of their supposedly extravagant and unpredictable nature.[22]

*　　　*　　　*

By the end of January 1934, O'Duffy had completed his first six months as leader of the Blueshirts. It had been an eventful and highly successful period. His arrival had seemed to infuse new spirit and enthusiasm into the movement; it had grown rapidly and gave every appearance of becoming a major political force.

More than that, it had survived a series of governmental

attempts to outlaw it—two direct bans and a number of court cases and arrests.

Its meetings had been spectacular, especially those addressed by O'Duffy, though it does now seem that there was an element of stage-management involved in some of these meetings from the way bus-loads of Blueshirts were often brought in—apparently at considerable expense and often from long distances.[23] However, the Fine Gael Ard-Fheis on 8 February saw a striking display of Blueshirt strength, and morale generally was high.[24] The movement had also succeeded in espousing a controversial issue in its support for those farmers who were suffering from the rigours of the economic war. The worsening effects of this war were to be in some way responsible for the sudden upsurge of violent opposition to the payment of rates by farmers, especially in the south, south-east and midlands. This was a form of activity which was soon to be fully supported by many Blueshirts.

The government measures against the Blueshirts had been singularly unsuccessful, but it was clear that the government had no intention of letting up in its efforts. The only question was one of method. This point was clarified in February when it was announced that the government was about to introduce a Bill which would make illegal the wearing of the blue shirt or uniforms of that nature. The Bill—the Wearing of Uniforms (Restriction) Bill—was introduced in the Dáil on 23 February 1934. It would prohibit the wearing of uniforms and badges and the use of military titles in support of any political party or its ancillary associations, and it would also prohibit the carrying of weapons, including sticks, at political meetings.[25]

The Bill was moved in the Dáil by the Minister for Justice who elaborated on the reasons for the need for such a bill. He claimed that there had been grave breaches of the peace for some months past and the object of the Bill was to preserve peace and maintain order.[26] Later, at the second stage of the Bill, he said that its object was 'frankly, to deal with the Blueshirt position in this country'. He went on to justify the government's decision to ban the wearing of uniforms: 'the wearing of uniforms in this country, as in other European countries, has resulted in the creation of disorder, and a strain that the authorities cannot adequately deal with.' The movement, he said, 'has created bitterness and tended to bring about a perpetuation of bitterness'.

He strongly attacked the Blueshirt claim that it existed primarily to help the police and to ensure the protection of free speech. He alleged that he had ample evidence from his police reports to show that the behaviour and tactics of Blueshirts at meetings throughout the country were 'dictatorial and provocative'. Blueshirts were being supplied with batons, and were committing acts of assault and battery on people attending their meetings. These 'bully tactics' were, he claimed, a very evident aspect of Blueshirtism.[27]

Ruttledge also devoted considerable attention to the European situation. He claimed that conditions similar to those in the Free State 'have arisen in most European countries. No doubt deputies are aware that these ideas about uniforms and blue shirts are not original in this country. The uniform, and indeed the objects of the organisation, seem to be copied, without practically a comma being changed, from similar organisations in continental countries.' He stated emphatically that the establishment of a Fascist state was very clearly one of the objects of the Blueshirts and he alleged that there was a close analogy between Mussolini's March on Rome and the banned National Guard parade of the previous August.

He ranged over the experience of a number of European countries which had, he claimed, to deal with a similar type of situation and with 'what has been described as militarisation in politics'. He detailed some of the legislative sanctions invoked against shirted movements in other countries and told the opposition: 'You may complain of the Bill being unreasonable, but remember, you copied your methods and your uniforms from other countries, and if we are to adopt the same methods in order to preserve peace that these other countries had to adopt, to deal with the position, can you complain?'[28]

Seán Lemass too, dwelt on the alleged similarity between events in Ireland and on the continent, but felt that in Ireland the memories of the Civil War would add an extra dimension of bitterness. He said that legislation had been introduced in other countries and was being introduced here 'because as a post-war development there has been a tendency in many countries towards the militarisation of politics, which it is very necessary to arrest if democratic institutions are going to be preserved. We can see in many European countries this development of militarisation of politics at its various stages; its incipient stages, its half-developed stages, and its completed stage'. The proposed legislation would retard these developments in Ireland.[29]

Unlike a number of other speakers who accused O'Duffy of having adopted the ideas and organisation of Italian Fascism, Lemass felt that O'Duffy's ideas were very confused: 'He does not appear to know very much about the type of political association he wants to establish in this country. His knowledge of Fascism appears to have been acquired during a fortnight's cruise on the Mediterranean. But he has made it quite clear that Fascism of some kind is the type of political association he wants to establish in the state.'[30]

Lemass also reiterated the government's determination to see that the democratic institutions were defended:

It is not for us to criticise the actions taken in Italy or Germany. The people in these countries are entitled to have whatever type of institutions they like. But we are going to see to it that in this country similar institutions are not going to be imposed upon the people, and that if they come into existence it will be by the development of existing institutions and the free will of the people. If the deputies opposite have the same views they can strip themselves of their shirts, disband their military organisation and confine themselves to political activity of the ordinary kind, because that is all that will be necessary.[31]

Other Fianna Fáil speakers stressed this point, that the aim of the Bill was to preserve parliamentary democracy against the dictatorial designs of the Blueshirts. De Valera also stressed the danger of civil war posed by the Blueshirts, but felt that the army, police and civil service were firmly loyal to the government. He dismissed completely the Blueshirt allegations about the strength of the Communist movement in the Free State. He gave a county by county breakdown of the extent of Communism, as supplied to him from confidential police reports, and concluded that in only three areas was there any evidence of the existence of Communist cells: Dublin, Kilrush and Castlecomer, and even in these areas, the danger was insignificant.[32]

De Valera also mentioned during his speech that he had no objection to the colour blue, or to the Blueshirt salute— 'I always thought it was a manly salute, a much better salute than the mere doffing of one's hat, so if people want to use that salute I have no objection, not the slightest.' But he reiterated the government's determination to prohibit uniformed parades in public and accused the opposition of 'using the courts to hamper the Executive.'[33]

Not surprisingly the Fine Gael interpretation of the Bill was completely different. The majority of speeches were concerned with the accusation that the government was determined to smash all constitutional opposition and establish its own dictatorship. It was alleged over and over again that the government was 'soft' on Communism and cowardly in the face of I.R.A. violence. The Blueshirt movement was represented as a spontaneous reaction to the government's negligent failure to give proper protection to speakers at public meetings, and a number of speakers described meetings which they claimed had been broken up by I.R.A. and Fianna Fáil supporters. The Blueshirts were described as being a totally democratic and constitutional movement and it was denied that the movement owed anything to, or sought to emulate any of, the continental movements.

John A. Costello saw the Bill as the 'culmination of the

illegal activities of the government over the past six months —illegal activities which were brought to an end by the operation of the constitutional courts'. He alleged that the police had been intimidated by the government into assaulting private citizens and that the protection given to political opponents of the government was inadequate. The A.C.A., he declared, had come into existence because of the disorder prevailing throughout the country, and the blue shirt was merely a symbol of comradeship.

He stressed the fact that the League of Youth was, in its methods and objectives, an entirely lawful and constitutional organisation, and went on to deal with the government's attempts to outlaw it and with the new proposals in this regard:

The Minister gave extracts from various laws on the Continent, but he carefully refrained from drawing attention to the fact that the Blackshirts were victorious in Italy, and that the Hitler shirts were victorious in Germany, as, assuredly, in spite of this Bill and in spite of the Public Safety Act, the Blueshirts will be victorious in the Irish Free State.[34]

It was not a statement that was to be easily forgotten by his political opponents.

Fitzgerald-Kenney, described during the debate by the Attorney-General, Conor Maguire, as the 'gloomy Dean of the Dáil',[35] in addition to attacking the Bill on the grounds already mentioned, saw further sinister implications in what it proposed. Under the new Bill, he said, 'a guard sees a girl wearing the banned blue blouse, and that guard has authority there and then to strip that article of clothing off that girl'. He was fairly confident that most of the older guards would not carry out their instructions and 'see public decency violated'. But he was 'not so sure as to the members of your new force', and felt that to give to a guard 'the power to tear the clothing off a respectable, decent Irish girl, to tear off her blouse in the public street or the public place, is a monstrous power to put in any Bill'.[36]

And so the debate continued, with charge and counter-charge and without any possibility of agreement. Dillon claimed there was absolutely no danger to the institutions of the state in any part of the movement and that 'not a single man sitting on these benches would continue in support of a movement that contained the possibility or prospect of a civil war, or aimed at upsetting the elected government by a dictatorship'.[37] Cosgrave saw the Blueshirts as being manned mainly by farmers and farmers' sons—whose livelihoods were in danger of being wrecked by the government.[38]

After scenes of great bitterness, the Bill passed all its stages in the Dáil on 14 March by seventy-seven votes to sixty-one.[39] It was then referred to the Senate, where it quickly became clear it was going to meet with resolute opposition. On 21 March, a week after it had been introduced in the Senate, that House, by thirty votes to eighteen, refused to give it a second reading.[40] This effectively meant that it would now be at least eighteen months before the Bill could reach the Statute Book. From the government's point of view, this action of the Senate completely emasculated the Bill and rendered it virtually useless.

The importance of the Senate's action lay in the fact that once again a direct attempt by the government to eliminate the Blueshirts had been thwarted. But in preserving the Blueshirts the Senate also signed its own death warrant. Government displeasure with the Senate now boiled over into open hostility, and, on the day following the rejection of the Uniforms Bill, de Valera introduced a Bill into the Dáil to abolish the Senate. On 24 May the Bill was passed in the Dáil but, not surprisingly, was rejected by the Senate.[41] However, like the Uniforms Bill, it would become effective after an eighteen-month moratorium.

Thus, as 1934 entered its second quarter, the third and most determined direct attempt by the government to outlaw the Blueshirts was, to the great and obvious chagrin of Mr de Valera, thwarted once more. O'Duffy could look back with satisfaction on his first six months as leader of Fine

Gael. It has been a breathless and exciting period and it had seen a rapid and sustained growth in Blueshirt numbers and in their involvement in the political life of the state. O'Duffy's leadership was as yet unquestioned, his movement united. His first electoral test as leader of a political movement was due in June in the form of the local authority elections and there seemed to be every reason for O'Duffy to look forward with optimism to this test. The coming months were destined to be even more turbulent and violent than those which had gone before.

8   The Local Elections and After

THE action of the Senate in defeating the Uniforms Bill
ensured the continuation of the Blueshirts as a legal organisation for at least a further eighteen months. It was in the
light of this—the most determined attempt yet by the
government to eliminate the Blueshirts—that Fine Gael welcomed the announcement made in early April that the local
authority elections would be held on 26 June.[1] This would
be the first electoral test for the new party and an excellent
opportunity to demonstrate at once the extent of the support
which the new party had attracted and the unpopularity of
the government's policies. The Fine Gael decision to contest
these elections represented a break with the old Cumann na
nGaedheal practice. Cumann na nGaedheal had refrained
from directly contesting and had hitherto argued that party
politics should have no place on local authorities. Fianna
Fáil, on the other hand, had from its foundation contested
these elections on a party basis seeing them both as useful
training ground for politicians and as a means of consolidat-
ing local support. In addition Fianna Fáil had claimed that
the Cumann na nGaedheal policy on this question was
merely a hypocritical facade—arguing that Cumann na
nGaedheal supporters had always stood, but under the guise
of Business or Independent candidates. In any event Fine
Gael had no hesitation in deciding to contest the 1934
elections and the spring and early summer months were to see
all parties making extensive preparations for these elections.

Public meetings were organised in all parts of the country
by all parties, and political disturbances—mainly at Fine

Gael meetings—continued to be frequent. Some of the most serious of these disturbances, when rival 'armies' of Blueshirts and Fianna Fáil supporters met head-on, took place at Bagenalstown on 17 March, Tullamore (8 April), Mohill, Waterford and Enniscorthy (29 April). At Mohill, O'Duffy's meeting was completely wrecked—all roads to the town were blocked, the platform was burned down, shots were fired and there were numerous police baton charges. Cronin's meeting in Enniscorthy the same day suffered a similar fate. Meetings at Urlingford, Ballybunion and Listowel in early May led to serious fighting and numerous police arrests and on 27 May, meetings in Midleton, Cork city, and Drogheda were disrupted. Before the election campaign ended, seven further meetings were seriously disrupted—at Castlebellingham, Ballinalee, Mullingar, Claremorris, Tallaght, Newcastlewest, and Kells.[2]

In addition to the traditional animosity between Blueshirts and members of both Fianna Fáil and the I.R.A., the rift between the government and the I.R.A. was now complete. By the end of 1933 thirty-four members of the I.R.A. had been convicted by the Military Tribunal and the rate of arrests and convictions increased during 1934. On 23 April an I.R.A. ammunition dump and landmine were discovered in County Dublin.[3] On 2 May, two members of the I.R.A. were sent to prison for three years following an explosion at Carrigtwohill, and on 3 May General Tom Barry, a prominent member of the I.R.A. and one of the most famed and colourful guerrilla fighters of the Anglo-Irish war, was sent to jail for a year for being caught in possession of arms and ammunition. He refused to recognise the court and attacked Fianna Fáil for its attitude to the Republic and its betrayal of the I.R.A.[4] Earlier, on Easter Sunday, Seán Russell, one of the top I.R.A. leaders, had declared his organisation's complete loss of confidence in Fianna Fáil. 'Constitutionalism has failed in Ireland' and only by military force would the Republic be realised. He also announced a new I.R.A. recruiting campaign.[5]

Despite this worsening of relations between the I.R.A. and the government and the increasingly strong I.R.A. tendency to resort to force, the bulk of cases heard before the Military Tribunal in 1934 related to the Blueshirts. More and more Blueshirts were appearing and being convicted both on charges of general violence and on charges arising out of economic war/anti-rates activity. Among those convicted were some very prominent members of the organisation. On 24 April, Colonel Jerry Ryan, a member of the Fine Gael national executive, was charged at a special court in Thurles Hospital with the attempted murder of a rate collector.[6] On 4 May, the Director of the League of Youth in County Clare was charged with attempted murder. The charge arose out of incidents that had taken place during a Blueshirt-I.R.A. clash in Ennis. The accused was found guilty of 'manslaughter under extreme provocation'. The bullet which he had fired in the air had apparently rebounded off a wall.[7] On 1 June, Captain P. Hughes, a prominent Dublin Blueshirt, was sentenced to two years by the Military Tribunal under the Official Secrets Act.[8]

However, the bulk of Blueshirt activity during these months was to be found more and more in the anti-rates campaign, which in the summer and autumn of 1934 dominated all other activity. The adverse effects of the economic war were being felt with increasing severity, especially in the cattle-farming counties of the south and midlands. In these areas, the movement against the payment of rates was strongest and in early April over forty per cent of the rate warrant was outstanding.[9] In four counties, where the county council had a strong anti-Fianna Fáil majority, the councils refused to co-operate fully in the collection of rates and were dissolved by an order of the Minister for Local Government. These counties were Kilkenny, Waterford, South Tipperary and Laois. The government alleged that enquiries into these councils' failure to collect rates had disclosed evidence of an organised attempt to prevent payment and that these attempts were being strengthened by the attitude of the councils in question.[10]

The government responded to the non-payment of rates by drafting in large forces of police to protect the bailiffs who were seizing cattle and goods from the farms of those who refused to pay. In many cases local farmers co-operated to frustrate the bailiffs by having stock and goods removed to a neighbouring farm or hidden away before the arrival of the bailiff. In other instances, roads and railway lines were blocked and telegraph wires cut, either to prevent the bailiff and his force getting to the farms or to prevent the goods from being removed from the area. Sometimes also, local farmers and Blueshirts would form a human barrier in an attempt to prevent the seizures. These activities led to numerous clashes and further difficulties arose when the bailiffs attempted to dispose of the seized goods in order to raise the amount owing for the rates. Usually in these cases, the bailiff would convene a special auction to sell off the goods. Local people would rarely bid for goods seized from their neighbours, though occasionally a farmer would buy back his goods for the amount owing. Usually government agents—generally a 'Mr Brown' or a 'Mr Smith'—would be present and the goods would be knocked down to them at very low prices: no one else would bid. The goods would then be taken away and sold elsewhere. Not surprisingly, the presence of these agents aroused tremendous resentment and they were in need of constant police protection. Frequent attempts were made to manhandle them and to hinder their movements.

The following is an account of a fairly typical sale of seized cattle, and gives some idea of the temper of the country. This incident took place in Thurles in April 1934—a few months before the agrarian unrest reached its highest point:

Exciting scenes were witnessed here today when three horses seized from local farmers for non-payment of rates were put up for auction by Superintendent R. Muldoon of the Garda Siochana. About three hundred farmers were present, many of them wearing blue shirts. About thirty gardai and twelve detectives were present.

The debts in each case were under five pounds and the seizures were made by gardai two days ago.

When the first horse was put up for sale, the Superintendent said there was a bid of ten shillings and shortly afterwards one pound. There was almost continuous cheering from the crowd and cries of 'Who is the bidder?' 'He is a German and Briscoe the Jew'. The second horse was also sold for a pound. When the third horse—a good-looking half-breed filly by St Dunstan—was led in, a continuous din was kept up and the owner, Jack Harty, Ballyvoneen, stated the bridle was his and proceeded to take it off the horse. Two Guards rushed towards the animal, but Harty succeeded in pulling the bridle away. At this stage, a portion of the crowd approached the rate collector, James Kinnane, who was struck several blows. Guards surrounded Mr Kinnane to save him from further blows. Mr Kinnane drew a revolver and immediately three guards caught hold of him and put the revolver back in his pocket. There were cries of 'We'll see this is your last seizure'.

The crowd afterwards marched to the main street where they were addressed by Colonel Jerry Ryan. It was announced that a victimisation fund was being opened. Three other horses were produced, on which the farmers were mounted. They then rode through the town followed by a cheering crowd.[11]

This type of activity tended to concentrate mainly in the counties of the south and midlands where the farms generally were bigger and where the cattle population per acre was higher. The counties most affected were Cork, Kilkenny, Limerick, Tipperary, Waterford, Westmeath, Meath, Wexford, Carlow and Kildare. Cattle exports had dropped catastrophically, while the cattle population had remained almost constant. No new export markets had been found, the farmers could see little possibility of any being found and felt their whole livelihoods were being threatened. Thus judging by the type of activity engaged in and by the areas in which it occurred, there is little doubt that economic deprivation was the driving force behind much—if not most—of the Blueshirt activity during 1934.

Despite some highly optimistic claims made in 1932, the

government had failed almost completely to find alternative markets for Irish exports.[12] Europe in 1934 was still in the throes of the great Depression and with the international scene so very unsettled, the time could scarcely have been less propitious for the seeking out of new markets for agricultural produce. This failure was posing some very serious problems for the government. For while the discomfiture of the bigger cattle farmers—the 'ranchers'—fitted in with the government's long-term strategy of breaking up the large farms and replacing grazing with tillage, and while also the government could be reasonably sure that this policy would not lose it much electoral support as the bigger farmers were regarded as strongly pro-Fine Gael, nevertheless, the glut of unsold and unsaleable cattle did pose an immediate problem. Given the nature of the international situation and the ideological conviction behind the dispute with Britain, there was probably little that the government could do in the circumstances and the major scheme put forward by the Minister for Agriculture, James Ryan, to alleviate the situation illustrated vividly the government's impotence on this point. In April he introduced the Calf Slaughter Scheme with the objective of reducing the cattle population of the Free State by slaughtering 200,000 calves.[13] It was a simple, brutal and futile solution. To encourage farmers to slaughter their calves, a bounty was paid for each calf slaughtered. Introducing the measure, Dr Ryan admitted the extremity of the scheme: 'Perhaps it is a calamity to see the calves slaughtered, but if there is no other way out of it, if we cannot consume the beef ourselves, if no other country is prepared to take it from us, the only solution is to cut down the numbers of our cattle, and the only way we can do that is by slaughtering up to 200,000 cattle in the year.'[14]

The government offered a compensation of three pounds for each cow slaughtered and thirty shillings for each bullock or calf.

By the end of April it was reported that calves were being slaughtered at the rate of 25,000 a week, and it was alleged

10

that in parts of the country beef could not be given away.[15] Certainly, the episode of the slaughtered calves was to become a part of Irish political folk-lore, and more than one anti-Fianna Fáil speaker was later to recall the 'ghosts of the slaughtered calves'. The government also introduced a free beef scheme whereby those entitled to certain social welfare and unemployment benefits were given free beef.[16]

This then was the background leading up to the holding of the local elections: bitterness in the Dáil, frequent and sometimes serious rows at political meetings, the persistence of violence and unrest throughout the country, the jailing of both I.R.A. and Blueshirts by the Military Tribunal and the prospect of economic collapse facing the agricultural population.

*　　*　　*

As election day approached, the contest took on a significance rarely associated with such elections and out of all proportion to the importance of the seats to be filled. For a start, this was the first electoral test for the new party and O'Duffy's very first essay in electioneering. He campaigned throughout the country and as election day approached, he became more and more confident that Fine Gael was going to score a spectacular success. His meetings attracted, for the most part, large and enthusiastic crowds and it may have been the euphoria generated by these meetings which led him on 24 June—on the eve of the election—to predict that Fine Gael would win control of twenty of the twenty-three councils being contested.[17] It was clear that for O'Duffy, success in the local elections was to be but the prelude to an even more resounding success for Fine Gael in the next general election and a triumphant vindication of his leadership. In addition, the election would help answer two further questions. It would demonstrate whether or not Fine Gael had succeeded in picking up any new supporters, or had merely held on to the Cumann na nGaedheal and Centre

Party support. The results would also give some indication of the actual strength of the Blueshirt movement. The swirl of activity which surrounded the affairs of the movement— the parades, meetings, O'Duffy's whirlwind tours—gave the impression of great strength and there were conflicting accounts as to the actual size of the movement. O'Higgins had claimed 29,000 members for the A.C.A. at the end of 1932.[18] O'Duffy had given a figure of 62,000 after the foundation of the National Guard,[19] and by the end of 1933 this figure had risen to over 100,000.[20] Finally, in 1934, O'Duffy was to estimate the size of the movement at over 120,000 members.[21] O'Duffy did not indicate how these figures were ascertained and Ruttledge was to claim in 1934 that the movement never numbered more than 20,000—information he claimed he had from 'official sources'.[22]

The result

The landslide which O'Duffy had been predicting—against, it seems, the advice of some of the other Fine Gael leaders—failed to materialise and when the results were in, it quickly became clear than Fianna Fáil was still—and securely—the majority party. It emerged as the biggest party on fourteen councils, while Fine Gael was biggest on only six: Carlow, Cork, Dublin, Sligo, Wexford and Wicklow. On three councils—Kildare, Limerick and Westmeath—the parties were equal in strength. The Fianna Fáil-Labour alliance ensured Fianna Fáil control of fifteen councils while Fine Gael controlled seven. In terms of seats won on all councils throughout the country, the result could be represented as follows:[23]

FIANNA FÁIL	728
Fine Gael	596
Labour	185
Others	371

This was, incidentally, the last Local Government election to be held on a register of rated occupiers. A government Bill providing full universal suffrage for these elections did

not become law in time for the 1934 elections. It was generally felt that Fine Gael would derive most benefit from the
operation of the rated occupier franchise.

At another time, the Fine Gael performance might have
been regarded as highly satisfactory, but after O'Duffy's
predictions, his confident assurances of success and the very
extensive campaign he had fought, the result could only be
seen as a decisive defeat. For in spite of the severities of the
economic war and the championing of the farmer's cause by
the Blueshirts, the results demonstrated the extent of de
Valera's popular support—and his ability to retain it even
in the face of adverse economic conditions. Thus, in the first
direct contest between de Valera and O'Duffy, de Valera
had won comfortably.

*   *   *

The elections had been regarded by O'Duffy and Fine
Gael as a show of strength between them and the government and as an opportunity to demonstrate to the government the unpopularity of the economic war policies and
those policies aimed at eliminating the Blueshirt movement.
O'Duffy and his party lost and while it is difficult to gauge
with any certainty the precise effects of this set-back on
Blueshirt behaviour, the period following the election saw a
definite and perceptible increase in anti-rates activity and
evidence of a new note of extremism in some of O'Duffy's
speeches and in those of some of his subordinates. The
worsening economic situation may also have been to some
extent responsible.

The number of Military Tribunal convictions during 1934
gives some indication of the extent of this unrest. 451 convictions were made and of these, 349 were Blueshirts and
102 were members of the I.R.A.[24] The summer months also
saw two further Blueshirt deaths. On 30 June a County
Tipperary Blueshirt, Patrick Kenny, died from injuries
sustained in a scuffle with some Fianna Fáil and I.R.A.

supporters.[25] The second incident occurred on 13 August during the sale of seized cattle at Marsh's yard in Cork. A lorry, carrying about fifteen men, crashed through a police cordon and through the closed gate of the sales yard. The lorry was followed into the yard by a group of supporters, and immediately a number of armed police opened fire—without, apparently, having been ordered to do so by the Superintendent present. A youth, Michael Lynch, was killed and seven other people injured. The action of the Special Police in firing on the crowd was later severely censured by Mr Justice Hanna of the High Court, who described them as 'an excrescence upon that respectable body' (the Civic Guard).[26]

The Cork shooting aroused tremendous Blueshirt indignation throughout the country. The youth of the dead man, the dramatic nature of the whole incident and the excessive and arbitrary manner in which the police had reacted, all combined to raise Blueshirt anger to a new level. The funeral of Michael Lynch saw a huge gathering of Blueshirts in Cork city and O'Duffy's graveside oration had all the elements of an emotional clarion-cry to Blueshirts to intensify their resistance.[27]

As the summer months passed and as the spate of agrarian unrest and violence showed no signs of abating, government speakers began to step up their allegations that the Fine Gael leaders were deliberately fomenting unrest for unconstitutional purposes. The Minister for Justice, for example, claimed in August that there was a definite Blueshirt conspiracy against the payment of rates.[28] And, indeed, while there may not have been any conspiracy as such, the prominent involvement of Blueshirts and of some Fine Gael T.D.s could well have given this impression.

In October 1933 Sidney Minch, the Fine Gael T.D. for Kildare, had advised farmers not to pay their rates.[29] During 1934 four Fine Gael T.D.s—Fagan of Longford-Westmeath, Curran of Tipperary, Bennett of Limerick and Wall of Waterford—had goods and livestock seized by bailiffs for non-payment of rates.[30] Another T.D., Edward O'Neill, was involved in the Marsh's Yard incident.[31] Some prominently placed Blueshirts went to jail during the campaign. Captain Padraig Quinn, a member of the Fine Gael national executive and probably the leading Blueshirt in County Kilkenny, was sentenced to three months in October 1934.[32] Another member of the national executive, Lieutenant Patrick Quinlan, was sentenced to nine months in December.[33] Colonel Jerry Ryan, who had been appointed Deputy Director of the League of Youth in October, was sent to jail for nine months for his part in an armed attack on the house of a Tipperary rate collector in April 1934.[34]

Speeches by Blueshirt leaders were becoming more and more reckless, and in the Dáil in August, Ruttledge read extracts from some of the more extreme instances. For example, Commandant Cronin speaking in Tipperary on 14 July 1934 said:

We have members of the police force earmarked, and when we get into power we will know how to deal with them, to relegate them to their proper place. I warn the police now that any of them that are doing the dirty work for a tyrannical government will find themselves where they are now trying to put others. If we are persecuted and driven to it, we may have to resort to arms, and what we did in three months in 1922 we can do again and teach them a lesson they will never forget.

De Valera has spoken about a dictatorship, but I say here to-night if a dictatorship is necessary for the Irish people we are going to have one.[35]

Or there was the speech on 23 July by Captain Quish, a prominent Limerick Blueshirt; after a sale of seized cattle he declared:

I say this and I understand fully what I say. We used guns before and if necessary we will use them again on the 'John Browns'. The government are a crowd of Spaniards, Jews and Manxmen. If necessary we will use the guns again to redeem the people.[36]

Another speaker, a member of the county council, spoke at the same meeting as Quish:

These are the men who are now going to strike a rate. I went behind the ditches and shot innocent members of the R.I.C. but I did not yet go behind them to shoot the 'John Browns' or the bailiffs, but the time is coming when action will have to be taken and we will have to shoot the 'John Browns'.[37]

Ruttledge also quoted from a speech of O'Higgins on 23 June which was reported in the *Leinster Leader*:

They were going on the offensive and if Blueshirt meetings were to be broken up, then next time Mr de Valera held a meeting that would also be broken up.
They would see that every man could express his opinion in public without fear. They did not want any blackguardism, but if there was, and if the other side broke gobs, they would also break gobs. They had the material and they would use it.[38]

It seems clear that by the middle of 1934, with the defeat in the local elections behind them, with a perceptible worsening in the economic situation, with the feelings of the farmers exacerbated by the brutal futility of the calf slaughter scheme, control of the Blueshirt movement was firmly in the hands of the more extreme elements—both at national and local level. Now, with an increase in anti-rates resistance and agrarian unrest, with the almost daily convictions of Blueshirts by the Military Tribunal and with the increase in inflammatory and sometimes almost hysterical speeches, the earlier vehement claims that the Blueshirts would always operate strictly within the law was more and more open to question.

However, despite the claim which would later be made that, by this time, there was a growing amount of unrest within Fine Gael with the leadership, there was as yet no signs of any real dissent or of any move to oust O'Duffy and reassert a more moderate type of leadership. This may have been due in part to the strike of Dublin newspapers which lasted for the months of July, August and September and which meant that many parts of the country were without newspapers and consequently many of the speeches and incidents may have gone unnoticed. But more important perhaps was the feeling among Fine Gael people of the absolute necessity of maintaining unity in face of the Fianna Fáil-I.R.A. opposition. For while the more moderate Fine Gael leaders might well deprecate the rural violence and the role being played by the Blueshirts, it is nevertheless very plausible that, in the circumstances, this could be seen as the natural and spontaneous reaction of a group facing financial ruin as a result of the misguided and vindictive policies of a hostile government, and most especially because of the government's insistence on collecting the rates at the very time its policies were destroying the only market the farmers had for their produce. Thus, whatever dissatisfaction with the leadership and methods existed within Fine Gael—and it does seem that some did exist—it had as yet found no public expression, partly perhaps because as yet no suitable opportunity presented itself, but more likely because, whatever reservations might be held about Blueshirt tactics and the manner in which the movement was developing, the majority of people in Fine Gael were convinced of the justice of the cause being espoused by the Blueshirts.

However, the two newspapers most hostile to Fine Gael and the Blueshirts, *The Irish Press* and *An Phoblacht* frequently suggested during these months that a split in Fine Gael was imminent. *The Irish Press*, like a number of Fianna Fáil politicians, had been pointing out a number of alleged discrepancies between the O'Duffy policy and that of his vice-presidents, and had been devoting some attention to alleged inconsistencies in some of O'Duffy's speeches.[39] Indeed it was later claimed that *The Irish Press* was quick to see that O'Duffy was often indiscreet in his public speeches, and consequently the paper had a special reporter instructed to cover in detail even his most minor speeches.[40] But, like the other Dublin papers, it was affected by the strike and consequently had no comment to offer on the events of August-September 1934. *An Phoblacht*, however, came to an agreement with the strike committee—whose cause it actively championed—and appeared twice weekly during the strike. As will be shown later in this chapter, it devoted during this time considerable attention to the internal workings of the Fine Gael leadership.

On 18 and 19 August, the first annual Blueshirt Congress convened in Dublin. In February of 1934 the Blueshirts had played a prominent part in the first ever Fine Gael Ard-Fheis, when O'Duffy, the Fine Gael president, had appeared wearing his blue shirt. But the holding now of a separate Blueshirt Congress emphasised the quasi-separate existence of the Blueshirts and attracted an attendance of over a thousand delegates. The timing of the congress too was important—it convened just five days after the Cork shooting incident and at a time when Blueshirt anger was very great. The occasion of the congress was marked by violent scenes in various parts of Dublin. A number of Blueshirts were attacked and had to seek refuge, while a Blueshirt dance in Dawson Street necessitated such police protection that the street had the appearance of being under military occupation.[41]

O'Duffy's congress speech was a marathon affair, in the course of which he traced the foundation and development of the movement, examined the policies of the Blueshirts and finally devoted a great deal of his attention to the agricultural crisis. He outlined the corporate policy of Fine Gael 'which we brought with us as our chief contribution to the policy of the united organisation, and which was unanimously accepted and which is now the chief plank in the policy of Fine Gael for the rehabilitation of Ireland'. Hardly surprisingly, most of his attention was taken up with the rates and the agricultural question. He singled out for special praise five prominent Blueshirts who were then serving prison sentences for their part in various violent incidents: Cronin, Captain Hughes, Captain Quish, Colonel Jerry Ryan and Seán McNamara, the director of the Blueshirts in Clare. He promised the farmers the wholehearted and unqualified support of the Blueshirts in their struggle for existence and told them that 'the attitude of the Blueshirt movement towards the farmers in their present desperate plight will be clearly shown in the discussions on the resolutions which will be submitted to the Congress for consideration'.

The central resolution was a three-pointed one which O'Duffy himself introduced. The motion:

  (i) called upon the government not to collect the Land Annuities during the present agricultural depression;
  (ii) called upon the government to set up an independent Tribunal, presided over by a judge to examine the farmer's position generally;
  (iii) called upon the farmers throughout the country not to pay the Land Annuities, or rents on labourers cottages in the event of the government's failing to agree to either of the first two requests.[42]

Despite the implications of the third point—an open directive to engage in unconstitutional activities—the motion was passed with the enthusiastic support of the delegates. No opposition was reported but it does seem that Colonel O'Higgins sought to prevent the motion being debated and to have it withdrawn.[43] However, the motion was passed and—partly at least due to the newspaper strike—did not occasion any public comment.

One further—and again largely unnoticed—incident of importance took place in late August, this time concerning the question of Northern Ireland. O'Duffy had strong feelings on Partition. A native of County Monaghan, a border area, he had done much of his soldiering in that area and had been O.C. of a northern brigade. He was on record as having advocated a forceful takeover of the North in 1922 with his famous 'Give them lead' speech.[44] He maintained close ties of friendship with many prominent Nationalists in the North and rarely made a speech which did not contain some reference to Partition and to the need to work for its removal. The National Guard had been banned from the start in Northern Ireland—partly, it would seem, because of the background and views of its leader and ostensibly because it sought the ending of Partition. In any event, in August 1934, O'Duffy declared in County Cavan that England was fortifying her outposts in the Six Counties. If this meant war, he said, then he would be in it, and so would ninety-five per cent of the Blueshirts: 'The other five per cent should give up their shirts.'[45] This statement, like the annuities motion, attracted very little attention, perhaps again because of the newspaper strike. In all probability it was little more than a typical piece of O'Duffy hyperbole but it was soon to lead to dramatic and unexpected consequences.

As already mentioned, *An Phoblacht* had been suggesting, in its special strike editions, that the Fine Gael-Blueshirt movement was heading for a major crisis. This newspaper, frankly and totally hostile to Fine Gael, had from the start been prophesying the disintegration of that movement. Previously its stories had tended to be general and somewhat fanciful. Now, however, they began to appear with a new frequency and a new attention to specific detail, such as to indicate that something was possibly afoot in Fine Gael. The stories merit some examination.

On 14 August the paper alleged that a top Blueshirt official had disappeared with £6,000 of the association's money. The story claimed that this had thrown the Blueshirt headquarters into complete disarray and would contribute further to the movement's decline—a decline which was being daily accelerated by events on the continent. A week later, O'Duffy denied this story, albeit in a rather odd manner. The story was untrue, he said, as they had no money in the funds.[46]

On 18 August *An Phoblacht* suggested O'Duffy was moving closer and closer to the Fascist movements of other European countries. It carried a news report of the visit to Britain and Ireland of the prominent Norwegian Greyshirt, Terje Ballsrud. Ballsrud, it appears, was to have talks in London with Sir Oswald Mosley and in Dublin with O'Duffy.

On 25 August the paper carried a report from the Belfast

Nationalist paper, *The Irish News*, which described some in-
itiatives O'Duffy had been taking concerning the Border.
The report said that recently a representative of the O'Duffy
wing of the League of Youth had visited important Nationalists to ascertain their views on matters across the Border.
This representative had 'confessed that the merger of the
League of Youth, Cumann na nGaedheal and the Centre
Party had not worked out altogether well.' Funds were low,
O'Duffy's insistence on weekly meetings and the bringing
in of contingents of Blueshirts to areas where they were weak
had proved very costly. The funds of the United Ireland
Party had vanished and the League of Youth was now
anxious to break free. The article claimed also that Cosgrave
had of late been critical while MacDermot had gone adrift
on his own from both of them. *The Irish News* claimed that
O'Duffy's representative was told that there was no support
for his party in Northern Ireland even though he 'pleaded
O'Duffy's soft spot for the North' and promised to reverse
the policy of Cosgrave and Blythe on the North. The article
ended: 'It was made evident during the interview that the
break [between Fine Gael and the League of Youth] could
not be long off.'

The same issue of *An Phoblacht* carried two further items
on the question of the coming dissension within Fine Gael.
A news report alleged that there had been severe criticism
of Cosgrave at the secret session of the Blueshirt Congress. It
claimed that Cosgrave's 'cautious methods' had been assailed
and went on to anticipate a trial of strength at the next
meeting of the Fine Gael executive. It anticipated an align-
ment of O'Duffy, Blythe, Mulcahy and Cronin in opposition
to the Cosgrave, MacDermot and Dillon forces.

A further article in the same issue, signed by Frank
O'Brien, also forecast an inevitable split, but gave rather
different reasons. The chief reason would be that 'O'Duffy
was going Fascist'. The campaign of agrarian violence was
his idea—he wanted martyrs. He was modelling himself on
European movements and was in league with Mosley. The

article claimed that O'Duffy's behaviour had 'disgusted the wily and more pacific Cosgrave clique'. It went on to cast Cronin as 'the new arch-henchman of O'Duffy' and forecast that Blythe would also side with O'Duffy.

Three days later, the emphasis had changed somewhat although the paper claimed, 'we can now state definitely that the split in the Blueshirt party is now complete'. However, the break would be on the specific issue of the unconstitutional activities of some of the more extreme Blueshirts. Again, it was anticipated that Cronin and Blythe would side with O'Duffy.

These *An Phoblacht* items, with one exception, drew no reported retort from O'Duffy. This is not surprising in itself as the Fine Gael leaders never bothered to conceal the contempt with which they regarded *An Phoblacht*. The stories may have been largely speculation and certainly it is difficult to see how *An Phoblacht* would be privy to the inner workings of the Fine Gael leadership. At the same time, the persistence of the stories, their apparent detail and insistence, would seem to indicate that something was afoot and that certain strains were becoming all too evident—predictions which were soon to be shown to be by no means without foundation.

9 The Split

On 30 August, eleven days after the Blueshirt Congress had ended, the national executive of Fine Gael held its regular meeting at the party's headquarters in Merrion Square, Dublin. Apart from routine matters, discussion at the meeting centred around two main topics—the motion on the non-payment of land annuities passed at the Blueshirt Congress and which O'Duffy now sought to have adopted as official Fine Gael policy and, to a lesser extent, the views expressed by O'Duffy on the Northern Ireland question.[1]

Both issues were fraught with pitfalls as far as the Fine Gael leaders were concerned. O'Duffy's motion on the non-payment of annuities was in effect calling for a campaign of civil disobedience which could be represented as striking at the financial foundations of the state. For Fine Gael to support O'Duffy's motion would be to unequivocally sanction the use of unconstitutional methods and could be seen as an endorsement of the speeches and actions of the more extreme Blueshirts. The motion touched upon a particularly sensitive area. Cosgrave and his associates had always been proud to regard their complete adherence to constitutional and democratic methods as one of the distinguishing features of their movement. The Civil War had been fought on this principle. Great sacrifices had been made in the twenties to uphold it and the peaceful transfer of power to Fianna Fáil in 1932 had seen this principle triumphally, if painfully, vindicated. Now, however, the government was charging Fine Gael with the violation of these very principles. The government could point to the active part being played in the anti-rates agitation by a number of Fine Gael T.D.s. It could point to the part being played by the Blueshirts in the entire campaign. It could point to the praise lavished by O'Duffy on those Blueshirts whose zeal had landed them in jail.[2]

Thus the existence of what looked like a conspiracy and the apparent association of certain elements of Fine Gael with it, placed Cosgrave and company in a very invidious position. However much they might regard the economic war as vindictive, provocative and ruinous—and they did—and however much sympathy they might have for the farming community, the fact remained that to adopt the Blueshirt motion would be to opt for a course of action blatantly unconstitutional, potentially violent and alien to the principles which had activated both the Cumann na nGaedheal Party and the Parliamentary Party tradition of Dillon and Mac-Dermot. On the other hand, for the executive to reject O'Duffy's motion would be to acknowledge openly that the party leadership was split on a policy issue of major importance—and more precisely that there was a major difference between the Blueshirt leaders and those in the parliamentary party. In the same way, to reject a motion, already championed in public by the party's president, and on which he appeared to have strong feelings, would be, in a sense, to cast doubts on his leadership.

Although the annuities motion was more important and of more immediate urgency, the Northern Ireland question also arose. What would mainly seem to have been at issue here was O'Duffy's style of leadership. He had made a major statement of intent, with little evidence to support his assertions, and had in fact committed the Blueshirts to a line of action little different to that of the I.R.A.

In the event, the main discussion at the meeting of the executive centred around the annuities motion and after a lengthy, confused and at times acrimonious debate, O'Duffy withdrew the motion. But not before one of his principal opponents on this question, Professor James Hogan, a party vice-president, resigned. Hogan said he was resigning from the executive 'as the strongest protest I can personally make against the generally destructive and hysterical leadership of its President, General O'Duffy'. He went on to be more specific. He said that he had had many opportunities of seeing General O'Duffy at close quarters during the past year but two things had immediately decided him in his decision to resign. These were 'O'Duffy's connection at a recent convention with the policy of universal non-payment of annuities and rents on labourers' cottages' and 'his destructive pronouncements on Ulster, which I regarded at the very least from the moral point of view as fatal to the policy of national unity, for which, by its very name the United Ireland Party stands'. He went on:

The United Ireland Party is full of the most high-principled and able men. It is one of the last hopes of democratic and ordered government in this country. That party can have no future as long as it retains at its head as its leader General O'Duffy. Whatever his good qualities may be, in politics I have found him to be utterly impossible. It is about time the United Ireland Party gave up its hopeless attempt of saving General O'Duffy from his errors.[3]

The resignation of Professor Hogan did not appear as a major sensation, nor did it look as if it would have the repercussions so gleefully forecast by *An Phoblacht*. This may have been partly due to the newspaper strike, but perhaps more to the fact that Professor Hogan was not a well known figure nationally. He had taken part in the War of Independence, but from the early twenties on, his main preoccupations had been academic. He held no public elective office and was best known for his contributions to the corporate policy of Fine Gael and for his writings on the relationship between the I.R.A. and Communism. Certainly, *The Cork Examiner*, the only daily paper unaffected by the strike, was 'clear that there was no question of a split in Fine Gael'.[4]

Nor did the resignation in any way appear to ruffle O'Duffy. The personal attack which Hogan had made on him would, he said, 'urge him on to greater efforts in the accomplishment of the national work he had undertaken'. He went on to deprecate the position of Hogan in the movement:

The national executive had been discussing an important national question during the past two days without making much progress because of Professor Hogan's criticism and obstructionist tactics. . . . It is significant that we were able to arrive at unanimous agreement a few minutes after he left, and all danger of a split on our ranks immediately disappeared. . . . Professor Hogan was merely a nominated member of the executive . . . and the public would be able to estimate his loss to the party by reading his hysterical statement.[5]

Nor did the national executive of Fine Gael appear to place any great importance on the resignation. In a statement on the day after the resignation, it declared that Hogan had resigned for 'personal reasons' and that O'Duffy had the full confidence of Fine Gael and the League of Youth.[6] During the next few days, Fine Gael speakers continued to deny any suggestions of a split. At Beal-na-Blath on 2 September, O'Duffy declared that 'there is no split and will be no split' while on the same occasion Cronin was just as emphatic— 'There is no split and never shall be.'[7] And James Dillon in Mitchelstown on 9 September emphasised that there was no split in Fine Gael.[8]

However, this display of public solidarity was to prove to be more apparent than real. It concealed for the moment the fact that Hogan's resignation had succeeded in bringing to a head the dissatisfaction with O'Duffy's leadership which existed at the upper levels of the party—which may indeed have been the very purpose Hogan had in mind when resigning. Although the details of what exactly happened during the next few weeks are cloudy and confused, it is clear than on the days following Hogan's resignation, a series of conferences were held between O'Duffy, Cosgrave, Dillon and Cronin. MacDermot was absent because of illness.

It is not clear who exactly called these conferences, but according to Cronin, the main topic discussed at them was 'the imprudent and contradictory character of O'Duffy's speeches, which had been lowering his own prestige as a leader, and shaking confidence in the movement'. It appears that O'Duffy was asked to agree to a number of proposals outlined by Cronin. These proposals, again according to Cronin, were:

1. O'Duffy and his vice-presidents were to meet weekly.
2. Policy was to be clarified at a big meeting in the Mansion House in October.
3. O'Duffy's speeches were to be delivered only from prepared and approved manuscripts.
4. Interviews to the press were to be given only after consultation, and in writing.[9]

These conferences were held in secret and certainly *The Cork Examiner* was unaware of their existence. While they were going on, O'Duffy continued to speak at Blueshirt meetings in the country, at which he was to make some apparently contradictory statements which would seem to have put him at variance with the official policy of the party he was leading. On 3 September:

Mr de Valera could not proclaim a Republic for twenty-six counties, as if he did he would go down in history as perpetuating partition.[10]

And six days later:

Mr de Valera had a perfect right to declare a Republic for the Twenty-six Counties and if he did I do not believe England would interfere.[11]

And in the course of the first of these speeches, the leader of the party committed to membership of the Commonwealth declared:

I suffered and risked my life for the Republic . . . I was sentenced to death for the Republic, and I have not changed since.

In addition, he appears during this time to have had some consultations with the Ulster Blackshirts with a view to some form of co-operation. The report of these tentative moves appeared in the *Derry Journal*—an organ hostile to O'Duffy, and it does seem somewhat strange that at a time when O'Duffy was protesting his allegiance to the Republic in terms which any member of the I.R.A. would have been pleased to use, he was at the same time exploring the possibility of co-operation with an Irish body whose motto was 'loyalty to King and Empire and the building of the greater Britain'.[12]

The circumstances surrounding the leadership conferences were, as has been mentioned, rather cloudy and many contradictory claims were later to be made about what actually went on. These meetings were, of course, held in secret, and there is no reason why there should have been any public awareness of their existence. Indeed, as far as the general public was concerned, there was no indication that things were other than usual in Fine Gael and party meetings continued to be held at various places throughout the country. Professor Hogan's resignation had been seen as an event of minor significance, and in any event, the public was in receipt of scanty political information because of the newspaper strike.

The apparent calm which had surrounded Fine Gael during these weeks was shattered at the next meeting of the party executive on 21 September, when, without warning, O'Duffy tendered his resignation. O'Duffy's decision came as a bombshell, and the suddenness of his resignation, with no apparent warning of impending change to the rank-and-file, was to be one of the main reasons for the utter confusion which followed.[13]

From the outset, the executive handled the crisis badly. The statement issued after the meeting was bald and terse. It announced the resignation but gave no reason for the decision. It merely regretted O'Duffy's decision and paid a warm tribute to the work he had done for Fine Gael. It

announced too, that at the same meeting Commandant
Cronin was 'unanimously selected by the Central Council of
the League of Youth as the new director-general of that
organisation'. When he was interviewed immediately after
the meeting, O'Duffy would give no reason for his resignation. He merely said he was glad to be out of politics and
he hoped that 'members of the League of Youth would
supported Edmund Cronin in the same unswerving way they
had supported him'.[14]

The next couple of weeks were to see the whole Fine
Gael-Blueshirt movement thrown into indescribable chaos—
with an unprecedented leadership crisis, with almost total
confusion, vacillation of support and absence of information
at local level, with a new and bitter note of acrimony and
with the whole movement seemingly bent on its own destruction. The confusion which followed was due in large part
to the manner in which O'Duffy's resignation took place,
but before examining this and before discussing in some
detail the circumstances of the resignation, it is proposed to
see the controversy first through the eyes of an impartial
observer and then as some of the main protagonists
viewed it.

One of the best informed commentators on Irish politics
at this time was the Irish correspondent of *The Round Table*,
John J. Horgan. He could be fairly expected to have a good
knowledge of what was happening in Fine Gael, and certainly his analysis of the situation is of interest. Writing in
the March 1935 issue:

The gallant General, it has turned out, has not only no political
experience, but little discretion. He is one of those people pos-
sessing boundless energy but ill-directed enthusiasm, who so often
come to the top in a revolutionary struggle but who are unable
to adjust themselves to the more prosaic requirements of ordinary
political life. He is also much too genial to fill the role of a
Mussolini, which his admirers thrust upon him . . .
Though it is obvious for some time that his speeches were severely
edited by more experienced politicians, he frequently managed

to escape his mentors' control and to make extempore speeches of an irresponsible and exuberent kind.

These outbursts were a constant source of embarrassment to Cosgrave and the more sober and experienced leaders of the United Ireland party and it was plain for some time that relations were becoming strained between the two elements.

But the final differences, Horgan felt, were due to more than O'Duffy's personal idiosyncracies. It was because of the fact that during the months of August and September, sections of the younger Blueshirts were getting out of hand, and were using direct action to impede the officials who were trying to collect the overdue land annuities and rates by legal process in the shape of forced sales of seized cattle.This growing violence, followed by the League of Youth motion on the annuities and the resignation of Professor Hogan had brought matters to a head. The accumulation of these factors was responsible for the growing dissatisfaction in the upper levels of the party, but Horgan felt that the immediate reason for O'Duffy's resignation was the insistence of the Fine Gael executive that he should not make unauthorised speeches.[15]

This, then, was the opinion of an impartial if not altogether detached observer. In the months which followed the split, each of the principals involved had something to say about the reasons for O'Duffy's resignation. Cosgrave, who had obviously been involved to a large extent in the entire episode, was more reticent than most. Possibly his temperament made him reluctant to attack a former colleague who did have some appealing personal qualities. Perhaps he felt that enough damage had already been done to the movement and that after all, the real enemy was Fianna Fáil and not one's former comrades. In any event, he was not prepared to elaborate in public on the circumstances surrounding the resignation. He claimed that the resignation had come as a surprise to the vice-presidents. He was vague about the conferences leading to the resignation. The only purpose of these conferences was, he said, 'to consolidate our forces, strengthen our positions where they were considered weak, and establish unity of purpose and effort'. Which does not really tell very much about the origin and nature of the conferences. And, the real cause of all the trouble, he felt, lay in the fact that 'O'Duffy confused his symbolic with his real personality'.[16]

MacDermot was not much more specific. According to his account, O'Duffy's resignation had come about because he was 'not a practical statesman'. His speeches had been injudicious and not in accordance with party policy. Mac-Dermot claimed that since O'Duffy's resignation, his speeches had been completely incoherent.[17] Writing about the controversy at a much later date, MacDermot was to claim that it was O'Duffy's reacceptance of Fascist models and methods which was the basic cause of the crisis—the fact that after the first few months of his leadership of Fine Gael were over, O'Duffy was moving back to some of the ideas he had promised to abandon when he merged the National Guard with the constitutional political parties.[18]

Cronin, who replaced O'Duffy as director-general of the League of Youth, was prepared to go into greater detail. He claimed that O'Duffy had resigned, not because of any fundamental difference of policy, 'but because he thought it was an insult to ask him to prepare his speeches. This he felt was an attempt to put him into a strait-jacket'. Cronin went on to claim that it was the 'imprudent and contradictory character of many of O'Duffy's speeches which had been lowering his own prestige as a leader and shaking the confidence of the movement' which forced the other leaders to impose these restrictions on O'Duffy. He claimed:

From the time this arrangement was first made, O'Duffy told me on several occasions that he was going to resign . . . and that he was in fact going to leave the country. Several of us prevailed on him not to retire, and after three weeks we succeeded in holding his hand. Eventually he did send in his resignation without consulting any of us.[19]

O'Duffy offered two main reasons for his resignation. The

first and more important was that there were fundamental differences of policy between himself and the majority of the executive, and in fact he later wrote a pamphlet outlining these differences.[20] The differences he claimed to be numerous, but the two most important were on the annuities and on the corporate policy. He felt that as far as the agricultural crisis was concerned, 'Fine Gael were talking but doing nothing, while the farmers starved'. He was proud to claim that he had prepared the controversial Blueshirt motion himself and would stand over it. On the question of the corporate policy he claimed that 'Fine Gael had only nominally accepted it'. He went on: 'It was like putting old wine into new bottles.' The other main reason which had led to his resigning was the increasingly irksome position he was finding himself in—'whenever he wanted to decide an issue, he was threatened with the instant resignation of either Cosgrave or MacDermot'. Thus he was later to claim that by 15 September he had made up his mind to resign.[21]

Patrick Belton, T.D., who supported O'Duffy during the controversy, broadly agreed with this interpretation. Without being too specific, he claimed that fundamental differences of policy were the main reason for the disagreement. He went on: 'It was obvious that O'Duffy was expected to be a tool, but when he proved to be a man of ability, with a constructive national outlook, he must be got rid of.'[22]

Captain Walsh, who was O'Duffy's private secretary at this time, and who was at all times an ardent admirer of the General, treats of this episode in his unpublished *General Eoin O'Duffy—His Life and Battle*. He claims also that it was a fundamental difference of policy which led to the resignation though his emphasis is different. According to Walsh, O'Duffy stood for:

. . . an independent and united Ireland, whether under a Republic, a Kingdom of Ireland, or an all-Ireland Free State with the sovereign right to withdraw from partnership in the Commonwealth at the earliest time advantageous to do so.
That vice-presidents MacDermot and Dillon could not or would

not agree everybody knows, for like others of the Fine Gael party they are irretrievably bound up in membership of the British Commonwealth—'Long live the British Empire' being their motto.[23]

This, says Walsh, was the main area of policy disagreement which led O'Duffy to resign. But he also suggests that Cronin had become jealous of O'Duffy and was working against him. He claimed that he remembered well when O'Duffy took over the leadership, Cronin's bitter resentment at having to preface all official correspondence: 'I am instructed by the director-general' etc. He went on to say that 'Cronin had succumbed to the wiliness of ex-ministers and became their willing agent in sowing the seeds of discontent within the organisation of which he was the paid secretary'. He went on:

Private conferences between Fine Gael 'brass-hats' and Blueshirt officers were arranged and held in an effort to undermine General O'Duffy's authority with the result that certain disaffection set in, and the required element of suspicion was created. I might here add that it was Commandant Cronin who appealed to the delegates of the Fine Gael executive when General O'Duffy's resignation as president of that party was before them on 21 September 1934 to accept it, thereby throwing the Blueshirt members of that body into confusion. The secretary had urged it; so there must be some good reason.[24]

*　　*　　*

From these accounts and from other available evidence, two clear points would seem to emerge—there were important differences of policy between the O'Duffy and Cosgrave wings of the party and secondly, there was continued and growing criticism of O'Duffy and his style of leadership especially in mid- and late 1934. In the final analysis, it was probably this growing dissatisfaction rather than any policy difference which led to the leadership crisis.

First, the policy differences: as already indicated, these existed mainly on the questions of the corporate policy and on the land annuities issue. That there were differences is clear enough but their actual importance in precipitating O'Duffy's resignation is not so clear. The only real confrontation appears to have been on the land annuities motion and although Hogan resigned on this issue, his statement made it clear that his resignation had as much, if not more, to do with O'Duffy's style of leadership. He used phrases such as 'hysterical and destructive' to describe O'Duffy's leadership and said it was 'about time the party gave up its hopeless attempt of trying to save O'Duffy from his errors'. The differences between O'Duffy and his vice-presidents on the corporate policy would probably have had important long-term significance, but in the context of the Irish situation of 1934 they would seem to have been more potential than actual. Certainly had O'Duffy continued to make overtures to European Fascist movements—as he was beginning to do—had he continued to express admiration for Hitler as well as for Mussolini—as he did—then in all probability some form of break would have occurred on this point. Mac-Dermot had, as early as 1933, deprecated the nascent Fascism which he saw in the National Guard.[25] One of the conditions of O'Duffy's acceptance as leader of Fine Gael was that he abandon Fascist ideas and notions. In 1934, he appeared to be moving back to his National Guard ideas and it does seem likely that had he continued to develop along these lines he could have been faced with a revolt from his vice-presidents.

In the context of late 1934, however, the agricultural crisis over-shadowed all else in immediacy and urgency. The crisis was a major one and those most affected were the traditional supporters of Fine Gael. Violence was widespread and rural life was in danger of disruption. Because of the immediacy and because of the urgency, the whole question of the attitudes to be adopted and the tactics to be used was to high-light a difference between the two groups in Fine Gael deep enough to be almost fundamental. As far as the O'Duffy wing was concerned, this was virtually another round in the

Civil War and constitutional niceties mattered little in face of both the enormous damage done and the vindictiveness of the government. The Cosgrave position briefly was that a constitutional political movement must use constitutional methods—however painful or unrewarding this might prove to be. In many ways the issue was as simple as that; nor was it without its European parallels.

On the question of Ulster, there would also appear to have been some difference, although these were hardly of immediate importance. The Fine Gael Party sought reunification of the country—but as a free and equal member of the Commonwealth of Nations. O'Duffy, as already mentioned, had strong and emotional feelings about Partition. Unlike Cosgrave and McGilligan, who had been involved in External Affairs during the 1920s and who had a sense of the important role Ireland could play in the Commonwealth—and who indeed had seen in the *Statute of Westminster* concrete evidence of this, and unlike Dillon and MacDermot whose Parliamentary Party background predisposed them to Commonwealth membership, O'Duffy did not appear to have any strong feelings on the value of membership as such. He wanted unity with sovereignty and was probably in no way insincere when he declared that he was once ready to die for the Republic and that he had not changed since. It should be remembered that O'Duffy was very much influenced by Michael Collins and his initial acceptance of the Free State was very probably influenced by Collins' 'stepping-stone' philosophy. Without developing this point any further, it does seem that there was an important difference of policy on this point between O'Duffy and his vice-presidents.

That policy differences existed and that they were of importance does seem to be clear. What is not clear nor so easy to ascertain, however, is just how important these differences were in the events leading to O'Duffy's resignation. It is very possible that they were of rather less importance than O'Duffy was later to claim. As has already been suggested, the differences on the corporate policy and on Ulster, while undoubtedly important and of long term significance, were not of such pressing immediacy as to precipitate a leadership crisis on their own. If the land annuities motion was the crucial factor, why then did Cronin and many of the Blue-shirts most associated with the extremist line not side with O'Duffy?

There was no simple reason for the split and it does seem that the differences on policy were merely part, albeit an important part, of a wider problem—O'Duffy's personality and his style of leadership. It is clear that there was consider-able dissatisfaction with O'Duffy among some of the other Fine Gael leaders and this dissatisfaction came to a head at the conferences called after Hogan's resignation. Indeed the four headings supplied by Cronin would seem to give a good indication of the nature of this dissatisfaction.

Firstly, there was the demand that O'Duffy and his vice-presidents should meet weekly. This was felt to be necessary because O'Duffy was thought to be somewhat autocratic and high-handed and given to making decisions without con-sulting the vice-presidents. Certainly there often appeared to be a surprising lack of coordination among the party leadership, and the unpredictability of some of O'Duffy's statements seemed to catch some of the other leaders by surprise.

Secondly, there was the demand that policy should be clarified at a meeting in the Mansion House. This point has already been dealt with and indicates that the vice-presidents were aware of the widening gulf between O'Duffy and them-selves especially on the subjects already mentioned—the annuities and rates resistance campaign, Ulster, the cor-porate policy and relations with European Fascist move-ments.

Thirdly, there was the question of O'Duffy's speeches and the demand that henceforth they should be delivered only from prepared and approved manuscripts. In many ways this was probably the most important source of discontent.

Cronin attacked O'Duffy for 'the imprudent and contradictory character of many of his speeches'. Horgan had noted
the 'irresponsible and exuberant nature' of many of O'Duffy's
extempore speeches. MacDermot had described these
speeches as 'injudicious and not in accordance with party
policy'. James Dillon once remarked to O'Duffy: 'When
you stick to your notes, General, you're the greatest speaker
there is. But let some old women in the audience shout 'Up
Dev' and God knows what you will say next.'[26] Michael
Tierney instances the occasion of a big meeting in Cavan.
O'Duffy spoke from his prepared script and having finished,
launched off into an inflammatory, exuberent and contradictory speech of his own.[27] Certainly, an examination of
O'Duffy's speeches shows a peculiar combination of characteristics—his statements on Ulster reveal an exuberance
and a belligerency, his references to the economic war situation were often inflammatory, his attitude to corporatism
ambiguous and his attitude to European Fascism unpredictable. He was capable too of extempore statements which were
to prove very embarrassing—statements which a more experienced politician would never make. At one meeting, for
example, he was asked by a heckler about the Guards
who had been dismissed during his time as Commissioner.
O'Duffy immediately gave the number of such dismissals,
and went on to claim that the great majority of these dismissed Guards were now staunch Blueshirts. *The Irish Press*
a few days later gave a detailed breakdown of the offences
with which the dismissed Guards had been charged—theft,
drunkenness, assault, dereliction of duty, incompetence, de-
sertion.[28] The general picture to emerge was hardly of a
group that any political leader would boast of having among
his supporters. Indeed, it has been said that O'Duffy's
political opponents were quick to fasten on this aspect of
O'Duffy's leadership, and *The Irish Press* is believed to have
had a number of reporters assigned to O'Duffy alone, in the
hope of capturing his more extravagant and injudicious
statements.[29] They were to find plenty to occupy them.

The fourth demand—that O'Duffy should give interviews to the press only after consultation and in writing was made again largely for the same reasons.

These points make clear the main areas of dissatisfaction with O'Duffy. There was at least one other point of dissatisfaction. This was on the question of finance. O'Duffy's re-organisational drive had included major meetings in all parts of the country. O'Duffy had insisted that in areas where the movement was weak, supporters should be brought in from the adjoining areas to give the impression of strength and to attract more support. This had been done, but the cost in addition to the cost of paying the full-time and part-time officials in various parts of the country, was proving too much of a strain on the finances of the movement and O'Duffy himself admitted in August that there was no money left.[30] O'Duffy's extravagance was blamed by some of the other leaders for this state of affairs and this was a further cause of dissatisfaction with his leadership.

All of these accumulated dissatisfactions combined to show in brief that O'Duffy was the wrong person to be at the head of Fine Gael. He had been brought in to give the Fine Gael leadership a new vigour. This he had done, but at a very considerable cost. For in his enthusiasm he lacked judgement; his lack of a parliamentary background and training made him oblivious to the nuances and subtleties of parliamentarianism and an inappropriate leader of a largely parliamentary movement. His military background and his penchant for action predisposed him to direct methods, where often a more thorough grasp of the situation would have counselled a more constitutional or diplomatic approach. His natural restlessness and abundance of nervous energy made him at times an uncomfortable colleague to work with. His impetuosity and exuberance led him into making many exaggerated and contradictory statements. He was not a man of ideas and seemed unable to distinguish easily between the 'Quadragesimo Anno' corporatism of Hogan and Tierney and some of the blatantly Fascist regimes of contemporary Europe. He was too impetuous, too naïve, too forthright, and too muddle-headed to be a serious politician. Indeed, almost immediately after his resignation, he declared how pleased he was to be out of politics and said that he had never been at home among politicians.[31] Surprisingly, O'Duffy had never regarded himself as a politician, even though he was president of the main opposition party. He always retained his National Guard days distrust of politicians and tended to see them in a narrow and uncomplimentary light. He liked to regard himself as something of a crusader—a man with a mission. He disliked the compromises and accommodations which are an everyday part of political life. He was, in short, an unhappy choice as leader of a political party and many of the later problems of Fine Gael sprang from this fact.

One further point needs to be discussed and that is one on which there is a shortage of information although there was no shortage of controversy at the time. This is the manner in which O'Duffy's resignation was brought about. First there is the question of the daily conferences which followed Hogan's resignation. In all probability Hogan intended that his resignation should bring matters to a head, but the rapidity with which the conferences were convened suggests some degree of prior planning. Secondly, there is the question as to whether or not O'Duffy intended merely breaking with Fine Gael and continuing as head of the Blueshirts, as *An Phoblacht* had earlier suggested and as O'Duffy was later to claim himself, or whether he intended leaving public life altogether. O'Duffy was later to claim that he had left Fine Gael only and that he was still director-general of the League of Youth and that only a full meeting of the central council of the League of Youth could accept his resignation from that body. Thus, he would claim, Cronin's selection as director-general was irregular. O'Duffy was to claim that he had been tricked into appearing to resign from the League of Youth by Cronin and Blythe and this contention was to be at the centre of the very bitter controversy which followed.[32] There are a number of possibilities here. Either O'Duffy resigned with the intention of making a complete break, as his message to the Blueshirts when he said that he hoped they would give Cronin the same unswerving loyalty as they had given him would seem to indicate, and then changed his mind, possibly under pressure. Or there is the other possibility that he was pressurised by Blythe and Cronin (or others) into appearing to resign completely when he merely intended leaving Fine Gael.

A further point of interest about the resignation controversy concerns the conditions which the vice-presidents were attempting to impose on O'Duffy. These may well have been aimed at rectifying specific abuses but they were undeniably irksome and likely to prove intolerable to some one of O'Duffy's temperament. There is also the possibility that the vice-presidents were attempting to make the conditions so tough that O'Duffy would feel he had no alternative but to resign, and that under these circumstances a resignation could be effected without splitting the movement. Both Cosgrave and Cronin were to deny that this was the intention.

O'Duffy resigned behind closed doors. His resignation was unexpected and the reasons given were obscure. The whole event was clouded in secrecy and confusion. The haste with which Cronin was given charge of the Blueshirts had all the appearances both of being irregular and of being an attempt to forestall some possible split. The whole episode was to plunge the entire Fine Gael-Blueshirt movement into utter confusion, and to hasten a decline which quickly set in. The absence of information coupled with the effects of the newspaper strike was to mean that at branch and divisional level members were in a state of confusion and prey to the wildest rumours.

10 Division and Confusion

THE resignation of O'Duffy, however dramatic and unexpected, did at first appear to be straightforward and un-
ambiguous. But soon the whole event became shrouded in
confusion and mystery and the claims and counter-claims
led to bitter rows and angry recriminations which rocked
the entire Fine Gael movement. Confusion and bitterness
were to epitomise the affairs of the Blueshirts during the
coming months, and nowhere was this confusion greater than
at local level where an absence of reliable information and
a vulnerability to all forms of rumours were to produce
conditions of near-chaos.

The main point of contention concerned the leadership of
the League of Youth and its relationship with Fine Gael.
The question at issue was whether or not O'Duffy had
resigned as leader of Fine Gael and of the Blueshirts or
whether he had merely resigned as president of Fine Gael
and continued to control the Blueshirts. Certainly, the initial
assumption after O'Duffy's resignation on 21 September,
seemed to be that he was leaving politics altogether. The
Fine Gael executive which accepted O'Duffy's resignation
seems to have acted on this assumption in that Cronin was
selected as director-general of the League of Youth at the
same meeting. O'Duffy himself had called upon the members
of the League of Youth 'to support Edmund Cronin in the
same unswerving manner they had supported him'.

However, the speed with which the whole resignation
episode had been effected, the fact that it had been the Fine
Gael national executive and not the central council of the

League of Youth which had selected the new director-general, coupled with the dissatisfaction among some Blue-shirts concerning Fine Gael's 'softness' in the anti-rates activities and possibly also the rumours that O'Duffy was planning to secede with the Blueshirts from Fine Gael, was quickly to lead to a new and potentially disruptive situation. On the Monday following O'Duffy's resignation, a number of prominent members of the League of Youth met in Dublin to discuss the situation. After this meeting, a statement was issued by one of their members, Commandant Stack, which stated that the League of Youth had not accepted O'Duffy's resignation and that in fact it had not even voted on the matter. The statement went on to say that Fine Gael head-quarters was not competent to remove or elect a director-general. Stack claimed that the vast majority of the members of the League of Youth were loyal to O'Duffy and they de-sired an early opportunity of showing their loyalty at a duly summoned congress. In any event such a congress was neces-sary as 'this was the only body capable of accepting O'Duffy's resignation from the League of Youth'.[1]

On the following day, O'Duffy declared that he did not wish to start any controversy but that he had resigned only from Fine Gael and not from the League of Youth. Stack's statement of the previous day got its answer from Cronin when he suspended Stack and another prominent pro-O'Duffy Blueshirt, T. P. Gunning, from membership of the League of Youth. On the same day there were calls from a number of League of Youth branches for a congress to clear the air.[2] Cronin, however, appeared to be quite definite about the position and showed no likelihood of acceding to this call for a congress. On 26 September he declared that 'various groups of mischief-makers, including agents of Fianna Fáil are trying to cause dissension in the Blueshirt ranks by raising doubts as to whether or not General O'Duffy has resigned from the office of director-general'. He went on to point out that O'Duffy had resigned from Fine Gael and therefore by rule 10 of the Blueshirt constitution, which

12

stipulated that every Blueshirt must also be a member of Fine Gael, O'Duffy had automatically resigned from the Blueshirts, and not being a Blueshirt could not be director-general. He threatened with suspension all officers 'foolish enough or mischievous enough to associate themselves publicly with this incipient campaign of disruption'.[3]

So within a week of the resignation meeting, two incompatible points of view had emerged and each side had begun to dig in its heels. On 27 September Cronin followed up his statement of the previous day by publishing the letter of resignation submitted by O'Duffy to Fine Gael. In this letter, O'Duffy specifically resigned from leadership of the Fine Gael organisation: 'I regret I do not see any hope for harmony as long as I remain. I have come to the conclusion that I can no longer effectively serve in the Fine Gael organisation and accordingly I have decided to retire.'

Cronin went on to claim that O'Duffy's resignation had not been on policy grounds but because he felt himself constrained by the restrictions which the other vice-presidents wished to impose on his freedom of action. O'Duffy quickly claimed that the document from which Cronin had quoted was merely a draft which he would have issued in the event of his resignation being tendered to and accepted by the central council of the League of Youth. He accused Cronin of having committed a breach of confidence and trust in publishing extracts from his draft address.[4] O'Duffy returned to the attack two days later. He described Cronin's election as 'irregular in every possible way'. He elaborated:

His appointment was not proposed or seconded. The only motion which was regularly put forward, the motion of confidence in me as director-general, was refused by Ernest Blythe who was in the chair at the time, and on his own responsibility he stood up and declared Commandant Cronin elected amidst intense confusion. As a matter of fact, sixteen county directors called on me the following day and admitted they did not know what happened. They all agreed, however, that my resignation was not before the council meeting.

Later in the same statement, he renewed the attack on the part played by Blythe in the whole affair:

Mr Ernest Blythe has been a traitor to me. Damnable traitor he was, going around Roscommon saying that Monaghan was against me, but I will hold a county parade of Blueshirts in Monaghan soon and Blythe will get another answer.

Things had been said by scandal-mongers, and Ernest Blythe was the principal one. We want no hostilities, but if there is any fighting we will hit back with the spirit of our race.[5]

The controversy continued over the next few weeks. Both sides set about winning over the divisional and local branches and, to this end, delegates were sent to the main strongholds of the movement throughout the country. O'Duffy started his campaign in Monaghan where he told his supporters: 'I am still your leader. Anybody who stands in our way will be sent back in a very short time to the obscurity in which I found them twelve months ago.'[6]

Cronin also set about contacting various Blueshirt leaders throughout the country. He had two immediate and formidable advantages over O'Duffy. He had the unequivocal support of *United Ireland,* the Fine Gael and Blueshirt newspaper, and this would seem to have been invaluable to him, especially in the early stages when the national newspaper strike was still on. And although the initial post-resignation attitude of this paper to O'Duffy had been friendly, as soon as he began to claim the leadership of the League of Youth it immediately adopted a tougher attitude, stating emphatically that Cronin was the leader of the Blueshirts, that he was in fact the real founder of the movement and that the blue shirt was his idea.[7] Cronin thus had a propaganda advantage over O'Duffy at the time when it counted most and had an immediate means of contacting and of putting his case to almost all members of the League of Youth. Cronin's second advantage at this stage was the fact that almost all major Blueshirt figures sided with him. He already had the backing of the constitutional wing of Fine Gael—Cosgrave, MacDermot and Dillon, but now in addition he was supported by Lieutenant P. F. Quinlan, Captain Padraig Quinn, Colonel Jerry Ryan, Commandant Denis Quish and Captain John L. O Sullivan.[8] He controlled the headquarters buildings and had charge of the staff. His appointment, whatever one might think about its legality, had followed upon O'Duffy's apparent resignation. All these factors combined to confer upon him an aura of legitimacy and to present O'Duffy as a breakaway.

The controversy had exploded suddenly and not all members of Fine Gael were convinced that a split of such proportions was inevitable, or that the differences could not be patched up with some give and take on all sides. Patrick Belton T.D., who had been a member of Fianna Fáil up to 1927, then an Independent T.D. and later a member of the Centre Party before the merger, immediately set about initiating peace moves. On 3 October he urged the recall of O'Duffy[9] and was to repeat this plea over the next few weeks, during which time he sought to bring the principals in the controversy together. Belton's pleas, however, were destined to fall on stony ground. On the day he began his peace efforts Dr O'Higgins accused O'Duffy of stabbing the organisation in the back and of attempting to undermine the influence of the new leader. He also claimed that he had founded the Blueshirts while 'O'Duffy was still Chief of Police under a Fianna Fáil government'.[10] O'Duffy, for his part, while welcoming Belton's offers, continued in his efforts to whip up support for his cause in the country. On 5 October he announced that he was going west on an organisational tour; the following day, he announced a series of county conventions which would rival those organised by Cronin and on 8 October he announced the appointment of new officers.[11]

The Oireachtas party of Fine Gael had met on 4 October and had unanimously accepted O'Duffy's resignation. The meeting decided that the party would be led by Cosgrave, MacDermot, Dillon and Cronin until the next Ard-fheis.[12]

On the following day, Colonel Jerry Ryan was appointed deputy director of the League of Youth.[13]

On 4 October Commandant Stack, who had issued the first pro-O'Duffy statement, declared that he had been misinformed, that he was now convinced that O'Duffy had resigned, and that henceforth he was supporting the executive.[14]

O'Duffy attempted to counter the influence of *United Ireland* when on 6 October the first issue of a new pro-O'Duffy paper, *The Blueshirt,* appeared. The paper was published from O'Duffy's home at Wilton Place in Dublin, and the first issue was given over to an account by O'Duffy of the reasons which had led him to resign.[15]

While both factions jostled and competed for support, a new and mutually damaging trend was becoming apparent. *The Irish Press* of 10 October claimed with scarcely concealed glee that there was now great confusion in many Blueshirt branches throughout the country and that many other branches had become inactive as a result of the split. Not surprisingly, *United Ireland* took a very different view. On 13 October it said definitely that 'O'Duffy's attempts to split the movement had failed'. An editorial a fortnight later could say that the Fine Gael organisation 'had not been shaken or appreciably weakened by the whole controversy'. Fine Gael had merely 'struck a small patch of trouble and is experiencing some growing pains'. The same editorial added that O'Duffy might, at the outside, take up to ten per cent of the League of Youth with him, but it did not regard this as being of great importance as the majority of these were 'men of doubtful standing'.[16]

Belton's peace efforts were meeting with little success. His call for unity, with O'Duffy's reinstatement as leader, was obviously unacceptable to the Cronin wing, and on 16 October, Cronin rejected it outright.[17] On the following day, he warned Belton that 'there were to be no more peace moves'.[18] Belton ignored this warning and on the following day set about organising a conference to be attended by

O'Duffy.[19] This move seemed to exhaust the patience of the anti-O'Duffy wing, for on the day after Belton announced he was organising this conference, O'Higgins tabled a motion for the next meeting of the national executive of Fine Gael calling for Belton's expulsion.[20] Belton retaliated with a strong personal attack on Cronin, calling him a 'bully and a tyrant'.[21] The expulsion motion, proposed by O'Higgins and seconded by General Mulcahy, was discussed and passed at the meeting of the executive of Fine Gael on 30 October. In spite of the bitterness of the previous month and the controversial circumstances surrounding his expulsion, the parting of Belton from Fine Gael was amicable. Belton expressed his regret, but declared that there was no other course open to him, and shook hands with Cosgrave and the others present before leaving.[22] *United Ireland* felt that Belton was 'no serious loss', saying that he 'should perhaps never have been in the party' because of his 'natural inclination to play a lone hand'.[23]

A further and abortive effort at peacemaking took place on 23 October when a conference under Captain Tom Hyde of Kerry was arranged for Dublin. O'Duffy and Cronin were both invited to attend but Cronin turned down the invitation. The conference proceeded without Cronin, and after two days of private deliberation, came out in favour of O'Duffy.[24]

Side by side with these unsuccessful efforts at restoring unity, was a growing tendency for both sides to indulge in bitter personal attacks. Belton had already described Cronin as a 'bully and tyrant' and O'Duffy continued this attack in *The Blueshirt* of 20 October. The following day, Cronin accused O'Duffy of 'having deserted the Blueshirts at a very critical period—on the eve of the first Communist Congress in this country'—and went on to give his views on the real reasons for O'Duffy's resignation.[25] On 3 November, the three principals in the controversy—O'Duffy, Cronin and O'Higgins—came together at a Blueshirt convention in County Limerick. Cronin and O'Higgins did not know that

O'Duffy was going to attend and probably would not have been present had they so known. In the event, the meeting which lasted six hours was bitter, stormy and entirely inconclusive. On the same day, Patrick Hogan attacked O'Duffy for his views on the North ('If he is a Republican, why does he not join Fianna Fáil?') and for having praised Hitler in a recent speech. Hogan said that he was 'disgusted at a statement he read, wherein General O'Duffy said Hitler was the greatest man Germany ever had. Hitler stood for the crude militaristic dictatorship of Germany and O'Duffy stood for the same thing according to that statement'.[26]

Nor was the controversy between the two factions confined entirely to verbal abuse. After the Limerick meeting, the rival Blueshirt supporters came to blows, and at a meeting the following day in Limerick, presided over by O'Duffy, a number of Cronin supporters were ejected from the hall. Later in November, rival Blueshirts came to blows at Newcastlewest, Ballyshannon, Roscommon and Bandon.[27]

The confusion and indecision amongst the local and divisional branches of the Blueshirt movement continued until the end of the year but, surprisingly, after the initial sharp and acrimonious outburst, the leadership controversy seemed by the end of November to quickly lose much of its momentum. From that point on, events moved at a much slower pace with each group concentrating more and more on its own internal affairs and with a consequent marked decline in vituperation and squabbling. This change occurred for a number of reasons.

It occurred partly because much of O'Duffy's energy was now being channelled into other areas of activity. He had revived *The Blueshirt* and the writing and publishing of this consumed much of his time, in addition to providing a new financial worry. The paper appeared weekly and it was quickly evident that staff shortages were throwing the bulk of the work on to the shoulders of O'Duffy and a very small number of helpers. As a result, much of the paper was usually devoted to reprints of O'Duffy's speeches. About this time also, O'Duffy and Belton began to formulate plans for a new political party. Early in November Belton had been talking in terms of a new party, and on 19 November a group of North Kerry Blueshirts met and discussed the proposal that a new party should be set up with Belton as leader.[28] Three days later, O'Duffy announced that Belton and he had definite plans for such a party, though in fact the party—the National Corporate Party—did not appear until the following June.[29]

But most of O'Duffy's boundless energy was now, it would appear, being devoted to international affairs. In mid-December, he attended an International Fascist Congress in Montreux in Switzerland. The conference was attended by delegates from all the chief corporate and Fascist movements in Europe. Fourteen European countries were represented, with O'Duffy as the Irish representative. The other countries represented were: Italy, Austria, France, Spain, Portugal, Switzerland, Belgium, Holland, Denmark, Norway, Lithuania, Greece and Rumania. Interestingly, there were no delegates from Germany or Britain. O'Duffy was elected member of an international committee of seven which was to meet henceforth in Paris to discuss the position of labour in the corporate state. The other members of the committee included some very prominent European Fascists, including Signor Coselochi (Italy), Dr Clausen (Denmark), Marcel Jucard (France) and Colonel Quisling (Norway).[30]

Incidentally, O'Duffy's attendance at this Congress was strongly attacked by *United Ireland* which stated that O'Duffy's previous claims that he was not a Fascist must be seriously in question and in fact saw his attendance at Montreux as 'tantamount to a declaration that he is now a Fascist'. It went on to claim that the corporate state as advocated by Fine Gael and as based on the principles of *Quadragesimo Anno* could be carried into effect 'without what are regarded as the characteristic features of Fascism'.[31]

From O'Duffy's point of view, it was probably this increasing preoccupation with the affairs of international

Fascism and his involvement in the Labour committee which distracted his attention from the split and from the Irish situation and thus contributed to a lessening of the controversy and an easing of tension all round.

As far as Fine Gael and the Cronin wing were concerned, nothing was to be gained by continuing the controversy. O'Duffy had failed to attract any substantial number of Blueshirts to his movement. The majority of those who remained stayed with the Cronin-led faction, even if, as *United Ireland* was later to admit, there was a decline in zeal among local officers and the progress of the movement was hindered by 'the persistence of factionist activity'.[32] It quickly became clear that the O'Duffy movement was not going to be a serious threat and that the only group which would benefit by the continuation of the squabble would be Fianna Fáil. Certainly Fianna Fáil, through *The Irish Press,* made no attempt to conceal its glee at the discomfiture of Fine Gael and it may have been the realisation of this which contributed in some way to a general playing down of the controversy, especially after the initial shock had passed and information began to filter through. It was not to be expected that men whose comradeship in many instances extended back over the best part of two decades would easily turn to attacking and vilifying each other in full view of their mutual enemy. Rather than do this, it appears that many Blueshirts drifted from the movement altogether, while many of those who remained attempted to dampen the controversy and to transfer attention back to the main issue which had been agitating the attention of most Blueshirts during the earlier months of 1934—the arrests and seizures arising out of the economic war situation.[33]

Although the Blueshirt split had occupied the headlines during these months, the violence and agrarian unrest continued unabated during September and October. During October this violence—the blocking of roads and railway lines, the felling of trees and the cutting of wires, the forcible obstruction of cattle seizures, and attempts to disrupt the sale of seized stock—was very marked, especially in the large cattle-farming counties of Westmeath, Meath, Waterford, Cork, Kilkenny, Limerick and Carlow.[34]

But the circumstances surrounding this agrarian unrest were now quite changed. For a start, there was the position of the Fine Gael leaders following the rejection of O'Duffy's non-payment of annuities motion in September. Government speakers had long been calling upon the Fine Gael leaders to condemn the unconstitutional activities with which so many Blueshirts were associated. This was an extremely sensitive subject in that Cumann na nGaedheal had always prided itself on its total commitment to constitutional methods and had long castigated Fianna Fáil for its failure to use these methods in the 1920s. Now many of these former statements were being repeated and government speakers were calling upon Cosgrave and his associates to condemn the present violence as they had condemned the violence of the previous decade. Indeed, somewhat ironically, some I.R.A. members were calling upon the bishops to do likewise.[35]

From the Fine Gael point of view, the position was extremely difficult. Its leaders believed the economic war to be unjustified, they believed that the farmers were being provoked and were in danger of losing their livelihoods. Yet at the same time, it was difficult for them to condone the violence with which the Blueshirts were associated, the undermining of authority and the seditious speeches. The government and *The Irish Press* hammered relentlessly at this point knowing full well how very sensitive it was. For while O'Duffy might counsel his supporters in County Cork, encouraging them to resist at all costs and to hold tight: 'If any of you go out and cut a tree and are caught doing it, take your medicine,'[36] it was not possible for Cosgrave or Dillon or MacDermot to speak in such terms. Thus in October, Cosgrave condemned the incidents with which Blueshirts had been associated as 'deplorable breaches of the law'.[37]

Secondly, the attitude of the government to these incidents was becoming increasingly tough and uncompromising. In October it announced the formation of a new Garda 'flying squad' which would be geared specifically to deal with this problem. The squad was to consist of about thirty specially selected policemen; it was to be mobilised and its members were to be equipped with hatchets and other tools which would enable them speedily to clear obstructions. This new 'flying squad' was to spearhead a special county by county drive for the collection of annuities, working in conjunction with the local bailiffs.[38] It began its operations in County Westmeath on 7 October and after a few weeks of intense activity there, moved to County Waterford and from there to Cork by the end of November.[39]

In addition to the formation of this 'flying squad', and as part of a tougher government policy, arrests and detentions throughout the country on charges arising out of rates-resistance incidents were now becoming very widespread. In mid-October, there were over 100 farmers awaiting trial by the Military Tribunal.[40] In early November a further 140 were lodged in Mountjoy awaiting trial.[41] In the last week of November and the first week of December, the number of arrests in County Limerick alone exceeded sixty.[42] Amongst those sent to jail on these charges were such prominent Blueshirts as Captain Quinn of Kilkenny, sentenced to three months in October, Lieutenant P. F. Quinlan of the Fine Gael national executive, sentenced to nine months on an arms charge in early December, and following an armed attack on the house of a Tipperary rate collector, Colonel Jerry Ryan was sentenced to imprisonment early in the new year.[43]

This agrarian unrest seemed to reach its high point during the months of September and October 1934, and from that time on, there was a very definite decline in the volume and intensity of such events. This decline can be largely attributed to the reasons already mentioned—the confusion in the Blueshirt movement and the distraction of the leadership struggle, the lack of a clear and unequivocal backing from the Fine Gael leaders on the tactics which were being used, and the effectiveness and determination of the police, especially after the introduction of the 'flying squad'. Another factor, though more difficult to measure accurately, was that the plight of the bigger farmers was hardly likely to attract any widespread or deep sympathy in the towns or cities, or indeed among the non-agricultural groups in the country-side. Certainly there was no weakening of support for Fianna Fáil in the small-farm counties of the west, and the poorer groups in the towns and cities were the main beneficiaries of the lower food prices and of the free beef scheme. Indeed, it is hard to see how, in the context of the 1930s, the bigger farmers, however desperate their situation, could have been regarded as a deprived or oppressed group by the many thousands who were themselves very much worse off. Their cause could scarcely have attracted much support either amongst the city workers—who in all probability had little knowledge of or liking for the farmers—or amongst the small farmers and landless men who saw in the destruction of the cattle ranchers a quick step in the direction of a division of these lands and a move to tillage farming. Certainly the predicament of the farmers and their well-publicised prophecies of economic ruin did not attract any great measure of support to Fine Gael in the 1934 local elections, a point which emphasised that their cause was to remain a minority or sectional one, and was not to become a popular crusade. This was indeed a serious weakness.

In any event, it became obvious by the end of November that the campaign of resistance was quickly losing its steam and, while isolated incidents were to continue up to late 1935, Chief Superintendent Murphy of the 'flying squad' was able to state on 10 December that information which he had at his disposal led him to believe that the campaign was now coming to an end.[44] It was to prove to be an accurate prediction.

Thus as 1934 came to an end, the Blueshirt movement

was in almost total disarray—divided and confused. The legal victories won over the government, the rallies and the reorganisation now counted for little, as the movement set about its own self-destruction. The one big cause espoused by the movement—the plight of the farmers in the economic war—was ending in futility and embarrassment. A new note of disillusion was spreading, members were leaving and enthusiasm was in short supply. More firmly than at any time since 1932 de Valera was in complete control.

This new note of disillusion is best exemplified in a speech made by one of the vice-presidents of the movement, Frank MacDermot in late November. MacDermot had been out of the country during the leadership controversy, but had been kept in touch by Michael Tierney and James Dillon.[45] By mid-1934, he had become completely disillusioned with O'Duffy, and he supported fully the decision of the national executive. Speaking at a fair-day meeting in Boyle, Co. Roscommon, he said that he hated to have to say it, but at the present time the chief asset of the government was the opposition, and when he said the opposition, he meant the entire Blueshirts and United Ireland Party. He went on to implore O'Duffy to desist from tearing the party to pieces, for the sake of his reputation, and added that since he had resigned 'O'Duffy's speeches have been completely incoherent and I am not able to make out what policy he has got'. He went on to talk about the Blueshirt movement in general:

I deplore the fact that those who ought to know better were propagating the Blueshirts as if they were something separate and better than a political party. It is all nonsense. I regard the Blueshirts as the bulwarks of democracy. I hated to look at our party organ *United Ireland* because I could scarcely look at it without seeing something of which I disapproved. I hate scurrility. That scurrility however has disappeared. There was also too much of what I call flirtation with Fascism in it.[46]

It was on this note of disappointment and disillusion that 1934 came to an end. Although the recriminations and hostility were decreasing as both factions went about their separate ways it was very obvious that the whole Blueshirt movement had been dealt a series of very grievous body blows from which it would not easily recover. With its leadership discredited and with the definite assertion of supremacy by the government in the agricultural conflict, the high hopes of the past eighteen months had by now little likelihood of fulfilment. Recovery, if it was to be, would be more than difficult.

11 The Final Disintegration

1934 ended with the League of Youth in a state of great disarray and with the assertion of supremacy by the governmental authorities in the campaign against the payment of the rates. The closing months of the year also saw an even further deterioration in the relations between the I.R.A. and the government and this conflict was destined to become yet more bitter during 1935.

An Phoblacht was now referring to the Fianna Fáil government in terms as bitter and vitriolic as it had ever used about Cumann na nGaedheal. The I.R.A. felt it had much to be bitter about and its charge that it had been 'betrayed' by de Valera and Fianna Fáil grew ever more strident. Its activities were being hampered by the police; Republicans were being jailed by a 'Republican' government; the repressive legislation of the Cosgrave regime—indeed the very same Military Tribunal of that regime—was back in operation; the I.R.A.'s own economic campaign was being frustrated by the police; and the government had set itself firmly against any attempt to end Partition by use of force. In addition the government's decision to set up a Reserve Volunteer force and the setting up of the 'Broy Harriers' had attracted members and potential members from the I.R.A., and the awarding of I.R.A. pensions to old anti-Treatyites coupled with the ameliorative social legislation had dampened down social discontent. The I.R.A. felt cheated and this feeling was daily increased by the ever-growing security of tenure of Fianna Fáil in government and its clear ascendancy over its constitutional opponents.

The friendly relations which had existed between the I.R.A. and Fianna Fáil in 1932 had now, at official level at any rate. disappeared, and de Valera had on more than one occasion warned the I.R.A. that he had no intention of tolerating the existence of a private army in the state.

The activities of the I.R.A. and its involvement in violence continued through 1935, though now on a more spectacular level. The very fact that the I.R.A. was adopting more spectacular methods may well have been due, as one commentator suggested, to the growing weakness of the I.R.A. John Horgan of *The Round Table* suggested that because the government 'by a judicious combination of pensions, jobs and secret service expenditure' had sapped the morale and reduced the strength of the I.R.A., it was substituting assassination for insurrection.[1] A land dispute at Edgeworthstown, Co. Longford, in early 1935 developed into a serious affair and the I.R.A. intervened to support the tenants. The son of the agent for the property, Richard More O'Ferrall, was shot by four assailants who also attempted to shoot his father. While it was never conclusively proved that the murder was the work of the I.R.A., it is generally accepted that the four assailants were active members of the I.R.A.[2]

In March, a tram and bus strike began in Dublin, and was to continue for seventy-six days. The I.R.A. expressed its support strongly for the workers, and vigorously condemned the government's decision to use army transport.[3] Shortly afterwards, armed gunmen fired at policemen in Dublin, in Grafton Street and Burgh Quay, wounding two of them, and a similar incident took place in Tralee.[4] The government retaliated by arresting over forty members of the I.R.A., including Frank Ryan, Peadar O'Donnell and Con Lehane, and interning them in the Curragh.[5]

The government now obviously saw its greatest threat coming from the I.R.A. and the precautions taken to guard the President and ministers at the Easter commemoration ceremonies were an indication of the unease and uncertainty of the government in face of the threat.[6] A month later,

1 Blueshirt parade

Election scenes, 1933

Gerard Boland warned: 'We have tolerated it as long as we could. The limit of human endurance has been reached. We will not tolerate it any longer.'[7]

In June, one of the men involved in the attack on the Dublin policemen was sent to jail for ten years—a concrete indication of the government's increasingly severe attitude.[8] However, the government refrained for the time being from proclaiming the I.R.A. an illegal organisation, and a further year was to elapse before this happened.

Although most of the violence in 1935 was coming from the I.R.A., the agrarian violence of the Blueshirts also continued though it was by no means as extensive as it had been in 1934. The incidents were for the most part concentrated in County Cork. In February, three Cork Blueshirts were sent to jail for attempting to derail a train and in the same month fourteen Cork farmers were arrested and charged with obstruction and violence arising out of non-payment of rates.[9] In April, Blueshirts from Kilkenny and Kerry were jailed on wire-cutting charges and in the same month wires were cut in thirty-seven areas in Cork.[10] In May the house of a Fianna Fáil T.D., P. S. Murphy, was burned down and an attempt was made to burn the house of Martin Corry T.D.[11] Captain John L. O'Sullivan, one of the best known Blueshirts in Cork, was jailed by the Military Tribunal for five years, for having taken part in the burning of Murphy's house. (It was widely believed in Cork that O'Sullivan had been attempting to *prevent* the burning of the house, but his loyalty to his colleagues, however foolish he felt them to have been, prevented him from telling the full story at the trial. He served the greater part of the sentence in conditions of great severity.)[12] Two Cork Blueshirts were later sent to jail for three years for attempting to burn Corry's house and the incident was strongly condemned by *United Ireland* which deplored the involvement of Blueshirts in this type of activity.[13]

The second part of 1935 was surprisingly free from such acts of violence. The only incidents of note occurred on

13

1 August, when Captain Quish was jailed for a year by the Military Tribunal on obstruction charges, and on 6 November, when three Kilkenny Blueshirts were jailed, also on obstruction charges.[14] By mid-1935, the campaign of violence with which the Blueshirts had been associated had all but come to an end.

Apart from the reasons already discussed—the success of the 'flying squad', stern measures and the Blueshirt split— the decline in agrarian unrest was also to some extent at least influenced by the 'Coal-Corn' Pact negotiated between the British and Free State governments in January 1935. The main feature of this agreement—described by de Valera as 'a business transaction based on the mutual interests of the two countries'—was that the quota of cattle to be exported to Britain from the Free State would be increased by thirty-three per cent and there would be a similar increase in the amount of coal exported from Britain to the Free State. As far as the cattle trade was concerned, this in effect meant that cattle exports would increase by about 150,000 cattle a year. But perhaps the main significance of the Pact was not the immediate improvements it effected—which would mitigate only very slightly the effects of the economic war— bur rather the promise it held as the first step towards ending that dispute.[15]

All these factors contributed to ensuring that from early 1935 on, the Blueshirts would play a new and very subdued role. While the split was largely instrumental in bringing about this situation, with its demoralisation and confusion, there was also the fact that the Fine Gael leaders such as Cosgrave, MacDermot and Dillon, whose authority had been asserted after O'Duffy's departure, were now anxious to play down the importance of the Blueshirts and to direct the energies of the movement into different channels.

The Fine Gael leaders had had a surfeit of controversy and this was also a factor in ensuring that the dispute with O'Duffy was given as little prominence as possible. O'Duffy was now becoming more interested in international affairs and neither side appeared over-anxious to indulge in a conflict whose only beneficiary would be Fianna Fáil. The Fine Gael desire to minimise the conflict was probably strengthened by the fact that O'Duffy was taking only a small section of the League of Youth with him.[16] In fact one of the most surprising aspects of the Blueshirt split was the shortness of the ensuing controversy and the fact that from the end of 1934 both groups journeyed along very separate paths and did not again become entangled.

As has been already mentioned the majority of Blueshirts stayed in the Cronin-led section, and largely for the reasons already discussed—O'Duffy's initial confusion and vacillation, the sense of legitimacy which control of League of Youth headquarters and the backing of the Fine Gael leaders conferred and possession of *United Ireland* at a crucial period. It is not possible to estimate the actual number that left with O'Duffy. *United Ireland* estimated ten per cent, although it is not possible to verify this.[17] Far more damaging was the number which drifted out of the movement altogether either through confusion, a disinclination to support either side or through sheer dejection at the manner in which the movement was breaking up. Again, it is not possible to estimate with any certainty the number so affected, but it does seem to have been considerable. Indeed one of the most striking things about the Blueshirt movement from this point on is the very dramatic decline in zeal and enthusiasm at all levels. *United Ireland* refers to this on a number of occasions and 'Onlooker' makes several appeals for the return of the old spirit and enthusiasm.[18]

From late 1935 *United Ireland* published weekly lists of Blueshirt branches and members throughout the country. Intended to display the strength and activity of the movement as a whole, the series reveals the opposite to have been the case. An examination of all the lists clearly shows that the organisation was active in surprisingly few counties and these largely predictable ones: Cork, Limerick, Tipperary, Kilkenny, Waterford, Carlow, Meath, Westmeath and

Kildare. The lists of Blueshirt members also show that very many branches had as few as five or ten full members.[19]

The Fine Gael Ard-Fheis was held in March 1935. This was the first gathering of the party since the split but surprisingly the split was not discussed or debated. The reason for this, according to the *Round Table* correspondent, was the desire of the Fine Gael leaders to extend to O'Duffy 'the charity of their silence'.[20] Cosgrave was unanimously elected president of Fine Gael and Cronin and O'Higgins were elected vice-presidents along with Dillon and MacDermot. The Ard-Fheis was a quiet affair and lacked the spectacle and sense of excitement which had attended the 1934 Ard-Fheis. The future of the League of Youth was discussed and after an unreported debate, it was decided to continue the League of Youth as 'a permanent institution providing the youth of Ireland with opportunities of discipline, voluntary, national and social service'.[21]

The period following the Ard-Fheis was quiet and uneventful and this comparative calm, broken only by a few isolated incidents of violence, characterised the affairs of the Blueshirts during 1935, in sharp contrast to the highly charged tension which had prevailed just a year earlier. Blueshirts continued to attend Fine Gael meetings and to act as stewards at these meetings, though with no elections in sight, the number of public meetings was small. *United Ireland* stressed on a number of occasions that the emphasis in Blueshirt activity had now changed—that henceforth the main work lay in preparing for the next election.[22] Perhaps it was the sight of the government and the I.R.A. preparing for a showdown or perhaps the movement had simply run out of steam, but in any event the Blueshirt movement was now in a period of obviously declining activity and enthusiasm, and displayed neither the inclination nor the ability to revert to its former position of prominence. Also, perhaps surprisingly, *United Ireland* was referring to a new spirit of 'cordiality' between Fine Gael and the Blueshirts which 'did not exist in 1934'.[23] It was also noticeable that relations between government and opposition improved considerably during 1935.

In this atmosphere, the Second Annual Blueshirt Congress was held in Dublin in August, 1935. It was at this meeting a year previously that the motion had been passed which had triggered off the split. The temper of the 1934 Congress had been one of defiance and determination to fight. This time, the atmosphere was more subdued and business-like, or, as 'Onlooker' said, 'less effervescent than the previous year'.[24] The main business of the Congress was taken up with amending the constitution of the League of Youth with the intention of preventing the recurrence of a too autocratic leadership. A series of motions was passed democratising the constitution 'to alter the dictatorial status which had been given to the office of director-general by a former holder'. The main effect of these changes was to alter the method of appointment. Up to now, officials of the League of Youth had been appointed—the director-general appointed county directors and these in turn appointed district directors who appointed unit captains. From now on, all offices would be elective. The other big change was the replacement of the central council of the League of Youth—made up of nominated members—by a new, elected national council. *United Ireland* saw the changes thus:

The unanimity with which Congress accepted the proposals laid before it for democratising the constitution of the League of Youth showed that the scheme put into operation by General O'Duffy was either never really acceptable to the mass of the organisation or that after a trial it had definitely been found wanting. There is no doubt that the dictatorial set of rules under which the League of Youth has been operating had become a definite handicap to further progress. Consequently it will now be possible to have something like a new start and to make members feel more definitely than in the past that the organisation is theirs to make and mould into the form that they desire.

The most dangerous weakness of the old constitution was that, differing so fundamentally from the democratic constitution of Fine Gael, it inclined to create an over-specialised outlook amongst the members of the League of Youth and to raise up barriers between them and the members of the bigger organisation.

Under our new democratic constitution the task of keeping strictly in line with Fine Gael, though preferably a few paces in front of it, will become easier.

Cronin, proposed by O'Higgins and seconded by Austin Brennan and Jerry Ryan, was unanimously re-elected director-general. In his speech he praised the Blueshirts for their restraint in the face of an administration which was not impartial. His speech was largely concerned with the need for new agricultural methods. He reiterated the intention of the Blueshirts to establish a corporate state in Ireland—'a thoroughly democratic form of corporate organisation based on *Quadragesimo Anno* and working under the authority of the Dáil'. This, however, was the only reported Congress reference to corporatism and the League of Youth constitution, published in September, had no references at all to the setting up of a corporate state.[25]

The national council to replace the central council was elected by the Congress. Two prominent Blueshirts, then serving prison sentences, John L. O'Sullivan and Captain Denis Quish, were elected unanimously. The other members included P. F. Quinlan, General Mulcahy, Gerard Sweetman, O. Esmonde, T.D., and—making his return—James Hogan.[26] Obviously with O'Duffy gone, Hogan had no reason for not rejoining the League of Youth. The Congress marked a very significant structural change in the League of Youth and the workmanlike and unspectacular nature of the proceedings emphasised the fundamental changes which had occurred within the space of a year. Surprisingly, the changes attracted very little public attention—partly perhaps because of the lacklustre nature of the Congress and partly as a reflection of the diminution in importance of the Blueshirts as a political force.

The series of resignations and splits which had dogged the short life of Fine Gael were destined to continue for a while longer. It was becoming fairly clear that Frank Mac-Dermot was not completely happy in Fine Gael. He had entered Irish politics in 1932 as an Independent, and later that year attempted to found a party which could liberate Irish politics from the burden of the Treaty and Civil War. His efforts did not meet with any great success and his decision in 1933 to merge with Cumann na nGaedheal had brought him right back into the mainstream of Civil War politics, for it quickly became clear that to most people, Fine Gael was merely another name for Cumann na nGaedheal. He had never been enthusiastic about the Blueshirts and had early criticised certain aspects of that movement. After the merger he had not managed to establish any relationship of real trust with his leader, O'Duffy. His speeches in late 1934 reveal a note of disillusion and his outspokenness and attempts at objectivity—as when he had criticised *United Ireland*—had not increased his popularity in Fine Gael. He was perhaps too cosmopolitan for the insularity of Irish politics in the 1930s and too much of a dilettante to remain for long in an atmosphere obviously so uncongenial. In any event, it was no secret in 1935 that his enthusiasm for Fine Gael was on the wane and it was not altogether a surprise when he broke with Fine Gael at the end of the year. The issue which led to his resignation was, somewhat surprisingly, a foreign affairs one.[27]

In 1935, after the Italian invasion of Abyssinia, de Valera had made a striking speech at the League of Nations in which he stated that his country stood by its obligations under the Covenant and attacked the invasion. The Fine Gael leaders attacked de Valera's policy in a rather carping manner. O'Higgins attacked it saying 'if their assistance was pledged without any settlement of their own quarrel, it was an opportunity lost which might never return'. Cosgrave took the same line, describing de Valera's stand as another 'lost opportunity'. MacDermot immediately wrote to Cosgrave saying: 'this line of argument seems to me to offend against common sense and consistency and to make nonsense of everything we stand for. It is one that can be renewed every time that Mr de Valera behaves with ordinary decency in international affairs.' His resignation followed shortly after this letter and his parting from Fine Gael was both un-sensational and amicable.[28] He continued to sit as an In-dependent T.D. until 1937, and was nominated to the new Senate by de Valera in 1938.

Ordinarily the resignation of a senior vice-president of a political party would attract considerable attention but such was the position of Fine Gael by late 1935—and such also perhaps was the surfeit of excitement of the previous few years—that the event attracted little notice. Indeed, Mac-Dermot's resignation coincided with the virtual disappear-ance of the Blueshirt from the political scene, for at this time, with few political meetings and with an end to the anti-rates activity, the Blueshirts had certainly ceased to be of im-portance in the political life of the state. *United Ireland* at-tributed this to the change in circumstances of the past year: 'Conditions have in certain respects changed considerably since the inception of the (Blueshirt) movement. . . . In the beginning its role was to combat the attack of the forces of the I.R.A. and Fianna Fáil on freedom of speech. Now more emphasis is needed on the educational and cultural side and on the political propaganda side.'[29]

This quiet note was even more marked in 1936 and now almost all attention was concentrated on the I.R.A. and its duel with the government. The government warnings, the stiffer sentences, the opening of a detention camp in the Curragh and the banning of *An Phoblacht*, did not succeed in altering the policy or intentions of the I.R.A. Drilling, recruiting and violence continued through 1935, and on St Patrick's Day, Mr de Valera's broadcast was effectively jammed.[30] It was shortly afterwards that two murders oc-curred which were regarded as being the work of the I.R.A. and which finally persuaded the government to outlaw that association.

On the night of 24 March, Vice Admiral Henry Boyle

Somerville (a brother of Edith Somerville the novelist) was shot dead in the presence of his wife, and although nobody was arrested for this crime, it was generally regarded as the work of the I.R.A. or of some members of that organisation. Admiral Somerville was a popular and kindly man, whose only 'crime' was that he wrote letters of recommendation for young men from the locality who wished to join the *British* navy.[31] A month later, a young man in County Waterford, John Egan, who had once been a member of the I.R.A., was shot dead in his home town of Dungarvan.[32] A member of the I.R.A. was later found guilty of this crime by the Military Tribunal and sentenced to be hanged. The sentence was later commuted and in fact he was released in 1938, when Douglas Hyde became President.[33]

The brutality of these murders shocked public opinion, and the futility and pointlessness of the crimes—the killing of a retired naval officer and a harmless young man—in addition to the cold-blooded manner in which the crimes had been committed, emphasised very clearly that the I.R.A. was rattled and becoming desperate, that splinter groups within the organisation were going their own ways, and that unless the organisation's activities could be effectively curbed, further outrages could be expected. It was now only a matter of time before the I.R.A. would be proclaimed an illegal organisation, and on 18 June the Executive Council issued an order under Article 2A of the Constitution declaring the I.R.A. an unlawful organisation. A short period of grace was given to allow members to sever their connections. From July onward, there was no respite. Those sent to prison included Maurice Twomey, the I.R.A. Chief of Staff, who was sentenced to three years for his membership of an illegal association.[34] The wheel had come full circle.

* * *

The Fine Gael Ard-Fheis in March 1936 was quiet and unspectacular. Cosgrave, who was re-elected president, concerned himself mainly with economic and agricultural problems. He made no references to the corporate state nor was there any motion on this subject. A number of Blueshirts were present at the Ard-Fheis, although in very small numbers, and they did not take any special part in the activities. In its account of the Ard-Fheis, *United Ireland* was again to emphasise the changed nature of the situation in which the Blueshirts now found themselves, and the consequent alteration in their functions, especially now that the government was finally dealing with the I.R.A.[35]

The third annual Blueshirt Congress followed just two months after the Fine Gael Ard-Fheis. It was held in Cork on 26 May and was a very insignificant and subdued affair, virtually ignored by the newspapers. The attendance was small and even *United Ireland* paid very little attention to this Congress. Cronin was re-elected director-general. If evidence was needed of the changed status and importance of the Blueshirt movement, this congress provided it. Gone was the excitement and expectancy of the O'Duffy era, the mustering of Blueshirt delegates from all parts of the country, the impressive parades and flamboyant speeches.[36]

The summer of 1936 was to see yet another serious blow delivered to by now a much weakened Fine Gael. In July Patrick Hogan died in a car crash in his home county of Galway. As Minister for Agriculture from 1922 to 1932, he had been one of the big successes of the Cosgrave government and although he had all but retired from front-bench politics, he was still regarded as one of the most vigorous, forceful and practical members of the party.[37] His death, following on a series of varied and almost uninterrupted setbacks since the assassination of Kevin O'Higgins in 1927—Ernest Blythe's budget, defeat in two successive elections, the Blueshirt split, the resignation of Frank MacDermot—deepened yet further the sense of despondency surrounding Fine Gael.

More trouble was to follow. On 25 July the last edition of *United Ireland* appeared. The paper had been appealing for some time back for more support from Fine Gael members and it too appears to have been a casualty of the decrease in enthusiasm and activity. It ceased publication, ostensibly to allow all energies and effort to be devoted to fighting the East Galway and Wexford by-elections. However, it did not reappear after the election campaigns were over. Nor was its gesture very effective for Fianna Fáil won resounding victories in both contests. The unsuccessful Fine Gael candidate in East Galway was James Hogan.[38]

Mid-1936 saw the fortunes of the Blueshirts at their lowest ebb and without any obvious hope of improvement. Indeed all that remained for a movement which had known more than its share of dissension and quarrelling was a further and final split, which heralded the end of the movement.

The final row centred around Cronin's leadership and conflicting views on what the role of the League of Youth should be in the new political situation. Cronin, as founder of the Blueshirts and as leader of that movement, was anxious to retain as much independence as possible, to re-activate the enthusiasm of the O'Duffy days and to extend once more the scope of Blueshirt activities. He was a Blueshirt first, a Fine Gaeler second. The Fine Gael leaders, especially O'Higgins and Cosgrave, had different ideas. As far as they were concerned, the Blueshirts had achieved the purpose for which the movement had been founded—the vindication of the right of free speech at political meetings, and now with the I.R.A. banned, this Blueshirt function was no longer necessary. There was also the question of finance. The Blueshirts had proved enormously expensive and by the end of O'Duffy's tenure, Fine Gael was in serious financial straits.[39] O'Higgins and other leaders felt that there was unnecessary duplication of function involved with two separate organisations and two separate headquarters catering for more or less the same group of persons. It was felt that Fine Gael headquarters could satisfactorily do most of the Blueshirt administrative work.

There was also the question of personalities. O'Higgins, for one, was highly critical of the way in which Cronin was

leading the movement, and was later to claim that Cronin
was autocratic, and that 'some of his stated views were not
in accordance with Fine Gael policy'.[40] However, no open
criticism of Cronin was made, possibly because of a general
desire to close the ranks in face of the common enemy—
Fianna Fáil.

Cronin resisted the tentative suggestions that the Fine
Gael headquarters should take over some of the League of
Youth functions, and in August 1937 he resigned as director-
general of the League of Youth, becoming deputy-director-
general, and remaining a vice-president of Fine Gael. This
change attracted no attention or comment.[41]

The question of change was discussed at the September
meeting of the national executive of Fine Gael, and the
question of the role to be adopted by the League of Youth
in the altered political situation was examined. It was decided that the League of Youth should be reorganised.[42]

Matters came to a head on 8 October. On that day, a
meeting of the national council of the League of Youth under
the chairmanship of Cronin was boycotted by O'Higgins,
Jerry Ryan and thirteen other members who then announced
that they had withdrawn from active participation in the
work of the Council and issued a statement outlining their
case. They claimed that:

Time and experience have proved to us that the experiment
attempted of having an autonomous and self-directed political
organisation within another political organisation has been a
failure, and that the main cause of the failure lay in the machinery
centrally controlling the League of Youth.

The statement went on to say that the national executive of
Fine Gael had unanimously agreed on the need for some
form of internal re-organisation for the League of Youth.
To this end, they intended outlining proposals to the standing committee of Fine Gael, and advised members to await
these proposals.[43]

The new controversy broke with the same suddenness and

unexpectedness as the leadership crisis of late 1934. This time, however, the issue aroused little interest or excitement, an indication—if such were needed—of the new found obscurity and insignificance of the Blueshirt movement. Cronin reacted to the boycott of his meeting by issuing a statement outlining his case. He claimed that relations between the League of Youth and Fine Gael had not been harmonious during the previous eighteen months. He accused O'Higgins of plotting against him and alleged that he had made several secret attempts to have him (Cronin) replaced and to have himself installed as director-general pending the calling of a new Congress. He claimed that O'Higgins had unsuccessfully attempted to enlist the support of Colonel Austin Brennan and Lieutenant Patrick Quinlan. He claimed also that O'Higgins had intimated to him that the proposals which he was going to make to the standing committee of Fine Gael were 'intended to paralyse all future Blueshirt activity'.[44]

The standing committee of Fine Gael met on the following day—9 October—to discuss Dr O'Higgins' proposals for the 'internal re-organisation of the League of Youth'. Cronin, as a vice-president, was present, and his worst fears were soon to be confirmed. According to a statement issued afterwards, the meeting had under discussion 'changes in the internal organisation of the League of Youth designed to ensure efficiency and harmony'.

Dr O'Higgins' report to the standing committee suggested that henceforth the League of Youth should continue its work as heretofore in branch areas, and in the constituencies under its own officers, but that the duplication of headquarters should be terminated, and that in future, general control of the League of Youth should be exercised by the standing committee of Fine Gael through League of Youth officers appointed by them.

The standing committee then had a motion put to it by General Mulcahy and seconded by Colonel Jerry Ryan that this scheme be adopted in principle. The motion was passed with three dissensions—Cronin, Quish and Quinn. The three dissidents then walked out.

The standing committee then resolved that the activities of the headquarters staff of the League of Youth should be suspended, and that Dr O'Higgins should administer the League on behalf of the standing committee. It was decided also that the new scheme of organisation would be further considered by the standing committee and submitted 'at an early date' to the national executive for ratification.[45]

It is interesting at this point to note that this motion—which in effect ended the separate existence of the Blueshirts—had the support of some of those who had been actively involved in the movement from its earliest days—O'Higgins, Jerry Ryan, Blythe and Mulcahy.

Cronin strongly attacked this decision of the standing committee to terminate 'the system of an autonomous self-directed political organisation within another organisation'. After the standing committee meeting, he announced that he would 'resist every attempt to absorb or strangle the Blueshirt movement' and threatened to 'revert to our original position as an absolutely independent organisation'.

Cronin was supported in his stand by Austin Brennan, Captain Padraig Quinn, Lieutenant Patrick Quinlan, Captain Denis Quish—all of whom had been active members of the A.C.A. from its inception.[46]

The decision to wind up the movement as speedily as possible was acted upon quickly and with very little publicity. O'Higgins refused to be drawn into controversy saying that such would 'serve neither the public interest, nor the best interests of the League of Youth'. Cronin was told (12 October) that the doors of the League of Youth headquarters would be locked to him, and that Fine Gael would not be responsible for any debts he might incur.[47]

Cronin was not prepared to see his movement disappear without a fight, but he was to find even less support than O'Duffy was able to bring with him in 1934. He claimed that the decision to wind up the League of Youth was not taken on any grounds of disharmony, inefficiency or in-discipline within the League of Youth, but partly because of 'occasional criticisms of the policy and organisation of Fine Gael by some League of Youth members'.[48]

Cronin's refusal to accept the decision resulted in his being expelled from Fine Gael by the standing committee on 14 October. He was in Cork at the time of this meeting, but on his return to Dublin the following day, he attempted to enter the Fine Gael offices at 3 Merrion Square. The doors, how-ever, were closed against Cronin, and not alone that, but the handle was removed and the keyhole stuffed with paper. Cronin angrily blamed Cosgrave for this incident, calling him 'a small man, a little Hitler'.[49]

It was an ignominious moment and scarcely an appro-priate finale for a movement which two years earlier had been so full of life and promise. For in spite of Cronin's protests, in spite of his threat to found a new Blueshirt move-ment, the decision of the Fine Gael standing committee marked the end—the very definite end—of the Blueshirt movement.

Colonel Brennan and Lieutenant Quinlan, who had taken Cronin's side in the controversy, sought to have Cronin's expulsion lifted at the next meeting of the standing committee on 22 October. However, the expulsion was ratified by twenty-five votes to two. Brennan and Quinlan both resigned from Fine Gael in protest, but the party was spared the agony of yet another split.[50]

Just as the first appearance of the Army Comrades As-sociation in early 1932 had been quiet and unheralded, so now did the movement steal out of existence in a manner which was inauspicious, if not surreptitious.

The movement had thrived and grown on the heady ex-citement of the violent years 1933 and 1934, but in the changed and quietened circumstances of 1936, it could find no role. And so, under the leadership of O'Higgins—under whom the blue shirt had made its first appearance in Irish politics—the affairs of the movement were quietly wound up and, without fuss, fanfare or panegyric, the blue shirt disappeared altogether from the Irish political scene. The controversy generated by Cronin's expulsion died almost as quickly as it had started, and to all intents and purposes Fine Gael resumed in 1936 where Cumann na nGaedheal had left off in 1933.

*   *   *

The general election of 1933 was probably the most bitter in the history of the state The local elections of the following year had taken place in an atmosphere of tension and violence. After the disintegration of the Blueshirts, the collapse of the anti-rates campaign and the banning of the I.R.A., the surfeit of excitement which had characterised the politics of the first half of the 1930s was replaced by a calmer, more placid mood. As a result the general election which took place in 1937, coinciding with the plebiscite on the new Constitution, was the most peaceable since the founding of the Free State. The campaign was short, and free of most of the bitterness of earlier contests. Cosgrave described it as the 'most good-humoured election' he had fought, and this sentiment was repeated by the newspapers.[51] With the Blueshirts gone, and the I.R.A. banned, the election was fought between three totally constitutional political parties.

A number of those who had come into prominence through the Blueshirt movement stood as Fine Gael candidates. Colonel Jerry Ryan was elected in Tipperary and Captain P. Giles in Meath-Westmeath. Captain John L. O'Sullivan —then in prison—stood unsuccessfully in Cork West and Gerard Sweetman was unsuccessful in Carlow-Kildare. Commandant Cronin stood as an Independent candidate in North Cork where he was bottom of the poll with 3,700 votes. Patrick Belton, continuing on his maverick way, stood as an Independent in Dublin County. Here he lost his seat, but stood and won as a Fine Gael candidate in 1938. He was again an Independent in 1943 when he lost his seat. Blythe,

General Eoin O'Duffy

Election poster, 1933

Mr Ernest Blythe

COSGRAVE
winning this time
BACK THE WINNER
te CUMANN NA nGAEDHEAL

Young Blueshirts at Charleville, Co. Cork,
April 1934

Blueshirts at Coachford, Co. Cork, April 1934

Blueshirts at Coachford, Co. Cork, April 1934

who had been elected to the Senate in 1934, did not seek re-election to the Dáil.[52]

The election to the ninth Dáil provided a somewhat inconclusive result. This time the number of seats was reduced from 153 to 137. The result was as follows:[53]

		Seats	Votes	Percentage of Votes
FIANNA FÁIL	..	69	599,040	45·3
FINE GAEL	..	48	461,171	34·8
LABOUR	..	13	135,758	10·0
INDEPENDENTS	..	8	16,471	9·9

The Constitution—Bunreacht na hÉireann—was ratified by 685,105 votes to 526,945.

As in 1932 and 1933, Labour continued to support Fianna Fáil, and Mr de Valera became the first Taoiseach under the new Constitution.

The 1937 elections marked the beginning of normal relations between the two main parties. From that point on, each side accepted the democratic intentions of the other and elections were for the most part peaceful and uneventful. With the ending of the economic war in 1938, the main grievance of the farming community was removed and the universal acceptance of a policy of neutrality in 1939 at the start of the Second World War contributed to a further weakening of political animosities. Indeed, the acceptance of neutrality by the vast majority of the people made for a semblance of national unity, unknown since the halcyon days of the Irish Party, and as the country prepared to meet the rigours and common dangers of war-time, the blue shirt became more and more a symbol and a memory.

It finally remains to discuss the fate of O'Duffy and the group which followed him after the split.

AFTER the initial confusion following his resignation had died down and after it became clear that the Fine Gael leaders were not going to engage in controversy with him— a controversy whose only beneficiary would be Fianna Fáil —O'Duffy began to channel his energies into three main areas of activity. These were the editing of his weekly paper *The Blueshirt,* his new involvement in the affairs of an international Fascist organisation and his efforts towards the founding of a new political party.

The production of a weekly paper was burdensome from both the financial and the editorial points of view. Funds were short, circulation and advertising were small and there were few available writers. As a result, O'Duffy had often to write much of the paper in addition to editing it. Its lifetime was short.

He had regarded his election to the Labour committee of the International Fascist Congress as a major honour and his trips to the continent became more frequent though the exact nature of his activities on these trips remains unclear.

Some of the Fine Gael leaders saw in O'Duffy's enthusiasm for the European Fascist movements clear evidence that he was a Fascist at heart and unsuited to lead their party. 'Onlooker' was especially strong in his condemnation of O'Duffy on this score.

In the early days of the post-resignation controversy he had announced that Patrick Belton and he were about to found a new political party to be based on the nucleus of those who had followed them from Fine Gael, and to be more thoroughly committed to the corporate state and to the cause of the farmers than Fine Gael had been.[1] However, after this announcement had been made there was little apparent progress towards the initiating of this party. This was due partly, it would seem, to the frequent absences of O'Duffy from the country and partly also to the absence of any significant manifestation of popular support. It was not until May 1935 that O'Duffy got down to finalising plans and set about addressing meetings in the main Blueshirt strongholds of Cork and Tipperary. Plans for the party, he confidently declared, were now in the final stages and he was certain that it would be fielding candidates in the next general election.[2]

A specially convened Ard-Fheis was called for the Mansion House, Dublin, on 8 June to launch the new party. 500 delegates attended and were told by O'Duffy that it would be known as the National Corporate Party. The objectives of the new party were wide and comprehensive. They promised to 'abolish party politics' and to create a vocational form of government; they were opposed to Communism, capitalism and all forms of dictatorship; they would establish a regime of social justice for every class and section and were opposed to all interferences with individual liberty; all these objectives would be sought in an all-Ireland corporate state which would have a Republican basis. O'Duffy announced also that the members of his party would contest the next general election on the ordinary register in the normal way and if they got a majority there would be another general election in a year on a vocational or occupational register. It was also announced that members of the party would continue to wear blue shirts but would now wear green ties and in place of the black berets, Volunteer hats.[3]

The inauguration of the new party received little attention and was attended by scant publicity. Indeed, the tardiness and lethargy which surrounded its inception and the absence of any manifest strength or enthusiasm from the inaugural meeting were to be characteristic of its subsequent fortunes. Little noticeable progress was made during the remaining months of 1935. No attempts were made to organise branches on a nation-wide basis; no attempts were made to hold meetings throughout the country; nor were there any obvious attempts at publicity-seeking. All this contrasted strangely with the driving energy and boundless enthusiasm which O'Duffy had brought to his previous undertakings.

Apart from his support for Mussolini following the invasion of Abyssinia, O'Duffy remained extraordinarily quiet during the remainder of 1935. He declared that 'Italy had taken steps to end an intolerable situation and defend her prestige among the civilised nations'. He said also that several members of his party had volunteered for service 'for the corporate state'.[4] Apart from this, the only other event of any significance was the decision announced by O'Duffy in March 1936 that henceforth the uniform of his party would be a green shirt and that the blue shirt would be worn no more.[5]

The Spanish Civil War started in July 1936 and immediately attracted tremendous attention in Ireland. For the most part, the issue was seen in clear-cut Catholic versus Communist terms and the cry of the 'Church in danger' was frequently heard. Stories of Red atrocities were reported; the Catholic hierarchy made a national appeal for prayers and aid for Nationalist Spain; resolutions of support were passed throughout the country and a new organisation—the Irish Christian Front—was set up to collect money for aid and supplies for Spain. Patrick Belton was chairman of the Irish Christian Front and the association set about raising funds and organising huge rallies on an impressive scale.[6]

The Spanish situation was, from the outset, calculated to appeal to O'Duffy's enthusiasm and to his imagination. Here before his very eyes the conflict between the forces of Christianity and Communism was being fought out in bloody battle for possession of one of the oldest countries of Europe —a country moreover bound to Ireland by many strong ties of history and religion. Everything that was romantic and crusading in O'Duffy's restless nature was attracted to this momentuous conflict.

O'Duffy expressed strong support for the Nationalist cause and made a number of speeches urging aid and prayers.[7] Then in late August as he was about to leave Ireland for a holiday in the Hague, he received an appeal from a prominent Carlist in London asking him to organise a Brigade to fight in Spain. According to O'Duffy, his name had been given to this Carlist by 'a prominent Irish ecclesiastic' as the ideal man to organise such a brigade. O'Duffy claims that he was undecided at first but wrote to the Dublin newspapers suggesting the formation of an Irish Volunteer Brigade and asking men to volunteer their services to the Christian cause.[8]

Again, according to O'Duffy, the response to this appeal was dramatic. Speaking at a meeting in Beal-na-Blath in early September, he claimed that in the space of a week over 5,000 men had volunteered.[9] A week later, this number had risen to 6,000. 'The response', he said, 'was so prompt, so generous and so spontaneous that I can only regard it as a mandate to go ahead with the organisation of the Brigade'.[10] He immediately contacted General Franco by a special courier and on 21 September he left Dublin for Spain. There he met General Mola and then had talks with Franco. He was carried away, he said, with enthusiasm when he witnessed the celebrations which followed the liberation of Alcazar.[11] O'Duffy's decision to organise a brigade to fight in Spain was not viewed with any great favour or enthusiasm by the de Valera government. Although the government was not unsympathetic to the Nationalist cause, and although it was under strong Catholic pressure to declare its support for Franco, it decided that the war was a domestic one and that the Irish government's policy would be one of neutrality. Consequently, lest the presence of Irish soldiers in Spain give the impression that the government was supporting one side or the other, it enacted a Non-Intervention Pact which made participation in the Civil War an offence punishable by a fine not exceeding five hundred pounds or two years

in jail. It also enacted that no citizen might leave the Free
State for the purpose of proceeding to Spain without a
special endorsement on his passport, and the issue of a ticket
for such purposes was made an offence.[12] In addition,
questions were asked in the British House of Commons in
an attempt to prevent O'Duffy from using English ports to
ship troops to Spain.[13]

O'Duffy was not to be deterred by these signs of opposition. He was quite clear where his destiny lay and he saw
many compelling reasons for his action. For a start, there
were the many historical links between the two countries:

The men of the Irish Brigade of today had indeed a great historical background. They went to repay in some slight measure the
vast debt that their forefathers owed to their fellow-Christians of
Spain.[14]

But more important was the fight for the Faith:

Ireland is behind the people of Spain in their fight for the Faith.
Irish Volunteers are making ready to leave home to fight side
by side with the Nationalist forces, convinced that the cause of
Franco is the cause of Christian civilisation.[15]

And later:

It was only in July 1936, when all seemed lost, and the Red
flag seemed to have triumphed over the Cross, that God raised
up, in the person of General Franco, a patriotic and God-fearing
man to deliver Spain out of the hands of Satan and his Communist legionaries.[16]

The lethargy which had characterised O'Duffy's leadership of the National Corporate Party now disappeared and
was replaced by a burst of frenetic activity. The organisation
of the Brigade he saw as the 'most difficult job I have ever
undertaken but he added that 'with the help of willing
workers at headquarters all obstacles were gradually sur-
mounted'.[17] The facts, however, were not so optimistic.

The first task was to answer the 'six thousand or so' ap-
plications; to organise medical check-ups, character refer-

ences and transport. He suspended the activities of the National Corporate Party so as 'to maintain the non-political character of the brigade'.[18] The problems of organisation were made even more difficult by the short amount of time available, the very cold weather and, most important of all, the need to maintain secrecy because of the hostile attitude of the government.

Transportation was a major difficulty, but eventually Senor La Cierva, who was looking after Franco's interests in London, chartered a ship, the *Domino*, capable of taking 1,000 men. This ship was due to arrive in Passage East, Co. Waterford, on 16 October and O'Duffy immediately set about organising the volunteers. As already mentioned, the problem of providing uniforms and supplies and the organisation of transport was, especially in view of the secrecy and shortness of time, providing many headaches. In addition, there were many financial problems. O'Duffy was later to claim that by the evening of 14 October most of these problems had been solved and that arrangements had reached the final stages. But at seven o'clock that evening, he was informed that the *Domino* would not be sailing after all. Confusion immediately followed and it was necessary to send messengers to all parts of the country to inform the volunteers. All but the Mayo contingent were informed in time—that is, before they had set out for Passage East.[19]

This was the first of many disappointments. O'Duffy immediately set out for Spain to make alternative arrangments. He was told by Franco that the sailing had to be postponed because of the international implications. He stayed on in Spain for a couple of days as a special guest of Franco,[20] returning to Dublin on 5 November, where he immediately convened a meeting of his key men for 8 November. At this meeting he informed them that the period of service of the brigade would be for six months or for the duration of the war—whichever was shorter.

Arrangements were again set in motion, and on Friday 13 November the first party of ten volunteers left the North Wall in Dublin for Liverpool, en route to Spain, as ordinary passengers aboard the *Lady Leinster*. A week later, this advance party was followed by a larger group which included O'Duffy himself, Captain Padraig Quinn and Captain Tom Hyde, again travelling as ordinary passengers.[21] O'Duffy remained only a couple of days in Spain and then hurried back to Dublin to arrange for the embarkation of his brigade. A further eighty-four volunteers left Liverpool for Lisbon on 27 November and the embarkation of the remainder of the first contingent was scheduled for Galway on the morning of 4 December.[22]

Five hundred were scheduled to go on this trip but once again, the secrecy and shortness of time available resulted in a certain measure of confusion and some of the volunteers arrived too late. Under cover of darkness, the volunteers boarded the *Dun Aengus* which was to wait in Galway harbour for the arrival of the ship which would take them to Spain. In miserable weather, the *Dun Aengus* with its complement of volunteers waited all night, buffeted by the rough weather. The other ship did not arrive until noon the next day, and then the perilous task of transferring the volunteers was carried out. Some thirty-five volunteers, mainly from Dublin, had a last-minute change of mind and returned to shore on the *Dun Aengus*. O'Duffy offers no explanation for this unexpected change of mind. A few days later, the main group arrived in Spain.[23]

The next major embarkation was scheduled for Passage East on 6 January 1937. This time the government made no secret of the fact that it was fully aware of O'Duffy's plans, and police were present in considerable numbers in the tiny fishing village on the night of 6 January. Indeed it is difficult to understand how O'Duffy expected to keep the operation a secret. About 700 volunteers turned up only to wait in vain for a ship which failed to arrive. They waited through the bitterly cold night and into the next day, only to be told that their ship would not be coming after all.[24] It is not clear just what went wrong, but it is possible that O'Duffy, in his impetuosity, organised the embarkation before he had a ship. In any event no further attempt was made to get this group of volunteers to Spain and their adventure ended almost before it began.

It is clear that the execution of the first stages of this expedition was inept and somewhat chaotic. Making full allowances for the necessity for secrecy and the unfavourable conditions imposed by the Free State government and by the uncertain international conditions, it would seem that O'Duffy attempted too much in too short a time and without adequate resources. For, out of a reputed 6,000 applicants, only 700 actually got to Spain. And that 700 were quickly to find their uniforms inadequate and the food unsuitable.[25] In addition, the selection of volunteers appears to have been somewhat haphazard and this was to lead to a measure of internal dissension and squabbling.[26] O'Duffy was later to admit that 'a few undesirables' had found their way into the Brigade and that this had had an unfortunate and disruptive effect on the harmony and morale of the rest of the Brigade.[27]

It may well have been the apparent ineptitude that surrounded the organising of the venture which was responsible for the government's virtual non-interference with the arrangements of the Brigade. As the *Round Table* correspondent expressed it: 'The government is hardly likely to invoke the Foreign Enlistment Act against General O'Duffy and his merry men, as they probably realise that Spain is the most suitable place for our Irish Don Quixote.'[28] And when it became known that a number of members of the I.R.A. were also going to Spain to fight on the Republican side, the same writer had this acerbic comment to make: 'The Spanish Civil War would at least have served some useful purpose if it enabled us to get rid of some of our wild men of both varieties.'[29]

After a month's training in Spain, the Brigade prepared for action in early February. The ill-luck and misfortune which had been its lot all along showed no sign of disappearing. Its first main engagement was on 18 February and this was to prove a fatal and humiliating blunder. Before they had seen action against the Communists, the Irish side were fired on by a *bandera* of General Franco's army from the Canary Islands. The Islanders failed to recognise the strange uniform of O'Duffy's Brigade and did not wait to ask questions before opening fire. There were two Irish fatalities—both Kerrymen—Captain Tom Hyde and Volunteer Dan Chute. O'Duffy later claimed that as a result of this incident, the Island *bandera* was dissolved.[30]

From then on, the Brigade was engaged mainly in the trenches and before very long, the inadequacy of their clothing in addition to the bad trenches and the presence of lice in considerable quantities caused great discomfort. Further casualties were inflicted in 13 March when the Irish Brigade went 'over the top'. This time, there were four dead—three of them from Kerry.[31]

By April and May, the Brigade was in serious trouble, although mainly as a result of the unaccustomed diet and the conditions in the trenches. In Ciempozuelos, over 150 men were taken ill and four of these died.[32] This, in addition to the dissensions and to the fact that the Brigade had engaged in no worth-while fighting, was not good for morale and it seems that by this time many members were dejected.[33]

In early June the six-month period of service was up and the question of a second term was discussed. Under the circumstances it was not thought possible to organise a reserve brigade. The members of the existing brigade were given the option of staying or returning home. According to O'Duffy, a number of members were minors and there was legal pressure on them to return home. Others had to return to their jobs and a considerable number were—or had been—ill. In any event, when the vote was taken, 654 decided to return and only nine opted to stay. Of those nine, two had only just arrived and a further two returned almost immediately.[34] The virtual unanimity of the decision to return was hardly an indication of high morale or that the adventure had been an unqualified success.

The Brigade left Lisbon on the *Mozambique* on 17 June and arrived in Dublin on 22 June—in the middle of the general election campaign. Because of this, the return of the Brigade attracted little attention and the members returned to their homes almost immediately.[35] O'Duffy took no part in the campaign nor was any attempt made to revive the National Corporate Party.

As has been said, O'Duffy saw the Spanish Civil War as a crusade against Communism. Looking back on the entire episode he was later to write: 'Our little unit did not, because it could not, play a very prominent part in the Spanish Civil War, but we ensured that our country was represented in the fight against World Communism.'[36] And: 'We have been criticised, sneered at, slandered, but truth, charity and justice shall prevail and time will justify our motives. We seek no praise. We did our duty. We went to Spain.'[37]

Thus O'Duffy himself, usually so given to extravagant and exaggerated assessments, made no such claims in this instance. Looking back, this man of action saw his brigade more in the light of a gesture which had to be made than as an effective contribution. And who is to say that this gesture, however inept, chaotic, ineffectual and incompetent it may have been, was not born of generosity, high ideals and a crusading zeal?

*   *   *

This was the effective end of Eoin O'Duffy's political career although he did make two further brief appearances on the political scene. The first was so ironic as to be almost comic. On 3 February 1939 he was contacted by a German agent, Oscar Pfaus, who was attempting to enlist the support of the I.R.A. in Germany's war effort! Because of O'Duffy's pro-German sympathies and because of his past membership of the I.R.A. he was seen as an ideal intermediary. The realities of Irish politics were indeed very different and O'Duffy's attempt to contact the I.R.A. was turned down.[38]

A far cry from the hectic anti-I.R.A. days of 1933 and 1934!

Shortly after the outbreak of World War II in 1939, O'Duffy wrote to Mr de Valera, offering his services in any way de Valera thought fit during the Emergency. Mr de Valera thanked him for his offer and told him: 'I have placed your name on our list and it will not be overlooked should the opportunity arise for making use of your services in any special capacity.'[39] Apparently, however, the opportunity did not arise and his services were not called upon. He again interested himself in the affairs of the National Athletic and Cycling Association and in 1942 he was elected president of that association—a position he had last held in 1933.

Shortly after this, however, his health gave way and he died on 30 November 1944. He was then fifty-two years of age. A measure of the man perhaps is that although he had been engaged in many bitter and stormy controversies, he left few real enemies and was, without hesitation, accorded the final honour of a state funeral.[40]

Part 2

THIS part of the book is concerned with examining two related topics:

(i) the development of a distinctive political doctrine by the Blueshirt movement and

(ii) a discussion as to whether or not, or to what extent, the Blueshirt movement can be classified as Fascist.

Chapter XIII traces the development of a Blueshirt ideology and chapter XIV discusses the question of Fascism.

13 The Political Ideas of Blueshirtism

THE Blueshirt movement sprang directly from the Army Comrades Association. The foundation of Fine Gael, of which the Blueshirt movement was an integral part, was brought about by the merging of Cumann na nGaedheal and the Centre Party with the National Guard. These three movements have already been described in detail in the earlier part of the book, and at this stage it is proposed to briefly examine the political ideas or policies of each as these existed before the merger.

Both the Centre Party and Cumann na nGaedheal were conservative, pragmatic, moderate, constitutional, political parties. Both were total in their commitment to the principles of liberal democracy, moderate in their nationalism, cautious in economic and social matters. Cumann na nGaedheal's efforts in restoring conditions of normality and stability had won to it the support of the propertied and business classes, the confidence of the Catholic hierarchy and the trust of the British government.

Neither of these parties displayed any interest in new political ideas or doctrines or exhibited any impatience with the functioning of the democratic process after the elections of 1932 or 1933. The Cumann na nGaedheal paper, *United Irishman,* saw no reason during 1932 why the party should seek to change its policies. The electoral defeat of 1932 was seen as an act of national ingratitude by a fickle electorate which would soon be regretted. Political developments on the continent might not have been happening as far as *United Irishman* was concerned. The second electoral defeat in under a year for Cumann na nGaedheal did not in any way cause this paper to change its mind. As far as it was concerned, the policies of Cumann na nGaedheal were 'sound and adequate', but the party could do with some improvement in terms of organisation and efficiency.[1]

The A.C.A. at the time of its foundation took trouble to make clear its independence of all political parties and indeed its lack of interest in political doctrines. However, this independence of all political parties was not accepted by many, who clearly saw bonds of affinity and sympathy between it and Cumann na nGaedheal.

It has been alleged that the A.C.A. was out to subvert the government and carry off a *coup d'état*. The majority of members of the A.C.A. were ex-servicemen; many possibly had, or could get hold of guns; some may have had friendly contacts within the army; but even if the A.C.A. was, at this stage, out to overthrow the government—and there is absolutely no evidence that it was—it is clear that this overthrow would not have been followed by the imposition of a Fascist-type regime. At most it would have been some form of military dictatorship, but there is no evidence to suggest that in the first six months of its existence the A.C.A. had any political ambitions.

The reason given by the A.C.A. to explain its decision to extend the scope of its activities—and indeed to become a political force in August 1932—is in the circumstances of the time credible, and need have no sinister connotations. Even at this stage, if there were some within the A.C.A. who favoured a coup, there is no reason to believe that such a coup would have been in any sense a prelude to a Fascist regime.

The A.C.A.'s decision to reorganise 'for the protection of freedom of speech and assembly' and to act as a bulwark against the forces of Communism was accompanied by a new and aggressive note, especially in the 'Onlooker' column in the *United Irishman*. It may be that the bitterness and excitement of the election campaign led to an escalation of aggressiveness all round, and taken in the context of the vigorous attacks made by I.R.A. and Fianna Fáil speakers on their opponents, 'Onlooker's' exhortation to the members of the A.C.A. to 'return ten blows for every one received'[2] and his claim that democracy in the Free State would be preserved only 'by the strong hands and stout sticks of the A.C.A.[3] is understandable.

But what is not so easy to explain at this point is the appearance in 'Onlooker's' column of new ideas on the efficacy and role of political parties. Stressing the A.C.A.'s complete independence of all political parties, he could say (while writing in the newspaper of a political party) that: 'As matters are developing in the country, I think everyone will soon see how ridiculous it is to talk about any party running the A.C.A. The A.C.A. will be obliged to run the parties.'[4] He also claimed that a new line of thought was discernible among members of the A.C.A. According to him, the younger members of the A.C.A. were 'not interested in party squabbles. They think that all parties gabble too much, and they are not at all sure that the national will can be properly ascertained by merely counting heads. They are generally without respect for an electoral system which enables men without ability, industry, patriotism, reputation or common honesty to become members of the nation's parliament, more easily than the best men in the community.'[5]

This type of remark was beginning to appear just at the time the blue shirt was being adopted, and shortly after Cumann na nGaedheal's second electoral defeat in under a year. Clearly at this stage an anti-democratic strain could be discerned among the Blueshirts and from this point on, Ireland, like virtually every other country in Europe, had its distinctive and shirted movement. It is important to remember too that all this was happening against a background of severe internal and external instability, at a time when the democratic structures which had mushroomed after Versailles were being increasingly blamed for the economic depression and political instability of Europe. It is important

15

to remember also that at this time the ideas on the vocational organisation of society, expounded by Pius XI in *Quadragesimo Anno*,[6] were percolating through. At this time too, a number of European countries had been or were in the process of experimenting with new forms of government; these countries were, for the most part, Catholic.

It is clear that changes in attitude were occurring within the A.C.A. and that these changes were in part due to continental influences, and in part to the fact that many within the Saorstát felt themselves in danger of physical attack, others feared the possibility of economic collapse, and for some the spectre of Communism loomed large. But it is also interesting to note at this stage that this new movement was still fairly peripheral, and the traditional Cumann na nGaedheal continued on its way. The first mention of any form of corporation did not appear in the *United Irishman* until April of 1933—the same month as saw the adoption of the blue shirt—and it evoked an interesting response. The article was written by 'M. G. Quin', who argued that the parliamentary system of government was inadequate and advocated in its place what he called a diastal system—'an organic democratic state adapted to Irish conditions'. Under this system, the role of parliament would be lessened and the task of examining details of legislation would devolve not on deputies, but on organisations representing economic and professional interests.

It is the reaction to this article which is of most interest. An editorial note which accompanied the article stated: 'The proposals made are so far away from anything that could be adopted by Cumann na nGaedheal that we are afraid we cannot give our contributor much, if any, further space for them.'[7] The paper again referred to Quin's ideas in its next issue. It made clear that it was not banning discussion on them, but that it considered them unreal in the context of Irish politics and in view of the traditions of Cumann na nGaedheal. It added: 'It should be obvious that a proposal for a revolutionary change in the Constitution of the state which is likely to commend itself as being practical politics to relatively few people cannot be allowed to occupy any substantial fraction of our very limited space.'[8] The position would seem to be that at the formation of the Blueshirts, a difference in attitude and outlook was becoming evident between the traditionalists in Cumann na nGaedheal and those who were leading the A.C.A. along new and untried paths. These differences were to become more pronounced with the founding of the National Guard and the accession of O'Duffy to the leadership.

*   *   *

The National Guard: With O'Duffy as leader, a change in name and an extension in membership and activities, the Blueshirts entered a new and significantly different phase. It was now an independent, autonomous organisation with a number of specifically political objectives. Many of these objectives were common to all Irish political parties at this time—national unity, opposition to Communism—but there were also some important innovations advocating the establishment of agricultural and economic corporations with statutory powers. In fact, the publication of the National Guard policy in July 1933 is the first definite commitment by an Irish political movement to some form of corporatism.

The first few weeks of life for the National Guard saw the rapid unveiling and elaboration by O'Duffy of his ideas on parliament and political parties. O'Duffy's assertion that political parties had outlived their period of usefulness and his views on the restructuring of parliament was one of the factors responsible for the banning of his parade to Leinster Lawn. It is interesting to note at this point that O'Duffy was prepared to admit that what he was proposing was in some respects Fascist. He defended this adoption of continental ideas and claimed that for the most part the scheme he was advocating was closer to the 'old Irish system', whereas the present parliamentary system (which would be replaced under the new dispensation) was 'English'.[9] Another interesting development at this time was a great increase in the number of parades and marches, a rapid spread in the wearing of the blue shirt and a further toughening of attitude in writings and speeches.

The National Guard had a separate existence of just over a month, and this makes it difficult to speak of it with any great certainty—its lifetime was too short to allow it to develop fully along the lines it was going. It is clear, however, that as it was developing, it had many of the hall-marks of a Fascist movement—in its appearance, its impatience with traditional parliamentary institutions, its distrust of political parties, its adherence to some form of corporate policy, its obsessive anti-Communism, in the fact that many of its members were ex-servicemen, and in that it could draw support from a section of the middle classes who felt their economic livelihood threatened. Had it continued to develop along these lines, it would almost certainly have become a fully Fascist movement.

However, the decision to merge with Cumann na nGaedheal and the Centre Party to form Fine Gael made for some important changes in the Blueshirts. The National Guard was no longer an autonomous body, independent and scornful of all political parties: it was now part of a constitutional political party, one of the conditions of which (and of O'Duffy's being made leader) was that he abandon whatever Fascist ideas he had been developing and henceforth work strictly within the constitutional framework. The decision of the National Guard to become part of another movement, to abdicate its independence, is probably the most important single decision in the history of the Blueshirt movement. It ensured that henceforth there would be considerable curbs on O'Duffy's freedom of action and that he would be obliged to work within a fairly rigidly defined constitutional framework. It meant, too, that the trend towards Fascism was at least temporarily arrested. In short, it ensured for the constitutionalists a position of dominance within the movement, deprived O'Duffy of the freedom of manoeuvre which his independence of parties and position of unquestioned authority within the National Guard permitted him. It also ensured the eventual disintegration of the movement by attempting to mould into one cohesive organisation groups with such disparate and conflicting attitudes.

* * *

Fine Gael: The incorporation of the Blueshirts in the new political movement, Fine Gael, did mean, however, that that party adopted as part of its official policy an allegiance to some form of corporate idea. One of the major points in the new Fine Gael policy stated that the party favoured 'the planning of our national economic life with a view to increased industrial efficiency and harmony by the organisation of industrial corporations with statutory powers, assisted by industrial courts and functioning under the guidance of a national economic council; the improvement of the conditions of the workers by the establishment within the corporations of contributory schemes for family allowances and retiring schemes'.[10] This was new, and had not previously found any place in the policies of Cumann na nGaedheal or the Centre Party.

The founding of Fine Gael was to coincide with or spark off considerable interest in the development of corporate ideas and their application to Irish politics. The columns of *United Irishman*, which had a short while before dismissed M. G. Quin's ideas as having little relevance, were now devoting a growing amount of space to the exposition of corporate ideas. It seems clear that an influential group within the National Guard which favoured these ideas was now attempting to 'educate' the Fine Gael Party and Blueshirt movement. O'Duffy was clearly in favour of the new ideas and it does appear as if an influential group was attempting to confer its own distinctive ideology—or to impose it—upon a movement which had grown up for entirely

different reasons, attempting, as it were, to give the movement an intellectual *raison d'être*.

The change in the attitude of the *United Irishman* can be
clearly seen in a review of Mussolini's book *The Political and
Social Doctrine of Fascism*, which appeared in November 1933.
In the course of the article, the reviewer, 'J. O'M', claimed
that Mussolini was 'the greatest statesman which this age
has produced' and saw Fascism as 'the greatest movement
of our age'. He also saw clear analogies between the Irish
and Italian scenes:

When we think of the striking similarity of the Italy to which
Mussolini came as a leader and our own present-day Ireland we
realise that this book will have more than a passing value to
those who are interested in rescuing our country from weak
government, civil unrest and the encroachment of Communism.
This is not to say that Ireland can be rescued only by Fascism,
but we would be fools were we to shut our eyes to the fact that
behind Fascism in Italy, and responsible for its phenomenal
success is that same spirit which is now making the Blueshirt
movement the biggest political movement that Ireland has ever
known.[11]

Late 1933 and 1934 saw a spate of articles and comments
on various aspects of corporatism, and the topic is more and
more frequently mentioned in the speeches of Fine Gael and
Blueshirt speakers. The most important and lengthy articles
on this subject came from Professor James Hogan and Professor Michael Tierney. Each of these wrote long articles in
late 1933.[12] In 1934 there were serialised articles from
both, Tierney writing under the title 'Fine Gael to adopt
Pope's social programme'[13] and Hogan on 'Corporatism'.[14]
O'Duffy's Ard-Fheis speech in March 1934 was devoted
largely to a reiteration of ideas on corporatism similar to
those being outlined by Hogan and Tierney.[15]

At this stage it is necessary to examine the source of
O'Duffy's ideas. He was later to embrace a fairly extreme
form of Fascism, but his printed speeches at this time followed

fairly closely along the lines being expounded by Hogan and Tierney.

There is no evidence to suggest that O'Duffy was deeply interested in political ideas before 1933. He was, however, highly impressionable and on his visit to Italy in 1929 he had met and been very impressed by Mussolini and by what he saw of the Fascist experiment in that country.[16] His European cruise following his dismissal as Chief of Police was also said to have been in some way responsible for turning his attention to Fascism. It is probable that the appeal of Fascism to O'Duffy was emotional and instinctive rather than intellectual. The organisational flamboyance, the colour and drama of the movement appealed to his restless temperament; the obvious Catholicism and anti-Communism appealed to his crusading spirit. He lacked subtlety and discrimination in his handling of ideas and he was in no way perceptive in distinguishing between the various movements. In his later days, he was completely indiscriminate in his endorsement of Fascist regimes and ideas. Even in his last days as leader of Fine Gael this aspect was becoming more noticeable and once the curbs were removed he wholeheartedly supported the Fascist movements of Europe, and saw himself as the Irish Fascist leader. However, by that time his movement was small and virtually impotent, and very much on the periphery. More important were the ideas he was expounding while leader of Fine Gael and here he would seem to have been very much under the influence of Professor Hogan and Professor Tierney. His major policy speeches during 1934 clearly reveal this influence.

Partly because of their influence on the thinking of O'Duffy and partly also because it was in their writings that the Blueshirt policy on corporatism received its fullest development, it is necessary to examine in detail the ideas being proposed by Hogan and Tierney. Although they were in agreement on many points, there were also some differences in emphasis between them, and for that reason it is necessary to examine the proposals of each separately.

*   *   *

Michael Tierney had been involved in Irish politics since the early 1920s. He was a son-in-law of Eoin MacNeill and had been a Cumann na nGaedheal T.D. during the 1920s. He had been close to the centre of Cumann na nGaedheal activity during the 1920s, during which time also he was a frequent contributor on scholarly and political matters to the influential periodical *Studies*.

His writings at this time reveal a sense of disillusionment at the spirit of hostility and bitterness which permeated political life during the first decade of the Irish Free State. He argued that this bitterness and the concentration on con-stitutional and nationalistic issues had resulted in the shelving or obscuring of the more fundamental problems of social and political re-organisation. He went on to argue that in many ways the democratic state as it existed in Ireland and Britain at this time was ill-equipped to deal with the great social and economic crises of the post-war world.[17] This is a view which was being aired by many political figures at this time, and even such a political sophisticate as Harold Nicolson could feel that the problems were too enormous to be solved without some drastic re-structuring.[18]

Tierney's analysis of Irish society led him to the conclusion that it had inherited most of the disorders and defects which were 'inseparable from individualist capitalism'. These de-fects he saw as: the partial and unequal organisation of Labour; the lack of any real organisation of productive forces, except for individual and profit-making purposes; the fact that the country had only an elementary system of law to regulate relations between employer and worker, or between both and the public; the fact that great inequalities still existed—and this he saw as the chief source of the 'current endemic unrest'; the fact that a Christian society still had all the 'social sub-divisions and snobberies that were the hall-mark of Victorian capitalism in its hey-day'.[19]

These he felt to be deep-seated problems, remediable neither by *laissez-faire* 'which has created conditions of more appalling cruelty and callous neglect than the worst days of the old regime in France', nor by 'the Soviet method of all round interference and universal state ownership which has established a tyranny unique in human experience'. Between these two extremes stood 'representative democracy as we know it', and about this he was almost as pessimistic:

From the philosophical standpoint there could be nothing funnier than the spectacle of a piebald and in general unintelligent and uneducated assembly of public representatives chosen by most defective methods claiming or having thrust upon it the whole enormously complicated and very subtle task of conducting the march of a complicated and subtle civilisation. Yet it is the exact spectacle with which philosophic observers of politics are presented in the countries which yesterday were regarded as the leaders in political wisdom.[20]

He regretted very much that the securing of national independence had not been accompanied by an attempt to develop 'native or organic institutions of government' and felt that the existing system was 'an exaggerated form of parliamentarianism, brought further than even in England or France by our anxiety in 1922 to preserve so-called Republican forms'. Under the structure of that time, he saw power and function divided between 'a bitterly sundered and frantically partisan committee of politicians whose only qualification is too often the noisiness of their own ambition' and 'an ever increasing class of irresponsible civil servants whose specialised knowledge is generally rendered nugatory by the fact that they are doomed forever to remain anonymous'.[21]

Because of the manner in which the state was constituted he felt that it tended to usurp gradually all the functions of society 'and to claim the final authority almost of a divinity'. Between the state and the individual there was no organic intermediary. The life, work and welfare of the citizen were coming more and more to depend on 'this lopsided combination of mediocre partisans and specialised, but intangible and often incredibly mechanised inspectors and clerks'. The result was that the citizen had no function except to vote and obey and 'when voting time comes around, every effort is made to make him think with his appetite rather than with his intelligence'.[22]

This was the dilemma as Tierney saw it, and he was clear that the solution to the problem could be provided neither by *laissez-faire* nor by Communism. The whole civilised world was being driven to face 'the necessity of some third course, between the individualism which produced Kreugers and the Communism which produces Lenins'.[23]

Dr Tierney felt that the solution to many of the problems was to be found in the social programme outlined by Pope Pius XI in the encyclical *Quadragesimo Anno*. He stressed as fundamental that passage in the encyclical which declares: 'the principal duty of the State and of all good citizens is to abolish conflict between classes with divergent interests, and thus foster and promote harmony between the various ranks of society. The aim of social legislation must therefore be the re-establishment of vocational groups.'[24]

This point is frequently emphasised in Tierney's writings —that the essence of the corporate programme must be the re-establishment of vocational groups, or as he described it on another occasion 'the medieval guild system brought up to date'. The ideal of this system he saw as: 'the harmony of differentiated functions in society, which has always been the dominant ideal in sound Christian and indeed even in pre-Christian political philosophy'.[25] Two of the major objectives of society were, he felt, the attaining of economic and social equality. But these were 'prizes in the gift of neither the state nor the individual'. '. . . They can only come from a more complex source—from a society highly organised and functioning with accurate certainty in all its varied parts.' This would be done by organising the whole society and economic system on new lines—'the re-establishment of vocational groups, and the creation of a system of national and local economic corporations'.[26]

He saw no reason whatsoever why either a civil war or

a dictatorship should be necessary as a prelude to such a system here. He felt there was 'no other or better means in Ireland for carrying our policy into effect than to persuade the majority of the people that it is desirable'.[27]

Corporatism would not involve the suppression or abolition of parliament. It would, however, involve a diminution in the business of parliament, and make possible a reduction in the number of deputies. It would mean also that 'Politicians would have to recognise that much more influence in the shaping of industrial and economic policy ought to be given to the ordinary citizens, organised in their various associations and professions than is now given.'[28]

Instead of a state organised only at the top, Tierney wanted a state organised all the way down in which the ordinary citizen would be given a chance to pronounce on matters within his competence and matters closely concerning his life and work: 'Parliament must cease to monopolise all national activity and we must abandon the grotesque idea that the whole work of rebuilding the nation can be done by a combination of ignorant ministers and mechanised civil servants.'

Under the present system, there was no place for the real representation of economic groups in parliament, but under the new system there would be full representation for both agriculture and industry.[29]

Tierney wanted the creation of workers' and employers' syndicates. The workers' organisation would be based on the present trades union structure. As far as the employers were concerned, he wanted all those in a given district and a given industry brought together as one group for the purpose of regulating their relations with their workers. These separately organised groups would be legally joined together in one institution which would have many other functions besides the mere regulation of wages and working hours. It would also be expected to play an important part for the workers in the securing of various amenities in both apprentice instruction and adult education. He felt that the existence of syndicates and their legal recognition and regulation would justify the total prohibition of strikes and lock-outs.

Farmers would also be organised on syndical lines, and he saw such a syndicate involving itself in such things as rural education, improvement of methods, co-operative purchase and sale of commodities, the organisation of rural amenities and the raising of standards of taste and culture.

The initiative in forming the syndicates would rest with the workers and employers themselves. But once formed, the syndicate would have to comply with certain mandatory principles. Again, individuals would not be compelled to join anything, but the syndicates once formed would be the legal representative organisations of the workers and the employers in their districts and trades.

The main difference as Tierney saw it between the medieval system and the proposed new system would be that the syndicate system would be thoroughly organised, and its parts would be inter-related.[30]

Continental influence on his thinking: Dr Tierney constantly stressed in his writings that there was nothing wrong with borrowing ideas from the continent. He often pointed out that neither the concept 'Republic' nor that of 'Parliament' were of Irish origin. He was always very emphatic that the corporate movement was not a 'Hitlerite' or Fascist one.

He felt it was very questionable if the corporate ideals had any place at all in the doctrine of German National Socialism 'whose extravagant nationalism and preoccupation with military prestige have in fact more in common with Fianna Fáil's curious jingoism and thirst for volunteer armies, than with genuine Fascism in its present phase'.[31] He approved of Dr Dollfuss, whom he regarded as being the great enemy of German Nazis. 'Dollfuss', he wrote, 'was engaged in putting the Papal plan for social reform into effect in his own country.'[32] He also felt that there were many similarities between the policy of Dr Dollfuss and that of the party led by Senor Gil Robles in Spain.[33]

It was the Italian system, however, which involved most of his attention. Italy he saw as 'the only country in which there is a sign of an attempt to create out of the wreckage, both of parliament and of party, a really well designed and complex machinery for dealing with a complex situation'.[34] And Italian Fascism was not 'merely a crude individualist or party dictatorship' but 'the product of peculiar Italian conditions, unknown elsewhere, which has gradually evolved a scheme of social and political organisation, which is quite certain as time goes on to be adapted to the needs of every civilised country'.[35]

He minimised the importance of the dictatorship within the Italian system. He claimed it was giving place to 'a new, and more intelligent, because more subtly organised kind of democracy. Mussolini, when his time comes to retire, will be succeeded not by another dictator but by a new entity suited to the needs of modern civilisation—the Corporate State'.[36] He approved of much that was being done in Italy, but this approval was not unqualified. He did not think that it would be 'either necessary or desirable for us here in Ireland to follow at all closely the details of the whole national structure as it was being put together in Italy'.[37]

In many ways conditions here were completely different from Italian conditions. For example, here there would be no need for a special confederation for sea and air transport; the agricultural organisation here would be different, and he would not contemplate giving any kind of constitutional functions to a more or less self-appointed body like the Fascist Grand Council.[38]

He was very definite that the corporate state here could be achieved 'under different historical and political conditions, without necessarily having recourse to all the accidentals of Italian dictatorship',[39] and he stressed that 'it was not in the least necessary to share Mussolini's rather drastic and in some ways excessive views on the exclusive rights of the state'. Tierney constantly emphasised that *Quadragesimo Anno* was the main source of his ideas, and that

Fine Gael's corporatism was an attempt to put the Papal plan into operation.

He regarded the movement for the reorganisation of the state and the restoration of vocational groups as a world-wide movement: 'It is the answer of civilised Europe to the Bolshevik heresy on the one hand, and the older individualist heresy of materialist *laissez-faire* on the other'.[40] And the object of corporatism he saw as 'the reintegration of Christian society, and its re-establishment on its old basis, strengthened and solidified'.[41] He was very certain that 'The Corporate State must come in the end in Ireland as elsewhere. Its inauguration need not be the work of any one political party, but the future is with those who honestly, intelligently and fearlessly will undertake its cause.'[42]

* * *

James Hogan, like Tierney, regarded the division of society into rival classes of employers and workers as one of the underlying causes of world-wide discontent. The mutual distrust and antagonism of these two classes, and the consequent tendency to class warfare was threatening, in greater or lesser degree, the internal unity of every civilised nation. He saw this social and emotional cleavage present in Irish society, although here 'an idolatrous nationalism is only too often a cloak for the ugly reality of class war'.[43]

He believed that the old type of capitalist civilisation could not continue to function much longer, and that the country was faced with many perils—political tyranny, economic collapse, revolutionary Socialism and acute dissension. There was, he felt, a danger of the country 'drifting into Socialism or some equally obnoxious form of Statism'. To prevent this from happening it was essential that some alternative 'that is as definite and as fundamental as the theories of Socialism be available'.[44] This practical alternative he saw as the concept of the corporate society: 'a practical alternative which is based upon the principles of

Christianity, not in the sentimental sense . . . but in the sense that it is the civil equivalent of Christian theology, the logical implication of its teachings.'[45]

He argued that from the standpoint of Catholic social philosophy the corporations or professional groupings of persons engaged in the same trade or activity were as natural as the family grouping. As the individual in his personal life is associated with the family, so in his larger, or social and economic life, would he be naturally associated with the larger family of the corporation, and they in turn would be brought into harmony by the council of corporations, working under the general supervision of the state.[46]

He went into rather more detail than did Tierney in outlining the manner in which these corporations would be organised, but there was little significant difference between the two structures. Like Tierney, he insisted that there would be no conflict between the council of corporations and parliament: 'It cannot be too strongly insisted upon that so far from contradicting or superseding political democracy, functional or economic democracy actually completes it,' and 'Surely it stands to reason that parliament has something to gain from the existence of an organisation with its finger on all the pulses of economic life, by which parliament can be advised on economic problems, and through which its policies can be carried out.'[47]

By advocating such a policy, they were not aiming at a dictatorship. Such an idea was alien to the Catholic concept of society, and Hogan argued that such a scheme had been expressly repudiated by the Catholic leader in Spain, Gil Robles, and by Dr Dollfuss in Austria.

The truth of the matter is that the corporate form of society is not wedded historically or politically to any particular form of government, whether by kingship, democracy or oligarchy. Neither Mussolini in Italy nor Dollfuss in Austria nor Gil Robles in Spain, nor Roosevelt in America, nor Mr Walter Eliot, the English Minister of Agriculture, has a monoply in the corporate idea, which they are trying out in different ways according to the special circumstances of their respective countries. In fact the corporate state was a brilliant afterthought of the Italian Revolution and had nothing whatever to do with the dictatorship which Communism rendered inevitable in Italy, as later in Germany.[48]

The corporations would be partly autonomous, administering their own affairs, partly working in co-operation with representative political institutions. There would be no corporatising of the entire life of the nation, no management of Church and state by the corporations.

Under the new scheme 'State politics and what we may call economic-social politics will be clearly distinguished, although associated, each being represented by its representative branch of the Legislature.'[49] Under the existing circumstances of the Free State 'The Second House might well become the supreme representative body of the corporation as a whole—an economic parliament. Thus will be realised the two democracies, the economic and the political, and the two democracies are the vital and necessary conditions for any democracy at all.'[50]

He felt strongly that the guild or corporative type of society was the normal type of society because 'It is the only type of society that can succeed in reconciling the conflicting claims of collective and individual life.'[51]

That in brief outline was the social and political doctrine of Blueshirtism as developed by Tierney and Hogan and as it appeared in O'Duffy's speeches during 1933 and 1934. A number of observations can be made.

The ideas and doctrine post-dated the emergence of the Blueshirt movement, and were of very little importance in helping the spread of the movement or in determining the nature of its activity. Clearly both Hogan and Tierney were hoping to use the Blueshirts as the vehicle for their ideas on the remodelling of the social and political order.

The dominant influence in their thinking is clearly the Papal encyclical, *Quadragesimo Anno* but they were also influenced by the example of some of the European Fascist leaders and movements—more especially the Catholic ones.

In all probability, their thinking was also to some extent influenced by the writings of the English Catholic school of Belloc and Chesterton, both of whom were at the height of their popularity at this time and were especially popular in Ireland, where their crusading Catholicism and glorification of a romantic Catholic past evoked an immediate and enthusiastic response.

While Tierney and Hogan were in the mainstream of contemporary Catholic social thinking and were both very conscious of happenings in Europe, they were also very discriminating in their perception of what the position was. They saw in the Blueshirts the Irish manifestation of a world trend, but were careful to stress that whatever adaptations were made would have to be geared to the peculiar Irish situation and circumstances.

It finally remains to discuss the impact of these ideas on the movement as a whole and the extent of the commitment of leaders and rank-and-file members to them.

O'Duffy's position is clear enough. He took the corporate ideas seriously and he wanted to establish a corporate state in Ireland—his political party founded in 1935 was known as the National Corporate Party. He saw the Blueshirts as part of a world-wide phenomenon and was quick to identify himself as its leader. He was pleased to call himself a Fascist and enthusiastically immersed himself in the affairs of international Fascism, supported Mussolini's invasion of Abyssinia and fought with Franco in Spain. His Fascism may have been emotional and instinctive rather than intellectual, but he certainly took it seriously. His crusading zeal and his view of Fascism as the Christian answer to the threat of Communism—indeed he went so far as to say that corporatism was 'the only programme which is compatible under modern conditions with Christian truths and teaching'[52]— may have blinded him to the ugly reality of many aspects of the Fascist movements he praised and hoped to emulate, and his natural muddle-headedness may have made it unclear what exactly he wanted, but in the final analysis, it is clear that he saw himself as being a Fascist leader of a Fascist movement, and that this is what he wanted.

The number of others in the movement who would fit into the same category as O'Duffy is difficult to estimate. After the split, none of the leaders and only a small segment of rank-and-file members followed him, and even this support did not prove very long-lasting. This does not mean that there may not have been a considerable number prepared to support a Fascist movement had it looked like being successful. All that can be said with certainty is that the number prepared to follow O'Duffy was small and the subsequent purging of the Blueshirts of any Fascist characteristics met with very little opposition.

Again, it is difficult to estimate with accuracy the degree of commitment of the Fine Gael leaders to the corporate ideas. Some such as Blythe, O'Higgins and FitzGerald devoted considerable attention to them and seem to have regarded them as being important. For many others, and especially it would seem Cosgrave, MacDermot and Dillon, the corporate proposals were seen as a detail of policy and not as being fundamentally important, or as an end in themselves.[53] O'Duffy, after the split, was particularly bitter on this point. He claimed that Fine Gael had never been serious about the corporate ideas or about setting up a corporate state. Fine Gael, he said, only nominally accepted the corporate state: 'It was putting new wine into old bottles to entrust the corporate state to them, and very annoying it proved to the bottles and very dangerous to the wine.'[54]

Certainly the speed with which the corporate items disappeared completely from Fine Gael policy after the split and the ease with which the old Cumann na nGaedheal patterns were reasserted would suggest that the commitment of the party was never deep or thoroughgoing. While the corporate ideas as developed by Tierney and Hogan did give to the Blueshirt movement a distinctive ideology, it is clear that for the great majority, both of leaders and rank-and-file supporters, this issue was largely an academic one. The issues which gave Blueshirtism its impetus, which concerned the minds and activities of its members and which determined the manner in which it developed, were far from academic. Blueshirtism was essentially the product of Civil War memories, fear and distrust, and the threat of economic collapse. Beside these, the promise of a new corporate state counted for very little.

14 The Blueshirts and Fascism

PROBABLY the most interesting and certainly the most controversial question raised by the Blueshirts is whether or not that movement can be meaningfully described as being a Fascist one.

This was a question on which there was violent disagreement in the 1930s. The opponents of the Blueshirts were clear and definite in their conviction that the Blueshirts were, and were intended by their leaders to be, a Fascist movement. This was particularly true of those on the left, the I.R.A. and the Labour Party, who saw in the Blueshirts the Irish manifestation of a world-wide phenomenon. Less emphasis seems to have been placed on this aspect of Blueshirtism by Fianna Fáil; nevertheless it is a charge which was frequently made.

The charge of Fascism was not confined to enemies of the movement. Frank MacDermot feared that during its National Guard days the movement was veering towards Fascism.[1] W. B. Yeats was pleased to see in the Blueshirts the Irish form of a world-wide movement—of which he heartily approved.[2] Of course, O'Duffy himself, especially in the later stages, was quick to identify himself and his movement with international Fascism.

Within Fine Gael, however, there was an equally strong conviction that the movement was in no sense a Fascist one; that it owed much of its inspiration to the Papal encyclical *Quadragesimo Anno,* that it was essentially a spontaneous reaction to counter the threat of anti-democratic forces, and that any of the trappings of Fascism which adorned the movement were wholly accidental and of no real significance.

*   *   *

The resolution of this question does involve a number of difficulties, the most important being that of definition. The term 'fascist' is imprecise—indeed, at the present time the word is so vague and used so indiscriminately and so comprehensively as to be almost meaningless except as a term of political abuse. Even during the 1930s, the term was used to describe a wide variety of movements, some of which had very little in common with others. It is probably accurate to say that the differences on the right during the 1930s were far more marked than those on the left.[3] As Professor Trevor-Roper observes:

Fascism may be limited in time and place, it may have a clear beginning and a clear end in public history, it may seem easily defined; but this unity, this definition was imposed upon it. Behind the one name lie a hundred forms. The abstraction, so convenient as a term of abuse, is singularly unhelpful as a means of definition . . .

That is not to say that Fascism has no distinctive, positive content, that it is merely a congeries of disparate national movements, artificially drawn or forced together by German power in the 1930s. There were some common features even in the early formative years, and afterwards, in the years of power, the various national movements, though independent in origin, borrowed ideas from each other and so helped to build up, retrospectively, a common ideology. But it is important to remember that Fascism, by its very nature being a movement of aggressive nationalism, began in a more disorderly fashion than Communism, and preserved that disorderly quality to the end.[3a]

However, having made this reservation, it is possible to say that the 1930s were the decade of Fascism. Virtually every country in the world had its Fascist party, and some had governments run on Fascist lines. Fascism was a real and identifiable political phenomenon—the various movements shared certain ideological, organisational and liturgical characteristics, and accorded a primacy and allegiance to certain values. Although each individual movement owed its peculiar shape and particular form to the social, economic, political and historical circumstances of its own country, Fascism was nevertheless a real and identifiable term in the 1930s, and it is in this context that the question of the Blueshirts and the relationship of that movement to Fascism must be raised.

Each of the Fascist movements had certain shared characteristics, and it was the sum of these which combined to make a movement 'Fascist'. It is proposed in this chapter to examine these characteristics, and see the extent to which they can be applied to the Blueshirts.[4]

* * *

Nationalism, usually of a very extreme variety, was an important characteristic of all Fascist movements. But as an aid to definition, the very universality of this phenomenon in inter-war Europe makes it of very little use. Soviet Russia was to prove itself no less nationalistic than Nazi Germany. Nationalism was so much a part of the general consensus of Irish politics that the differences between the various groups on this question were merely of degree and emphasis; not generic. The nationalism of the Blueshirts was moderate and certainly less extreme than that of Fianna Fáil and the I.R.A.

Likewise it can be said that *anti-Communism* was an essential characteristic of all Fascist movements, and was a determining factor in the origin and early development of a number of them. In almost all the European countries it was the presence of organised and easily identifiable Communist groups which accelerated the early growth of Fascism. In France, for example, the first real impetus which the nascent Fascist movement got was in November 1924, after the huge Communist-Socialist parades in Paris made clear to the middle classes the extent of the 'Red Menace'. After this,

Fascist movements in France sprang up, almost literally over-night. In the early days of its development, much of the energy of the movement that was to become the Austrians' Heimwehr-Frontkampfer Association was devoted to violent exchanges with Communist and Socialist groups in post-war Austria. One of Hitler's biggest initial advantages lay in the fact that the National Socialists appeared to be the only group capable of stemming the rising tide of German Communism. Much the same was true of Mussolini's movement. The growing strength of Communism in Spain had its reaction in the Spanish Falange. The Rumanian Legion of the Archangel Michael was strongly anti-Communist, though in this particular instance the dominant factor was probably fear of Soviet imperialistic expansion rather than of Communism as such. In all these countries Communism repre-sented a real threat—sizeable and easily recognisable—sufficient to provoke a reaction.[5]

The position in Ireland was very different. The Commun-ist movement was illegal, minute, not easily identifiable and did not seem to pose any immediate or obvious threat to the stability of the state. In this respect the position in Ireland was rather similar to that in Britain where the absence of any strong or obvious Communist movement was one of the reasons why Mosley's British Union of Fascists failed to make any real headway. The radical left in Britain was never sufficiently strong or coherent to provoke a reaction from the radical right such as happened in Germany, France, Italy and Austria.

Opposition to Communism was part of the general consensus of Irish politics, which was not surprising in an overwhelmingly Catholic country and at a time when Com-munism was being constantly and virulently denounced in Papal encyclicals and bishops' pastorals. The Blueshirts were strongly anti-Communist, but this opposition was largely theoretical, as was only to be expected in a country without any direct or practical experience of Communism. This would not have been admitted by some Blueshirts who claimed to see Communism as a real and immediate threat and for whom 'Communist' was a wide and comprehensive term; who saw the I.R.A. as being in the vanguard of Irish Communism, and who felt de Valera was playing the role of a 'Kerensky'. Professor Hogan is the best exemplar of this strain of Blueshirtism, and his pamphlet *Could Ireland Become Communist*[6] is sometimes almost hysterical in its expression of these fears. It is not surprising then that there were some among the Blueshirts—many perhaps—who were fanatical in their opposition to Communism, and who saw the Blueshirts as the strongest bulwark in the state against the spread of Communism. It was in the degree of Blueshirt opposition to Communism, and in its perception of itself as the only group fully alive to the reality of the Communist threat that it was different, or saw itself as being different to the other Irish parties.

All Fascist movements were explicit in their *opposition to democracy*. A list of European Fascist movements does not reveal one that was not avowedly anti-democratic. The position of Hitler and Mussolini, in both their doctrines and their practice, is sufficiently clear. Mosley's opposition to democracy was 'born of well-founded impatience'.[7] The Action Française from the very beginning made no secret of its opposition to democracy, as was the case also with the Spanish movements, the Falange and Jons, and the Austrian Heimwehr. In Hungary, Szalasi's Scythe Cross tirelessly campaigned for his dictatorship. Rumanian Fascism made no pretence of being democratic, nor did the ineffectual People's Patriotic Movement of Finland, nor Quisling's Najonal Sporling. The Belgium movements—Action Nationale, Legion Nationale, Rex and V.N.V.—though all making use of parliament did not hide the fact that they hoped to supplant parliament and set up a dictatorship. The position of the V.N.V. is interesting here because it attracted the support of some members of parliament who were convinced that its anti-parliamentarianism was a very minor part of its programme, and that the real issue was Flemish nationalism.[8]

The important point about all these movements is that they *openly proclaimed* their opposition to democracy, and their intention of setting up a dictatorship. In this regard, the Blueshirts differ profoundly from Fascist movements. Blueshirt leaders stressed their commitment to democracy and claimed that the movement came into existence in the first place to save the democratic freedoms which were being threatened by the I.R.A. and Fianna Fáil. They stressed their opposition to all dictatorships, disclaimed any intentions or designs in this direction, challenged their opponents to produce any evidence to prove their allegations and claimed that the corporate policy which they advocated would complement and fulfil the institutions of democracy.

Adherence to some form of *corporate* or organic organisation of society was part of the programme of most Fascist parties, although of course with considerable variation of degree and emphasis.[9]

The Blueshirts were committed to some form of corporate organisation. The Fine Gael policy never went further than advocating the establishment of economic and agricultural corporations with statutory powers, but individual Blueshirts including O'Duffy went much further than this. However, the degree of commitment of Blueshirt leaders or rank-and-file is not, at this stage, relevant. All that is necessary to note is that the Blueshirts were committed to some form of corporatism, and in this they had an affinity with the various Fascist movements.

All Fascist movements not only used *violence*, but regarded it as an absolute means to an absolute and necessary end. As Mosse observes, 'the Fasci, the German Storm Troopers, the Iron Guard in Rumania, all regarded their post-war world as an enemy which as shock troops they must destroy'.[10]

This belief in movement, in activism, in the great necessity for the purifying efficacy of violence, is a characteristic of all major Fascist movements, although of course with varying degrees of emphasis.

These characteristics apply, need it be said, to the movements of Hitler and Mussolini, but also to Mosley's 'brawling hooligans', to the Scythe Cross movement of Hungary, to the Iron Guard of the Legion of the Archangel, to the Action Française, to the Heimwehr and to the Falange. The same is true also, but not to the same extent, of the Legion Nationale, the Verdinaso and to a still lesser extent of the V.N.V., the Rexists and the Najonal Sporling. All these movements had their organised storm troops and certainly the first named movements believed that systematic violence was a necessary and a desirable means of obtaining their objectives. Thus, while the degree of commitment to violence, and the belief in its usefulness and necessity varied greatly from movement to movement it can be seen as a very definite characteristic of Fascist movements.[11]

This commitment to violence almost as an end in itself does not appear to have had any place in Blueshirt thinking. There are, it must be said, instances of Blueshirt leaders exhorting members to be prepared for combat; to be ready to exchange 'ten blows for every one received' and to 'break gobs if necessary;'[12] there are the speeches of Cronin and Quish which could be construed as inciting civil war; there is the undoubted military aspect of Blueshirtism—both in its origins and in its organisation; there is also the fact that the Blueshirt movement was frequently involved in incidents of violence.

In mitigation it must be said that the Blueshirt leaders always claimed that their involvement in such activity was purely defensive and the result of provocation; that had they not been prepared to resort to methods of violence, freedom of speech would have been wiped out and opponents of the I R.A. and Fianna Fáil would be at the mercy of vindictive thugs.

It should be mentioned also that the Blueshirt leaders never sought or hoped to gain their objectives through the use of force: adherence to the ballot-box was invariably stressed. Moreover, on this question of violence, it should be noted that it was participation by the Blueshirts in the anti-rates violence—hardly systematic or ruthless—which was one of the factors leading to the final disruption of the movement. The leaders expressly forbade members to engage in these acts of violence.

There would seem, therefore, to be little similarity between the Blueshirts and most of the European Fascist movements, either in their attitude to violence, or in the type of violence in which they engaged. However, it is not possible to be altogether clear about this aspect of Blueshirtism, but it might be accurate to say that the violence associated with some of their activities was a fairly incidental by-product of their political aims.

The most obvious aspect of all Fascist movements was the *liturgical* element—the outward trappings, the uniforms, salutes, marches, parades and monster meetings. Each movement had its own liturgy, and it is here that all Fascist movements have much in common. Although the ritual may have varied from movement to movement, both in intensity and in execution, its presence does establish a common bond between all Fascist movements.

If the sole criterion of Fascism was the adoption of this particular liturgy, then without question the Blueshirts could be classed a Fascist movement. For certainly they had all the essential trimmings—shirts, marches, salutes, and even O'Duffy's mass-meetings. On balance, this might seem to be the most obvious and real similarity between the Blueshirts and European movements.

Chiefly because of the crude and brutal manner in which *racism* and *anti-Semitism* found expression in the doctrine and practice of National Socialism, they are generally regarded as integral parts of Fascism. While Fascist movements could exist which were neither racist nor anti-Semitic—there was not anti-Semitism in Italian Fascism before 1936, and Leon Degrelle expressly repudiated racism—both these doctrines nevertheless were such integral parts of the principal forms of Fascism as to be regarded as usual Fascist characteristics. Germany, post-1936 Italy, the British Union of Fascists, the

Iron Guard, the Heimwehr, Action Française, the Falange, the Scythe Cross and the Najonal Sporling were all anti-Semitic.[13]

There is no evidence that the Blueshirts were in any way anti-Semitic. Certainly there was no good reason why they should have been—there was no tradition of anti-Semitism in Ireland and the Jews were a minute fraction of the population with no obvious or oppressive economic power.[14] Yet the position in Britain was somewhat similar and there anti-Semitism was one of the most marked aspects of Mosley's movement, but possibly because it was possible to find there areas of concentrated Jewish population.

The only nagging doubt on this question arises in connection with the proviso in the constitution of the National Guard, which confined membership of the movement to 'those of Irish birth or parentage who profess the Christian faith'. No explanation for this proviso was ever proffered. It may possibly have been designed to keep Jews out, or it may more probably have been a bit of pious rhetoric. It is a small point and one can say with certainty that neither in their practice nor in their ideology did the Blueshirts exhibit any traces of anti-Semitism. They never claimed or stated they were opposed to Jews, and more conclusive still, they were never accused by their enemies of being so.

Irredentism was a characteristic of many Fascist movements, and always a potent rallying cry. The most obvious examples are Germany with its restless, relentless quest for *lebensraum,* and Italy with its yearning for imperial conquest. This was a characteristic also of the Scythe Cross movement which sought the return to Hungary of lands lost after the First World War and of the People's Patriotic Party which sought a 'Greater Finland'. Both the British Union of Fascists and the Falange were avowedly imperialistic, but neither irredentism nor imperialism could be regarded as a characteristic of the Belgian movements or of the Blueshirts.

It is true that the Blueshirts, in common with the other political movements in the state, sought the unification of the two parts of Ireland. But this, like nationalism, was so much a part of the general consensus of Irish politics that it is scarcely of much value as a criterion of irredentism.

Appeal to youth: All Fascist movements stressed their youthful quality—youth signifying vigour, action and freedom from vested interest in the old and discredited system. Most Fascist leaders, in comparison to the elder statesmen they opposed and sometimes replaced, were comparatively young: 'Youth was the indispensable quality of the Rightist leader, for it promised vitality and dynamism, and created the expectation of a bright tomorrow, which was bound to be an improvement over the dreary present.'[15] In 1933, when most of the leaders of Europe's political destinies were in their sixties or older, the men who were prominent on the Right ranged from twenty-four (Degrelle) to forty-four (Hitler and Mussolini).

In terms of age, however, the Blueshirt leaders were neither appreciably older nor younger than their political opponents. Most of the leaders on both sides had been young men in the Sinn Féin movement, and had entered politics in the revolutionary period 1916–1922. The Blueshirts did, however, stress the importance of youth to the movement, which indeed was known at different times as the League of *Youth* and the *Young* Ireland Association. The leaders certainly set about organising youth sections in the association, though it is difficult to know how successful these efforts were. It is not possible to estimate the effectiveness of the Blueshirt appeal to youth, but the significant fact is that they placed great emphasis on the place of youth in the movement.

The charismatic leader is an important feature of Fascist movements and many Fascist leaders were men of outstanding ability, combining ruthlessness with strange flashes of brilliance and sometimes even nobility. Indeed, some of them, especially in the early stages, could be said to merit the Machiavellian title of 'Hero', and the awe and reverence which was shown to them by their followers can best be

understood from this point of view. It is not surprising that
Fascism produced this type of situation, for the emphasis
which Fascist theory placed on dictatorship tended to give
a unique status to the leader, and many of them were
talented enough to exploit this.

O'Duffy's leadership of the Blueshirts could not, by any
stretch of the imagination, be termed charismatic. He was
unsubtle, muddle-headed and contradictory, was not even
a good opportunist, was clearly unable to dominate his vice-
presidents and could take only a tiny segment of the rank-
and-file with him after the split. However, and especially in
the early days, it does seem as if strong attempts were being
made to build up O'Duffy into this type of leader and those
who persuaded him to join may have hoped that he would
develop along these lines, or at least that he would counter-
match de Valera more effectively than did Cosgrave. Whatever the hopes and plans may have been, O'Duffy very
clearly was not a charismatic leader.

It should be mentioned also that almost every one of the
European Fascist movements owed its origin, at least in
some part to the presence of organised *groups of ex-servicemen*,
dissatisfied with the existing post-war order. As S. J.
Woolf observes: 'The future Fascist parties in almost all the
countries of Europe traced their origins back to the numerous
groupings of patriotic associations which emerged or re-
emerged in strength after the war.'[16] In this respect there
is a definite similarity between the Blueshirts and the Fascist
movements, for it was from the A.C.A. that the Blueshirt
movement was to evolve.

There is one final point, and that is the one of self-
perception. To many there was nothing particularly repre-
hensible about being Fascist in the early 1930s—in some
respects it was new and fashionable and had a certain
respectability on account of its anti-Communism, supposed
efficiency and sometimes because of its Catholicism. Fascist
movements were proud to call themselves Fascist—indeed,
most gloried in the title. Certainly it is difficult to find any

Fascist movement which shied away from that description or vehemently denied that it was Fascist. As far as the Blueshirts were concerned, the word 'Fascist' was never officially used to describe the movement, or any aspect of it, and in fact, the majority of the leaders consistently denied that the movement had anything to do with Fascism. Again, it was partly because of the feeling that the movement was veering towards Fascism that the split arose.

On the other hand, there were some, and especially O'Duffy, who did see the movement in an international context and who would have been pleased to use the term 'Fascist', but as far as can be ascertained, this group was comparatively small and in all probability the majority of leaders and members did not see the movement as being a Facist one.

*   *   *

If the features outlined above are accepted as being sufficiently defining characteristics of Fascism, it is possible to come to at least a partial judgement on the question of whether or to what extent the Blueshirts can be termed Fascist. It is possible to say that the Blueshirts had origins similar to many Fascist movements, that this movement looked like and had many of the external trimmings of Fascism and that it exhibited such Fascist characteristics as a strong emphasis on the role of youth, attachment to some form of corporate policy and a fanatical opposition to Communism. On the other hand, it must be said that not all of these characteristics were the exclusive preserve of Fascist movements and that the Blueshirts lacked some of the basic features of Fascism—opposition to democracy, a commitment to violence almost as an end in itself, and a belief in dictatorship. It is probable that the majority of Blueshirts never saw their movement as a Fascist one.

In the final analysis, it is probably true to say that the

Blueshirts, as they were developing during the National Guard days, were on the way to becoming a Fascist movement. Certainly, many of the portents were ominous. The accession of Cumann na nGaedheal and the Centre Party halted this process and provided restraints which led to the disruption of the Blueshirts. From that time on, it could be said perhaps that the Blueshirts had much of the appearance but little enough of the substance of Fascism.

15 Postscript

THE Blueshirt movement, under its various names and phases had an actual life of four and a half years—from the founding of the Army Comrades Association in 1932 to the disbanding of the League of Youth in 1936. Its effective life, however, was far shorter and it can be seen as a major political force for just over two years—from the accession of O'Higgins to the leadership in August of 1932 until the split of late 1934. During those two years, however, it dominated Irish politics in a way that neither its friends nor its enemies will easily forget and ensured that the term 'Blueshirt' will long remain in the Irish political and folk consciousness.

And yet as far as Irish politics are concerned the Blueshirts were an aberration, the most fundamental explanation of whose origin lies in the fear and distrust harboured by the opponents of Fianna Fáil in 1932 and 1933. The fear of vindictive retribution and the distrust in the democratic intentions of Fianna Fáil may have had little justification, but it is certain that these were genuinely held fears in whose existence can be found the major explanation of the rapid spread of the A.C.A. in late 1932. The foundation of such a body possibly, the rapid spread of such a body certainly, with its assumption of a bodyguard role, would have been most unlikely under conditions of normality. Indeed it is virtually impossible to understand the Blueshirt phenomenon without keeping constantly in mind the fact that the Irish Civil War was but a decade past—and that decade was filled with bitterness and rancour as few other decades have been.

It is important to remember also that the movement made its appearance at a time of international unease and uncertainty when the new and fragile democracies were under increasing strain.

Although the lifetime of the movement was short, its existence can be seen as falling into a series of distinct phases. First there was the quiet, almost pre-political phase, from the foundation of the A.C.A. in February 1932 to the reorganisation that coincided with O'Higgins' accession to the leadership in August of that year. Under O'Higgins the movement burst dramatically on to the national scene—organising, stewarding meetings, holding parades, actively involved in the 1933 election, increasingly in conflict with Fianna Fáil and I.R.A. supporters—and then there was the sudden and unexpected adoption of the blue shirt in April of 1933. The next phase began in June with the adoption of O'Duffy as leader, the foundation of the National Guard, the increasingly-apparent impatience with democratic methods, the stepping-up of activity generally and the growing accusations of plans to carry out a *coup d'état*. This phase came to an end with the banning of the National Guard and the foundation of Fine Gael and the next phase covered O'Duffy's first nine months as leader of Fine Gael. During this time the government's persistent efforts to defeat the Blueshirts—by banning their meetings, attempting to jail O'Duffy and seeking to outlaw the wearing of the blue shirt—were continually frustrated, and O'Duffy appeared secure in the leadership of a vigorous and united organisation. The disappointment in the local government election results ushered in the fifth phase and it was during this time that discontent with O'Duffy's leadership grew, anti-rates violence escalated, the government attitude became tougher still, all culminating in the split which followed the resignation of Professor Hogan. The final phase was characterised by quarrelling and splits and by a massive decline in enthusiasm and activity as the movement petered ineffectually out of existence.

It is not possible to estimate with any certainty the size of the movement. No records exist and various conflicting estimates have been made. O'Higgins claimed 30,000 members in late 1932. By 1934 O'Duffy was claiming a membership of over 120,000, but Ruttledge was later to state that the Blueshirt movement even at its strongest numbered no more than 20,000.

It is possible to regard the development of the Blueshirts as influenced by five main factors: the inherited bitterness of the Civil War, the example of international Fascist movements, the economic war, the link-up with Cumann na nGaedheal and the Centre Party, and the personality of O'Duffy.

The Civil War memories ensured an atmosphere that was bitter and unforgiving; the European movements provided the idea and example of a distinctive uniform and style of organisation; the link with Cumann na nGaedheal and the Centre Party meant that the Blueshirts shared in a parliamentary role as well as having an extra-parliamentary one—in itself a conflict-laden situation; the economic war provided an immediate and ready-made issue on which to fight the government, mobilised support for the movement and dictated the type of activity into which much Blueshirt energy was to be subsequently channelled; in O'Duffy's personality can be found the key to his erratic and unsubtle style of leadership.

The Blueshirt movement failed and this failure is attributable to a number of diverse factors. O'Duffy's inadequacies as a leader certainly contributed to it—and almost certainly accelerated the process of disintegration. Important also was the lack of unity within the movement—the party leaders were not united and there was constant disagreement between the Fine Gael and Blueshirt sections on policy and methods. The movement failed also because it was able to capitalise on only one major issue—the economic war—and its stand here was unlikely to provide it with any great measure of *new* support. Almost certainly the majority of bigger farmers—those most hit by the economic war—were already supporters of Cumann na nGaedheal or the Centre Party and their allegiance to Fine Gael and the Blueshirts might have been expected, almost as a matter of course.

The movement failed, much as any movement might have failed in the Ireland of the 1930s, so great was the strength of Fianna Fáil's popular support. This party, highly organised, skilfully-led, implementing a wide range of popular policies and completely attuned to the extreme nationalism of the decade, would have been very difficult to beat even if Fine Gael had not been beset by the particular problems then facing it. Fianna Fáil had by this time established itself as the natural 'majority' party and with political issues and views so clear-cut, with attitudes hardened and unshakeable there were very few floating or uncommitted votes to be won by O'Duffy or Fine Gael.

The movement failed also because it carried within itself internal contradictions which could only work themselves out by disrupting the movement. For instance if the Blueshirts were to be effective in their anti-rates activity, then direct measures and violation of the law were necessary. Anything less was destined to be unsuccessful. But inevitably the use of direct methods resulted in conflicts with the law and this type of activity obviously could not be sanctioned by the constitutional wing of the party. Likewise there was unlikely to be any lengthy term of peaceful co-existence within the same party between those who gloried in the supremacy of parliamentary methods and those impatient with the practices and procedures of parliament.

The whole Blueshirt phenomenon can be seen as a final instalment of the Civil War saga. The demise of the Blueshirts was to coincide with the establishment of something approaching normal relations between government and opposition. After 1936 the bile seemed to go out of Irish politics with a general lowering of temperatures all round. Personal animosities and bitter memories persisted certainly, but not with the same intensity or pervasiveness. The Blueshirt episode was, in one sense, a last great letting off of steam, the working out of the system of some of the virulent forces let loose during the Civil War decade.

In another sense too the Blueshirt episode is of great interest for it may well have been the closest brush Ireland has had with a class war. Certainly it is very easy and plausible to represent it in these terms, with the Blueshirts identified with and defending the rights of the middle classes, the farmers and merchants against the I.R.A. and Fianna Fáil behind whom were ranked the men of no property or at least the men of little property. Had de Valera not been so essentially conservative in matters economic and social, the conflict might well have worked itself out in terms of social conflict.

The Fine Gael Party was born of the decision to bring the Blueshirts into the constitutional arena and the manner in which the Blueshirts disintegrated was to affect the subsequent development of Fine Gael. The controversies and wrangling which followed the split, coupled with the apparent invincibility of de Valera, seemed to knock much of the fight and much of the heart out of Fine Gael and from this point until 1948 it lost seats and votes at every successive election, attracting little new support and becoming in every sense a middle-aged, very conservative and declining party. It is one of the ironies of modern Irish politics that it was the intervention of Clann na Poblachta in the 1948 election which made possible the formation of an Inter-Party government that was to spark off a limited but definite revival in the fortunes of Fine Gael—a Clann na Poblachta Party which included in its ranks many of the I.R.A. veterans of the 1930s.

The fact that the Blueshirts were the only shirted movement to appear in Irish politics may have a certain other importance. The obvious lack of success of the movement and the fact that it was so closely identified with Fine Gael may well have ensured that no further—and perhaps far more dangerous—versions of shirted movements appeared, especially at a time when the appearance of such a movement could well have upset that very delicate balance on which Irish neutrality rested from 1939 to 1945.

This then was the Blueshirt movement—a movement whose main importance lies in its uniqueness. It was a movement which drew some of its inspiration and some of its practices from the continent—but essentially it was an Irish phenomenon, for most of the factors which influenced its growth and origin were the product of conditions peculiar to Ireland. And most of all it was an unsuccessful movement whose very lack of success emphasised at once the skill of de Valera as a political leader and the unwillingness of the majority—both people and politicians—to experiment with new and untried forms of political activity.

Sources and Bibliography

UNPUBLISHED MS.
General Eoin O'Duffy—His Life and Battle by Captain Liam Walsh,
   who was O'Duffy's private secretary.

BOOKS AND PAMPHLETS
O'Duffy, Eoin, *Crusade in Spain*, Brown and Nolan 1938.
O'Duffy, Eoin, *An Outline of the Political, Social and Economic
   Policies of Fine Gael*, Fine Gael Policy Series, pamphlet no. 1,
   1934.
O'Duffy, Eoin, *The Labour Policy of Fine Gael*, Fine Gael Policy
   Series, pamphlet no. 2, 1934.
O'Duffy, Eoin, *Why I Resigned from Fine Gael*, Blueshirt Series,
   pamphlet no. 1, 1935.
Hogan, James, *Could Ireland Become Communist?* Cahill and Co.
   1935.
Hogan, James, *Modern Democracies*, Cork University Press 1938.
Coughlan, Col. P. J., *The Truth: The Story of the Blueshirts*
   Skibbereen Star, 1935.

NEWSPAPERS
The Irish Times
   Irish Independent
The Cork Examiner
The Irish Press
   United Irishman
   United Ireland
   An Phoblacht
The Blueshirt
The Nation
   Irish Weekly Independent
   Nationalist and Leinster Times

The Anglo Celt
     Kilkenny People
     Limerick Leader

PERIODICALS
The Round Table.
The Leader.
Studies—and especially the following articles:
John J. Horgan, 'The Problem of Government', with comments
     by W. T. Cosgrave and Michael Tierney, Vol. 22, December
     1933.
Edward J. Coyne, S.J., 'The Corporative Organisation of
     Society', Vol. 23, June 1934.
Michael Tierney, 'Ireland and the Reform of Democracy', Vol.
     23, September 1934.
Michael Tierney, 'An Irish View of Irish Politics', Vol. 24,
     December 1936.
Denis O'Keefe, 'The Corporative Organisation of Society', Vol.
     25, June 1937.
Vincent Grogan, 'Irish Constitutional Development', Vol. 40,
     December 1951.

OFFICIAL SOURCES
Dail Debates.
Senate Debates
Statistical Abstract.
Iris Oifigiuil.
The Cabinet Papers in the British Public Record Office contain
     no direct references to the Blueshirts but are of value on such
     subjects as the economic war, the Oath of Allegiance and
     Anglo-Irish relations. The following Cabinet Papers for 1932
     are particularly important: Nos. 86, 114, 123, 156, 157, 198,
     206, 212, 227, 233, 235, 236, 242, 248, 257, 265, 278, 291,
     303, 324, 334, 339, 350.
And for 1933: C.P. Nos. 258, 281, 287 and 288.
Important references to official British attitudes and policy on
     these topics can be found in the following Cabinet Minutes:
     17(32)7; 19(32)13; 20(32)3; 21(32)6; 26(32)3; 27(32)4;
     28(32)3; 30(32)6; 32(32)4; 35(32)3; 37(32)3; 38(32)3;
     40(32)3; 42(32)5; 42(32)3; 48(32)10; 50(32)11; 55(32)11;
     58(32)11.

SELECT BIBLIOGRAPHY

Bromage, Mary C., *De Valera and the March of a Nation*, Hutchinson, 1956.

Carsten, F. L., *The Rise of Fascism*, Batsford 1967.

Cobban, Alfred, *Dictatorship: Its History and Theory*, Cape 1939.

Coogan, T. P., *Ireland Since the Rising*, Pall Mall 1966.

Coogan, T. P., *The I.R.A.*, Pall Mall 1970.

Cross, Colin, *The Fascists in Britain*, Barrie and Rockliff 1951.

De Vere White, Terence, *Kevin O'Higgins*, Methuen 1948.

De Vere White, Terence, *A Fretful Midge*, Routledge and Kegan Paul 1957.

Finer, Herman, *Mussolini's Italy*, Gollancz 1935.

Friedrich, Carl Joachim (ed.), *Totalitarianism*, Grosset 1954.

Gilmore, George, *1934—Republican Congress*, Dochas, Dublin 1969.

Gray, Tony, *The Irish Answer*, Heinemann 1966.

Gwynn, Denis, *The Irish Free State 1922–27*, Benn 1928.

Hancock, K., *Survey of British Commonwealth Affairs*, Vol. 1, Oxford University Press 1937.

Harkness, David, *The Restless Dominion*, Gill and Macmillan 1969.

Inglis, Brian, *West Briton*, Faber 1962.

Inglis, Brian, *The Story of Ireland*, Faber 1956.

Larkin, Emmet, *James Larkin*, Routledge and Kegan Paul 1965.

Macardle, Dorothy, *The Irish Republic*, The Irish Press 1937.

McCracken, J. L., *Representative Government in Ireland: Dáil Éireann 1919–48*, Oxford University Press 1958.

McManus, F., *The Years of the Great Test: 1926–39*, Mercier Press 1967.

MacManus, M. J., *Eamon de Valera*, Talbot Press 1962.

Mansergh, Nicholas, *The Irish Free State: Its Government and Politics*, Allen and Unwin 1934.

Meenan, James, *The Italian Corporative System*, Cork University Press 1944.

Moss, Warner, *Political Parties in the Irish Free State*, Harvard 1933.

Neeson, Eoin, *The Civil War in Ireland*, Mercier Press 1966.

Nolte, Ernst, *Three Faces of Fascism*, Weidenfeld and Nicolson 1965.

O'Brien, Conor Cruise, 'Passion and Cunning: The Politics of Yeats'—an essay in *In Excited Reverie: A Centenary Tribute to William Butler Yeats*, edited by A. K. Jeffares and K. G. W. Cross, Macmillan 1965.

O'Brien, George, *The Four Green Fields*, Talbot Press 1936.

O'Conor Lysaght, A., *The Irish Republic*, Mercier Press 1970.

O'Donnell, Peadar, *There will be Another Day*, Mercier Press 1963.

O'Sullivan, Donal, *The Irish Free State and Its Senate*, Faber 1940.

Rogger, Hans and Eugen Weber (eds.), *The European Right: A Historical Profile*, Weidenfeld and Nicolson 1965.

Rumpf, Erland, *Nationalismus und Socialismus in Irland*, Meisenheim am Glan 1959.

Ryan, Desmond, *Unique Dictator*, Barkei 1936.

Skinner, Liam C., *Politicians by Accident*, Dublin Metropolitan Publishing Company 1946.

Stephan, Enno, *Spies in Ireland*, Macdonald 1962.

Talmon, J. L., *The Origins of Totalitarian Democracy*, Secker and Warburg 1952.

Weber, Eugen, *Varieties of Fascism*, Anvil Books 1965.

Williams, T. D. (ed.), *The Irish Struggle: 1916–26*, Routledge and Kegan Paul 1966.

Woolf, S. J. (ed.), *European Fascism*, Weidenfeld and Nicolson 1968.

Younger, Carlton, *Ireland's Civil War*, Frederick Muller 1968.

The Story of Fianna Fáil, National Executive Council, Dublin 1960.

The Journal of Contemporary History, Vol. 1, No. 1, 1966: being a series of essays on *International Fascism 1920–45* including—

George L. Mosse, 'The Genesis of Fascism';

Robert J. Soucy, 'The Nature of Fascism in France';

Adrian Lyttelton, 'Fascism in Italy: The Second Wave';

Eugen Weber, 'The Men of the Archangel';

Ludwig Jedlicka, 'The Austrian Heimwehr';

Paul M. Hayes, 'Quisling's Political Ideas';

Erwin Oberländer, 'The All-Russian Fascist Party';

Hugh Seton-Watson, 'Fascism, Right and Left'.

Notes

CHAPTER I

1. For the best single work on the Civil War see Calton Younger, *Ireland's Civil War*, London 1968.
2. For an account of the foundation of Cumann na nGaedheal see Warner Moss, *Political Parties in the Irish Free State*, Columbia University Press, 1933, 28–30, 54–70 and 133–40. The short impressions of the Cumann na nGaedheal ministers are based largely on conversations with their surviving colleagues and opponents.
3. Cf. *Studies*, vol. 25, no. 353 (1936), article by George O'Brien.
4. For a full account of the part played by the Irish Free State in Commonwealth affairs during this time, and especially the part played by McGilligan, see David Harkness' excellent study, *The Restless Dominion*, Dublin 1969.
5. Moss, *op. cit.*, 136.
6. For a good account of the early years of Fianna Fáil, cf. articles by Peter P. Pyne in *Economic and Social Review*, vol. I, nos. 1 and 2 (1969).
7. See *I.I.* and *I.T.* 11 Mar. 1926; also Moss, *op. cit.*, 25–7.
8. See *I.I.* and *I.T.* 17 May 1926.
9. Cf. Terence de Vere White, *Kevin O'Higgins*, London 1948 and T. P. Coogan, *The I.R.A.*, London 1970.
10. The early years of the Labour Party are discussed by Arthur Mitchell in four articles in *The Irish Times*, 27 Feb.–2 Mar. 1967.
11. K. B. Nowlan in *The Years of the Great Test*, ed. Francis McManus, Cork 1967, 9.
12. T. D. Williams in McManus, *op. cit.*, 37–8.

CHAPTER II

1. For a good short account of the implications of the Statute of Westminster cf. V. Grogan, 'Irish Constitutional Development' in *Studies*, December 1951. For a more elaborate discussion cf. Harkness, *op. cit.*
2. T. D. Williams in McManus, *op. cit.*, 31.
3. See *I.I.* 30 Jan. 1932; also Donal O'Sullivan, *The Irish Free State and its Senate*, London 1940, 281–2.
4. See *I.T.* 13 Feb. 1932.
5. See *I.T.* 15 Feb. 1932.
6. See *R.T.* vol. 22, no. 87, p. 496.
7. See *I.I., I.T.* 30 Jan.–6 Feb. 1932. Until quite recently a copy of this poster could be seen in the Fine Gael national headquarters in Dublin.
8. See *I.P.* 9 Feb. 1932; also Moss, *op. cit.*, 183.
9. Among the gratuities to which most publicity was accorded were the

following: D. Hogan, £3,300; E. Cronin, £1,100; Austin Brennan, £1,300; T. F. O'Higgins, £3,034; Seán MacEoin, £3,300.

10. I.R.A. speakers were prominent on many Fianna Fáil platforms during the campaign.

11. Election figures from *Irish Parliamentary Handbook,* compiled by W. J. Flynn, Stationery Office, Dublin 1939.

12. See *I.T.* 27 Feb. 1932.

13. Gerald Bartley; see *D.D.* vol. 41 col. 228.

14. See T. D. Williams in McManus, *op. cit.,* 30. The allegation about the revolvers is denied by some, but most of those to whom I spoke and who were members of the Dáil at that time feel that there is some basis to the allegation.

15. See *I.T.* 10 Mar. 1932.

16. *An Phob.* 19 Mar. 1932.

17. See *I.P.* 10 Mar. 1932.

18. See *I.P.* 11 Mar. 1932.

19. See *I.P.* 14 Mar. 1932 and *D.D.* vol. 44 col. 949.

20. See *I.T.* 19 Mar. 1932.

21. See *D.D.* vol. 41 col. 250.

22. See *D.D.* vol. 41 col. 145–6.

23. Submissions made by the Irish High Commissioner, J. W. Dulanty to the British government, see *I.T.* 23 Mar. 1932. See British Cabinet Conclusions 20(32)3 and 21(32)6.

24. *House of Commons Debates,* cclxv, 1914.

25. See *I.T.* 20 May 1932.

26. See *S.D.* vol. 15 col. 1090–1101, 1424 *seq.*; *D.D.* vol. 43 col. 615–717.

27. See K. Hancock, *Survey of British Commonwealth Affairs* I, Oxford 1937. 334–50.

28. See *I.T.* 5 and 12 July 1932.

29. See *I.T.* 12–23 July 1932.

30. See *U.I.* 18 Feb.; 3 and 10 Mar. 1932.

31. See *I.I.* 10 Feb. 1932.

32. Based on conversations with former members.

33. See *Daily Mail* 14 Nov. 1930 and *The Nation* 11 Apr. 1931.

34. All survivors spoken to were definite that there was no connection between the two associations.

35. See *I.I.* 18 Mar. 1932.

CHAPTER III

1. See Flynn, *op. cit.,* 119.

2. *I.I.* 12 Aug. 1932.

3. *Ibid.*

4. *Ibid.*

5. *I.I.* 15 Aug. 1932.

6. See *I.I.* 16 Aug. 1932.

7. *I.I.* 22 Aug. 1932.

8. *I.P.* 20 Mar. 1932.

9. *I.P.* 3 Apr. 1932.
10. *U.I.* 16 May 1932.
11. See *I.I.* 24 Aug. 1932.
12. See *I.I.* 1 May 1932. It was widely believed that it was the events of this meeting which precipitated the decision to re-form the A.C.A.
13. See *I.P.* 16 Mar. 1932.
14. Every surviving Blueshirt interviewed bore witness to the reality of these fears.
15. *R.T.* vol. 23, no. 89 (Dec. 1932), 124–5.
16. Cf. O'Sullivan, *op. cit.*, 264–5.
17. Neither O'Donnell or Gilmore ever took any trouble to disguise their left-wing views. In addition O'Donnell had been to Russia and was shortly to be engaged in a bitter libel action against *The Irish Rosary*.
18. The Communist vote in the Saorstát in the 1932 election was as follows:

J. Larkin (Irish Workers League)	3,860	Dublin City North.		
J. Troy (Communist)	170	„	„	„
J. Larkin, jnr. (Communist)	917	„	„	South.
TOTAL	4,947			

19. *D.D.* vol. 41 col. 325.
20. These allegations of corruption which appeared most weeks in the *United Irishman* were concerned mainly with jobs at the local level, and especially to such appointments as road gangers.
21. Cf. ch. II note 9.
22. See *I.I.* and *I.P* 5 Sept. 1932.
23. See *I.I.* 8 Sept. 1932.
24. See *I.I.* 16 Oct. 1932.
25. See *I.I.* and *I.P.* 10 Oct. 1932, and *Limerick Leader* 14 Oct. 1932.
26. See *I.I.* 22 Oct. 1932.
27. See *I.I.* 7 Nov. 1932.
28. *I.I.* 3 Oct. 1932.
29. *I.T.* 5 Dec. 1932.
30. *Ibid.*
31. For a full if somewhat biased account of the Governor-General controversy, see O'Sullivan, *op. cit.*, 291–4, 330 and 482–4.
32. *Statistical Abstract*, 1932 and 1933.
33. *I.T.* and *I.P.* 16 Dec. 1932, and interview with F. MacDermot.
34. *I.P.* and *I.I.* 3 Jan. 1933.
35. Interview with G. Boland.
36. See *I.T.* 12 Sept. 1932.
37. See *I.T.* 28–30 Dec. 1932.
38. *I.T.* 3 Jan. 1932.
39. See *I.P.* 3–15 Jan. 1933; also Flynn *op. cit.*
40. *Ibid.*
41. *Ibid.*
42. *Ibid.*
43. *An Phob.* 14 Jan. 1933.
44. See *I.I.* 7 Jan. 1933.
45. See *I.I., I.P.* and *I.T.* 9 Jan. 1933.

alsh MS., 1664–5.

I. and *I.P.* 12 Jan. 1933.

ibid., 17 Jan. 1933.

49. *ibid.*, 23 Jan. 1933.
50. *D.D.* vol. 48 col. 2769–70.
51. Cf. *U.I.*, 10 and 24 Mar.; 8 Apr. 1932.
52. See *An Phob.* 24 Feb. 1932.
53. See *I.I.* 12 Jan. 1933.
54. *I.I.* 13 Jan. 1933.
55. See *I.I.* 14 Jan. 1933.
56. *I.T.* 21 Jan. 1933.
57. Flynn, *op. cit.*
58. See *I.T.* 9 Feb. 1933.
59. See *I.I.* 11 Feb. 1933.
60. *Ibid.*, 17 Feb. 1933.
61. *Ibid.*, 15 Feb. 1933.
62. *Ibid.*, 25 Mar. 1933.
63. Based partly on recollections of survivors.
64. See *I.I.* 25 Mar. 1933.
65. Based partly on recollections of survivors.
66. See *U.I.* 29 Apr. 1933.
67. See *I.I.* 10 Apr. 1933.
68. See *Irish Weekly Independent* 17 Apr. 1933.
69. *U.I.* 20 May 1933.
70. *U.I.* 20 May 1933. O'Duffy was later to claim that 'Onlooker' was but one of a number of names used by Blythe in *U.I.* See *The Blueshirt* 26 Jan. 1935.
71. *Ibid.*
72. *U.I.* 8 July 1933.
73. *U.I.* 17 June 1933.
74. *D.D.* vol. 48 col. 2777–90.
75. *An Phob.* 4 Mar. 1933.
76. *An Phob.* 18 Mar. 1933.
77. *D.D.* vol. 48 col. 2769–70.
78. *An Phoblacht* was particularly anxious to have O'Duffy and Colonel David Neligan dismissed. Cf. issues of 21 Jan., 4 Feb. and 4 Mar. 1933.
79. For I.R.A. attitude to 'Bass' cf. *An Phob.* Jan.–March 1933.
80. See *An Phob.* 18 Feb. 1933.
81. See *An Phob.* 1 July 1933 and 5 Aug. 1933.
82. See *I.I.*, *I.P.* and *I.T.* 27 Mar. 1933.
83. See *I.I.* 29 Mar. 1933.
84. See *I.I.* 30 Mar. 1933.
85. See *An Phob.* 27 May 1933.
86. See *D.D.* vol. 48 col. 2057.

CHAPTER IV

1. Walsh, *op. cit.*, 164–70.
2. See *An Phob.* 4 Mar. 1933.

3. *I.T.* 16 Mar. 1933.
4. See *D.D.* vol. 46 col. 33 seq. and col. 493 seq.
5. *D.D.* vol. 46 col. 33.
6. *D.D.* vol. 46 col. 758–814.
7. *D.D.* vol. 46 col. 796–7.
8. See *U.I.* 4 and 18 Mar. 1933.
9. See *D.D.* vol. 46 col. 765–6. Cosgrave cited as his sources the *Irish Catholic Journal* and another Catholic paper, *The Glasgow Observer*.
10. O'Sullivan, *op. cit.,* 330.
11. Walsh, *op. cit.,* 170.
12. *Ibid.,* 170.
13. *I.I.* 9 Nov. 1933.
14. Biographical details on O'Duffy mainly from Walsh, *op. cit.*
15. From interviews with O'Duffy's former colleagues.
16. See *I.I.* 21–28 Dec. 1929.
17. *I.P.* 8 Feb. 1932.
18. See *D.D.* vol. 50 col. 1195–6.
19. From an interview.
20. From interviews with former Fianna Fáil ministers.
21. See *I.I.* 16 Mar. 1933.
22. Walsh, *op. cit.,* 180 seq.
23. *Ibid.,* 134.
24. From interviews.
25. Based mainly on the recollections of O'Higgins' surviving colleagues.
26. *U.I.* 29 July 1933.
27. Interview with ex-Cumann na nGaedheal minister.
28. *U.I.* 15 July 1933.
29. See *I.T.* 17 July 1933 and *Sunday Independent* 18 July 1933.
30. *D.D.* vol. 48 col. 2770.
31. *Ibid.*
32. See *I.I.* 21 July 1933.
33. *Ibid.*
34. *U.I.* 29 July 1933.

CHAPTER V

1. *I.T.* 21 July 1933.
2. See *I.T.* 23 July 1933.
3. *Ibid.*
4. See *I.T.* 26 July 1933.
5. *The Blueshirt* 5 Aug. 1933.
6. See *I.T.* 31 July 1933.
7. *Ibid.*
8. *I.T.* 1 Aug. 1933.
9. See *I.T.* 2 Aug. 1933.
10. *D.D.* vol. 49 col. 1057–59.
11. See *D.D.* vol. 49 col. 1060–67.
12. *D.D.* vol. 49 col. 1068.
13. See *D.D.* vol. 49 col. 1030.
14. See *D.D.* vol. 49 col. 1068, 1072.

I.T. 3 Aug. 1933.

D.D. vol. 49 col. 1218.

I.T. 5 Aug. 1933.

18. See *I.T.* 7 Aug. 1933. The new police force were quickly nick-named the 'Broy Harriers'; cf. also Coogan, *The I.R.A., op. cit.,* 71–3.

19. See *I.T.* 9 Aug. 1933.
20. *Ibid.*
21. *D.D.* vol. 49 col. 1577–8.
22. *D.D.* vol. 49 col. 1581.
23. See *I.T.* 11 Aug. 1933.
24. See *I.T.* and *I.P.* 11 Aug. 1933. The I.R.A., according to Coogan, were determined to hinder the parade should it take place. Cf. Coogan, *op. cit.,* 73.
25. *I.T.* 12 Aug. 1933.
26. *I.T.* 9 Aug. 1933.
27. *I.T.* 14 Aug. 1933.
28. *Ibid.*
29. See *I.T., I.P.* and *I.I.* 14 Aug. 1933.
30. See *I.T.* 16 Aug. 1933.
31. See *I.T.* 19 Aug. 1933.
32. See *I.T.* 21 Aug. 1933.
33. *Ibid.*
34. See *I.T.* 23 Aug. 1933.
35. See *I.T.* 24 Aug. 1933.
36. See *I.T.* 25 Aug. 1933.
37. See *I.T.* 26 Aug. 1933.
38. *Ibid.*
39. See *I.T.* 28 Aug. 1933.
40. *U.I.* 26 Aug. 1933.
41. Details given by Cosgrave. See *I.T.* 9 Sept. 1933.
42. *I.T.* 11 Aug. 1933.
43. Walsh, *op. cit.,* 186.
44. *Ibid.*
45. *I.T.* 4 Sept. 1933.
46. See *I.T.* 9 Sept. 1933.
47. From an interview with Michael Tierney 29 Sept. 1967.
48. See *I.I.* and *I.P.* 11 Sept. 1933.
49. See *I.T.* 15 Sept. 1933.
50. *U.I.* 16 Sept. 1933.
51. See *U.I.* 6 May, 13 May, 20 May, 3 June 1933.
52. From interviews with Michael Tierney, Ernest Blythe and Frank Mac-Dermot.
53. Impression formed from interviews with surviving participants.
54. See letter to *The Irish Times* 3 Oct. 1950.

CHAPTER VI

1. See *I.T.* 4 Sept. 1933.
2. See *I.T.* 13 Nov. 1933.

3. See *I.T.* 3 Oct. 1950.
4. See *I.T.* 20 Nov. 1933 and 9 Feb. 1934.
5. List of meetings addressed by O'Duffy compiled from the three daily papers and from *U.I.*
6. See *I.T.* 28 Sept. 1933.
7. See *I.P.* 28 and 29 Sept. 1933.
8. See *S.D.* vol. 18 col. 408, 409, 450–60 and 1567–1628.
9. See *I.T.* 11 Sept. 1933.
10. See *I.T.* 16 Sept. 1933.
11. See *I.T.* 4–9 Nov. 1933.
12. See *D.D.* vol. 49 col. 1880.
13. See *D.D.* vol. 49 col. 1845.
14. *D.D.* vol. 49 col. 1927–29.
15. *D.D.* vol. 49 col. 1859.
16. *D.D.* vol. 49 col. 1818.
17. *D.D.* vol. 49 col. 1831.
18. See *I.T.* 1 Dec. 1933.
19. *D.D.* vol. 50 col. 710.
20. *D.D.* vol. 50 col. 859–70.
21. For instances of typical Bass raids cf. *I.T.* 5, 9, 10, 12, 13 and 14 Sept. 1933. Bass was singled out for special attention largely because of some insulting anti-Irish references made by one of the company's directors in the House of Lords.
22. See *I.T.* 9 and 22 Sept. 1933.
23. See *I.T.* 25 Sept. 1933.
24. See *I.T.* 1 Oct. 1933.
25. See *I.T.* 7 and 8 Oct. 1933.
26. *I.T.* 9 Dec. 1933.
27. See *I.T.* 23 Oct. 1933.
28. See *I.T.* 5 Jan. 1934.
29. See *I.T.* 6–11 Oct. 1933.
30. *An Phob.* 23 Sept. 1933.
31. *Ibid.*
32. See *Statistical Abstract,* 1930–1937.
33. See *I.T.* 17 Apr. 1934.
34. See *I.T.* 9 Dec. 1933.
35. *Ibid.*
36. *Ibid.*
37. *Ibid.*
38. See *I.T.* 11 Dec. 1933.
39. *Ibid.*
40. See *I.T.* 12-15 Dec. 1933.
41. See *I.T.* 15 Dec. 1933.

CHAPTER VII

1. See *I.I.* 15 Dec. 1933.
2. See *I.I.* and *I.P.* 17 Dec. 1933.
3. See *I.I.* 18 Dec. 1933.

18

4. See *I.I.* 21 Dec. 1933.
5. *I.I.* 23 Dec. 1933. Dr Morrisroe was probably the most openly partisan member of the hierarchy. His brother was a Cumann na nGaedheal T.D.
6. See *I.I.* 22 Dec. 1933.
7. See *I.I.* 24 and 31 Dec. 1933 and 2–3 Jan. 1934.
8. See *I.T.* 22 Mar. 1934.
9. *I.T.* 18 Dec. 1933.
10. See *I.T.* 5 Jan. 1934.
11. See *I.T.* 7, 20, 22 and 29 Jan. 1934.
12. See *I.T.* 12 Feb. 1934.
13. See *I.T.* 16 Feb. 1934.
14. See *I.T.* 21 and 24 Feb. 1934.
15. *I.T.* 1 Feb. 1934.
16. *Ibid.*
17. *I.I.* 1 Feb. 1934.
18. *D.D.* vol. 50 col. 2292.
19. *D.D.* vol. 50 col. 1153.
20. *D.D.* vol. 50 col. 1189.
21. *D.D.* vol. 51 col. 2318.
22. See *D.D.* vol. 50 col. 1637.
23. From interviews with former Blueshirts.
24. See *I.I.* and *I.T.* 9–10 Feb. 1934.
25. See *I.T.* 24 Feb. 1934.
26. See *D.D.* vol. 50 col. 2120.
27. *D.D.* vol. 50 col. 2213–23.
28. *D.D.* vol. 50 col. 2223–9.
29. *D.D.* vol. 50 col. 2290.
30. *D.D.* vol. 50 col. 2294.
31. *D.D.* vol. 50 col. 2295 seq.
32. See *D.D.* vol. 50 col. 2505–10.
33. *D.D.* vol. 50 col. 2510–38.
34. *D.D.* vol. 50 col. 2237 seq.
35. *D.D.* vol. 50 col. 2260.
36. *D.D.* vol. 50 col. 2254.
37. *D.D.* vol. 50 col. 2234.
38. See *D.D.* vol. 50 col. 2548.
39. See *I.I.* 15 Mar. 1934.
40. See *S.D.* vol. 18 col. 749–876.
41. See *I.T.* 25 May 1934.

CHAPTER VIII

1. See *I.T.* 5 Apr. 1934.
2. Accounts of these disturbances were given in *I.T.* and *I.P.* of 18 Mar.; 19 and 30 Apr.; 7, 8, 11, 15 and 28 May; 9, 11, 12, 18 and 25 June 1934.
3. See *I.T.* 24 Apr. 1934.
4. See *I.T.* 4 May 1934.
5. See *I.T.* 2 Apr. 1934.

6. See *I.T.* 25 Apr. 1934.
7. See *I.T.* 5 May 1934.
8. See *I.T.* 2 June 1934.
9. See *I.T.* 16 Apr. 1934.
10. See *I.P.* 8 Feb. 1934; *I.T.* 2 June 1934. An enquiry into the failure to collect rates in Tipperary S.R. showed evidence of an organised attempt to prevent collection (*I.P.* 8 Feb. 1934).
11. *I.P.* 13 Apr. 1934.
12. *Statistical Abstract*, 1933, 1934 and 1935.
13. See *I.T.* 21 Mar. and 4 Apr. 1934.
14. *Ibid.*
15. See *I.T.* 21 and 27 Apr. 1934.
16. See *I.P.* 13 and 22 Oct. 1934.
17. See *I.I.* 25 June 1934.
18. See *I.T.* 16 Sept. 1932.
19. See *I.T.* 9 Dec. 1932.
20. See *I.T.* 9 Feb. 1934.
21. See *I.T.* and *C.E.* 28 Aug. 1934; a *U.I.* editorial of 13 Oct. 1934 declared this estimate to be 'fantastic'.
22. *I.P.* 11 Jan. 1934.
23. Results from *I.I.*, *I.P.* and *I.T.* 4–6 July 1934.
24. From confidential police reports.
25. See *I.T.* 2 July 1934.
26. *C.E.* 14 and 15 Aug. 1934.
27. See *C.E.* 16 and 17 Aug. 1934.
28. See *D.D.* vol. 53 col. 2569.
29. See *D.D.* vol. 52 col. 818.
30. See *C.E.* 19 Sept. 1934; *I.P.* 24 Oct., 21 Nov. and 14 Dec. 1934.
31. See *C.E.* 14 Aug. 1934.
32. See *I.I.* 30 Oct. 1934.
33. See *I.P.* 6 Dec. 1934.
34. See *I.P.* 22 Dec. 1934 and 8 Feb. 1935.
35. Cited by the Minister for Justice, *D.D.* vol. 53 col. 2566–73.
36. *Ibid.*
37. *Ibid.*
38. *Ibid.*
39. This was especially noticeable after November 1933.
40. From ex-*Irish Press* journalists.
41. See *C.E.* 19 and 20 Aug. 1934 and *U.I.* 25 Aug. 1934.
42. *U.I.* 25 Aug. 1934.
43. From an interview with Colonel A. Brennan.
44. T. D. Williams in *The Years of the Great Test, op. cit.*, 36.
45. *The Anglo Celt*, 1 Sept. 1934.
46. See *An Phob.* 21 Aug. 1934.

CHAPTER IX

1. See *C.E.* 1 Sept. 1934.

2. Cf. *D.D.* vol. 53 col. 2567 and virtually every contemporary issue of *An Phoblacht.*
3. *C.E.* 1 Sept. 1934.
4. *Ibid.*
5. *Ibid.*
6. See *C.E.* 3 Sept. 1934.
7. *I.P.* 2 Oct. 1934.
8. See *C.E.* 10 Sept. 1934.
9. *I.I.* 2 Oct. 1934.
10. *An Phob.* 11 Sept. 1934.
11. *Ibid.*
12. *Ibid.*
13. See *I.I.* 6 Nov. 1934.
14. *C.E.* 22 Sept. 1934.
15. See *R.T.* vol. 25, no. 98 (March 1935), 155–8.
16. *U.I.* 13 Oct. 1934.
17. See *U.I.* 22 Nov. 1934.
18. See *I.T.* 3 Oct. 1950.
19. *C.E.* 28 Sept. 1934 and *I.I.* 2 Oct. 1934.
20. *Why I resigned from Fine Gael,* Dublin 1935.
21. See *I.P.* and *I.I.* 6 Nov. 1934.
22. *I.P.* 20 Oct. 1934.
23. Walsh, *op. cit.,* 189.
24. *Ibid.,* 193.
25. See *D.D.* vol. 48 col. 2769–70.
26. From an RTE interview (David Thornley) with John A. Costello, June 1969.
27. From an interview with Michael Tierney, 29 Sept. 1967.
28. See *I.P.* 19 Mar. 1934.
29. O'Duffy's own salary was £1,100 according to the general secretary of Fine Gael, Liam Burke. See *I.P.* 9 Nov. 1934.
30. The question of finance was raised by most of those interviewed. *United Ireland* was constantly appealing for funds.
31. See *C.E.* 25 Sept. 1934.
32. Walsh also makes this point, *op. cit.,* 192–3.

CHAPTER X

1. *I.I.* 2 Oct. 1934.
2. *Ibid.*
3. *I.P.* 2 Oct. 1934.
4. *Ibid.*
5. *Ibid.*
6. *I.I.* 2 Oct. 1934.
7. See *U.I.* 29 Sept. 1934.
8. *Ibid.*
9. See *I.P.* 4 Oct. 1934 *et seq.*
10. *Ibid.*
11. See *I.P.* 5, 6 and 8 Oct. 1934.

12. See *I.I.* 5 Oct. 1934.
13. See *I.I.* 6 Oct. 1934.
14. See *I.I.* 5 Oct. 1934.
15. See *The Blueshirt* 6 Oct. 1934.
16. *U.I.* 27 Oct. 1934.
17. See *I.I.* 17 Oct. 1934.
18. *I.I.* 18 Oct. 1934.
19. See *I.P.* 19 Oct. 1934.
20. *Ibid.*
21. *I.P.* 20 Oct. 1934.
22. See *I.I.* 31 Oct. 1934.
23. *U.I.* 27 Oct. 1934.
24. See *I.P.* 25 Oct. 1934.
25. See *I.I.* 22 Oct. 1934.
26. *I.P.* 5 Nov. 1934.
27. See *I.P.* 7, 13, 25 and 30 Nov. 1934.
28. See *I.P.* 20 Nov. 1934.
29. See *I.I.* 24 Nov. 1934.
30. See *The Blueshirt* 22 Dec. 1934.
31. *U.I.* 22 Dec. 1934.
32. *U.I.* 17 Aug. 1935 and 11 Jan. 1936.
33. Based in part on recollections of survivors.
34. For example, during the week 10–16 September the following incidents took place (see *C.E.* 11 and 15 Sept. 1934):

   Sept. 10: Wires cut and roads blocked in Kilkenny following the seizure of cattle. Fights same day between I.R.A. supporters and Blueshirts.

   Sept. 11: Cattle seizure incidents followed by forty arrests in Elfin, Co. Limerick. More roads blocked and wires cut in Co. Waterford.

   Sept. 12: Railway lines blocked at Kilsheelin, Co. Tipperary. Incidents following sale of cattle in Douglas, Co. Cork.

   Sept. 13: Roads and railway blocked and wires cut following the sale of cattle in Dungarvan. Fights between farmers and police. Seventeen men charged in Kilmallock following cattle seizures.

   Sept. 14: Fourteen farmers charged in Waterford because of incidents at a sale of seized cattle. Fine Gael supporter injured in a gun incident in Cooraclare, Co. Clare.
35. See *An Phob.* 28 Aug. 1934.
36. *I.P.* 30 Nov. 1934.
37. *I.P.* 29 Oct. 1934.
38. See *I.I.* 8 Oct. 1934.
39. See *I.I.* 27 Oct. 1934.
40. See *I.I.* 22 Nov. 1932.
41. See *I.P.* 6 Dec. 1934.
42. See *I.I.* 30 Oct., 6 and 22 Dec. 1934.
43. See *I.P.* 23 Oct. 1934.
44. See *I.I.* 11 Dec. 1934.
45. From an interview with F. MacDermot.
46. *I.P.* 27 Nov. 1934.

CHAPTER XI

1. *R.T.* vol. 25 no. 100, p. 557.
2. See *I.I.* and *I.P.* 11 Feb. 1935 *et seq.*; also cf. Coogan *The I.R.A., op. cit.*, 90–91.
3. See *I.I.* 4 Mar. 1935.
4. See *I.I.* and *I.P.* 19 and 25 Mar. 1935.
5. See *I.I.* and *I.P.* 27–28 Mar. 1935.
6. See *I.I.* 22 Apr. 1935, and *D.D.* vol. 56 col. 307 and 308.
7. *I.I.* 9 May 1935.
8. See *I.I.* 13 June 1935.
9. See *I.I.* 8 Feb. 1935 and 1 Mar. 1935.
10. See *I.I.* 19 Apr. 1935.
11. See *I.I.* 7 and 8 May and 6 June 1935; *U.I.* 11 May 1935.
12. See *I.I.* 12 June 1935: based also on interviews.
13. See *U.I.* 11 May 1935.
14. See *I.I.* 2 Aug. 1935 and 7 Nov. 1935.
15. See *I.T.* 4 Jan. 1935.
16. It is difficult to be any way precise in estimating the number of Blueshirts who left with O'Duffy—but clearly they were a small minority.
17. See *U.I.* 27 Oct. 1934.
18. See *U.I.* 12 Jan., 16 Feb. and 24 Aug. 1935.
19. Publication of the roll of members began on 16 Nov. 1935 and continued until *United Ireland* wound up in June 1936.
20. *R.T.* vol. 25, no. 99, p. 376.
21. See *I.I., I.P.* and *I.T.* 22 and 23 Mar. 1935, and *U.I.* 30 Mar. 1935.
22. Cf. *U.I.* 22 June, 7 Sept. and 2 Nov. 1935.
23. *U.I.* 31 Aug. 1935.
24. *Ibid.*
25. See *U.I.* 31 Aug. and 7 Sept. 1935.
26. See *U.I.* 31 Aug. 1935.
27. See *D.D.* vol. 48 col. 2769–70; also cf. ch. X p. 177 *supra*.
28. O'Higgins' speech *I.I.* 23 Sept. 1935; Cosgrave *I.I.* 5 Oct. 1935; Mac-Dermot's reply *I.I.* 8 Oct. 1935; his resignation *I.I.* 11 Oct. 1935 and *U.I.* 19 Oct. 1935.
29. *U.I.* 2 Nov. 1935.
30. See *I.I.* 18 Mar. 1935.
31. See *I.T.* 26 Mar. 1935.
32. See *I.T.* 27 Apr. 1935; cf. also Coogan *The I.R.A., op. cit.*, 91–2.
33. This was Michael Conway—sentenced to death but released 4 May 1938. He later became a Cistercian monk. For an account of Conway's career see Coogan, *The I.R.A., op. cit.*, 61, 92, 117, 132, 153, 232–3, 263–4.
34. See *I.I.* 20 June 1936.
35. See *U.I.* 14 Mar. 1936.
36. See *U.I.* 30 May and 6 June 1936.
37. See *I.I.* 14 July 1936; cf. also a commemorative article in *Studies* by Professor George O'Brien, Winter 1936.

38. See *U.I.* 25 July 1936 and *I.I.* 20 Aug. 1936. The votes went as follows:

Wexford	F.F.	23,263	Galway	F.F.	39,982
	F.G.	16,734		F.G.	23,264
	Lab.	4,296		Rep.	2,096
	Rep.	1,301			

39. Virtually every edition of *United Ireland* sought financial aid.
40. *I.P.* 9 Oct. 1936.
41. *Ibid.*
42. *Ibid.*
43. *Ibid.*
44. *I.P.* 9 Oct. 1936.
45. See *I.P.* 10 Oct. 1936.
46. *Ibid.* and *I.P.* 11 Oct. 1936.
47. See *I.P.* 13 Oct. 1936.
48. *Ibid.*
49. *I.P.* 16 Oct. 1936.
50. See *I.P.* 23 Oct. 1936.
51. See *I.I.* 6 July 1937.
52. For election details see Flynn *op. cit.*
53. *Ibid.*

CHAPTER XII

1. See *I.P.* 20 Nov. 1934.
2. See *I.T.* 18 May 1935.
3. See *I.I.* and *I.P.* 10 June 1935 and *The Blueshirt* 15 June 1935.
4. *R.T.* vol. 26, no. 101, p. 132.
5. See *U.I.* 7 Mar. 1936.
6. Cf. *I.I.* July-Aug. 1936.
7. *Ibid.*
8. See O'Duffy, *Crusade in Spain*, Dublin 1938, 12–14.
9. See *I.I.* 3 Sept. 1936.
10. O'Duffy, *op. cit.*, 15.
11. *Ibid.*, 24.
12. See *I.I.* 20 July 1936.
13. O'Duffy, *op. cit.*, 28–30.
14. *Ibid.*, 10.
15. *Ibid.*, 11.
16. *Ibid.*, 55.
17. *Ibid.*, 56.
18. *Ibid.*, 60.
19. *Ibid.*, 59–64.
20. *Ibid.*, 65–6.
21. *Ibid.*, 89–91.
22. *Ibid.*, 94–101.
23. *Ibid.*, 102; and *I.P.* 6 and 7 Jan. 1937.
24. *Ibid.* 147 and borne out by recollections of survivors interviewed.
25. *Ibid.*, 153.

26. *Ibid.*, 154.
27. *Ibid.;* borne out by recollections of survivors interviewed.
28. *R.T.* vol. 27, no. 105, p. 163.
29. *R.T.* vol. 27, no. 107, p. 365.
30. O'Duffy, *op. cit.*, 136–9.
31. *Ibid.*, 153.
32. *Ibid.*, 170.
33. From interviews with survivors.
34. O'Duffy, *op. cit.*, 236–9.
35. *Ibid.*, 247; and *I.I.* 23 June 1936.
36. *Ibid.*, 248.
37. *Ibid.*, 249.
38. See Coogan, *Ireland Since the Rising,* London 1966, 270. The meeting between O'Duffy and some of the I.R.A. leaders in the former Red Bank restaurant in Dublin when O'Duffy sought to act as intermediary is still remembered with amusement by some older members of the I.R.A.
39. Walsh MS., 222.
40. See *I.T.* 4 Dec. 1944.

CHAPTER XIII

1. See *U.I.* 11 Feb. 1932.
2. *U.I.* 10 June 1933.
3. *U.I.* 20 May 1933.
4. *U.I.* 10 June 1933.
5. *U.I.* 17 June 1933.
6. *Quadragesimo Anno* was published in 1931.
7. *U.I.* 15 Apr. 1933.
8. *U.I.* 22 Apr. 1933.
9. Cf. ch. V pp. 78 and 82.
10. Cf. ch. VI, pp. 99–100.
11. *U.I.* 25 Nov. 1933.
12. See *U.I.* 14 Oct., 1 Nov. and 16 Dec. 1933.
13. *U.I.* 24 and 31 Mar. and 7 Apr. 1934.
14. *U.I.* 19 and 26 May and 2 June 1934.
15. See *U.I.* 17 Feb. 1934.
16. From interviews.
17. Cf. *U.I.* 16 Dec. 1933.
18. See Harold Nicolson, *Diaries and Letters I,* London 1966.
19. See *U.I.* 6 Jan. 1934.
20. *Ibid.*
21. *U.I.* 24 Mar. 1934.
22. *Ibid.*
23. *U.I.* 16 Dec. 1933.
24. *U.I.* 6 Jan. 1934.
25. *U.I.* 24 Mar. 1934.
26. *U.I.* 6 Jan. 1934.
27. *U.I.* 31 Mar. 1934.

28. *Ibid.*
29. *Ibid.*
30. *Ibid.*
31. *U.I.* 24 Mar. 1934.
32. *Ibid.*
33. *Ibid.*
34. *U.I.* 16 Dec. 1933.
35. *Ibid.*
36. *Ibid.*
37. *U.I.* 24 Mar. 1934.
38. *U.I.* 7 Apr. 1934.
39. *U.I.* 24 Mar. 1934.
40. *Ibid.*
41. *Ibid.*
42. *U.I.* 16 Dec. 1934.
43. *U.I.* 19 May 1934.
44. *Ibid.*
45. *Ibid.*
46. See *U.I.* 26 May 1934.
47. *Ibid.*
48. *U.I.* 2 June 1934.
49. *Ibid.*
50. *Ibid.*
51. *U.I.* 14 Oct. 1933.
52. See *U.I.* 11 Aug. 1934.
53. Cf. in particular the speeches during the Dáil debate on the Wearing of Uniforms Bill, Feb. 1934.
54. O'Duffy, *Why I Resigned from Fine Gael, op. cit.*, 26; and he was later to say: 'Fine Gael only wanted the old time methods and the system they had grown used to', *ibid.*, 27.

CHAPTER XIV

1. See *D.D.* vol. 48 col. 2769–70.
2. Cf. Conor Cruise O'Brien, 'Passion and Cunning—the Politics of Yeats', in *In Excited Reverie* ed. A. K. Jeffares and K. G. W. Cross, London 1965.
3. Cf. *The European Right* ed. H. Rogger and E. Weber, London 1965.
3a. H. R. Trevor-Roper 'The Phenomenon of Fascism' in S. J. Woolf (ed)., *European Fascism*, London 1968, 19–20.
4. Characteristics instanced here are based on a study of the descriptions and analyses of Fascist movements in books cited in the bibliography, among which the following were particularly helpful:
   Rogger and Weber, *op. cit.*,
   Journal of Contemporary History, vol. I, no. 1: 'International Fascism 1920–45,' London 1966,
   Eugen Weber, *Varieties of Fascism*, New York 1965.
   S. J. Woolf, *European Fascism*, London 1968.
5. See note 4 *supra*.

6. James Hogan, *Could Ireland become Communist*, Dublin 1935.
7. See Weber, *op. cit.*
8. See Rogger and Weber, *op. cit.*
9. See Weber, *op. cit.*
10. George L. Mosse, 'The Genesis of Fascism' in *The Journal of Contemporary History*, *op. cit.*, 17–18.
11. See note 4 *supra*.
12. Cf. ch. V *supra*.
13. See note 4 *supra*.
14. There was no tradition of anti-Semitism in Ireland. There had been anti-Jewish incidents in Limerick in 1904–5 but these were isolated cases.
15. Hugh Seton-Watson, 'Fascism, Right and Left' in *The Journal of Contemporary History*, *op. cit.*, 194–5.
16. S. J. Woolf (ed.), *European Fascism*, *op. cit.*, 6.

Index